# THE
# CREAKY KNEES
# GUIDE

*The 75 Best Easy Hikes*

**PACIFIC NORTHWEST**
**NATIONAL PARKS & MONUMENTS**

# THE
# CREAKY KNEES
# GUIDE

## *The 75 Best Easy Hikes*

**SEABURY BLAIR JR.**

**SASQUATCH BOOKS**
**SEATTLE**

Editors: Gary Luke and Christy Cox
Production editor: Emma Reh
Design: Joyce Hwang
Interior maps: Marlene Blair
Copyeditor: Kristin Vorce Duran

ISBN: 978-1-63217-011-8

Sasquatch Books
1904 Third Avenue, Suite 710
Seattle, WA 98101

SasquatchBooks.com

23 22 21 20 19          9 8 7 6 5 4 3 2

Library of Congress Cataloging-in-Publication Data
Blair, Seabury.
  The Creaky Knees guide Pacific Northwest national parks and monuments : the best 75 easy hikes / Seabury Blair Jr.
     pages cm. -- (Creaky Knees guides)
  Includes index.
  ISBN 978-1-63217-011-8
  1. Hiking--Northwest, Pacific--Guidebooks. 2. National parks and reserves--Northwest, Pacific--Guidebooks. 3. Northwest, Pacific--Guidebooks. I. Title.
  GV199.42.N69B53 2016
  796.510979--dc23
                              2015027631

PHOTO CREDITS:
Front cover: A Jungle Experience by Sathish Jothiku-mar, www.flickr.com/photos/sathishcj/4789944363, CC BY-NC-ND 2.0; Page 22: Icerberg Point Vertical by Jeff Clark, Bureau of Land Management Oregon and Washington, www.flickr.com/photos/blmore-gon/15517399858, CC BY 2.0; Page 29: San Juan Islands 19 by Jeff Clark, Bureau of Land Management Oregon and Washington, www.flickr.com/photos/

blmoregon/8970070779, CC BY-SA 2.0; Page 211: Red Crossbill by Jason Crotty, www.flickr.com/pho-tos/46789814@N05/14487200986, CC BY 2.0; Pages 258 and 272: Courtesy of Marlene Blair; Page 282: Views from Cascade-Siskiyou National Monument -- Pilot Rock by Bureau of Land Management Oregon and Washington, flic.kr/p/sgzrj3, CC BY 2.0; All other photos: Courtesy of Seabury Blair, Jr.

IMPORTANT NOTE: Please use common sense. No guidebook can act as a substitute for experience, careful planning, the right equipment, and appropriate training. There is inherent danger in all the activities described in this book, and readers must assume full responsibility for their own actions and safety. Changing or unfavorable conditions in weather, roads, trails, snow, waterways, and so forth cannot be anticipated by the author or publisher, but should be considered by any outdoor participants. The author and publisher will not be responsible for the safety of users of this guide, and neither of them shall be liable or responsible for any legal liability, or any loss or damage or physical injury of any kind, allegedly arising from any information herein. Given the potential for changes to trail accessibility and hiking rules and regulations post-publication, please check ahead for updates on contact information, parking passes, and camping permits.

Certified Chain of Custody
Promoting Sustainable Forestry
www.sfiprogram.org
SFI-01268

SUSTAINABLE FORESTRY INITIATIVE

SFI label applies to the text stock

This guide is dedicated to all the workers and volunteers
who make certain our national parks and monuments
will always be the treasures they are

# CONTENTS

Hikes at a Glance                         viii
Acknowledgments                            xi
Introduction                             xiii
Using This Guide                           xv
Be Careful                                xix

## NORTH CASCADES NATIONAL PARK          1

1   River Loop Trail                        3
2   Thunder Knob                            7
3   East Bank Trail                        10
4   Rainy and Ann Lakes                    13
5   Cutthroat Pass                         17

## SAN JUAN ISLANDS NATIONAL MONUMENT    23

6   Iceberg Point                          25

## OLYMPIC NATIONAL PARK                 31

7   South Fork,
    Skokomish River                        33
8   North Fork,
    Skokomish River                        37
9   Shady Lane Trail                       41
10  Big Hump                               44
11  Dosewallips Road                       48
12  Lower Big Quilcene Trail               51
13  Camp Handy                             55
14  Royal Lake Trail                       59
15  Lower Gray Wolf Trail                  63
16  Dungeness Spit                         66
17  Hurricane Hill                         70

18  Elk Mountain                           74
19  Elwha Loop                             78
20  Spruce Railroad Trail                  82
21  Pacific Ocean Beaches                  86

## MOUNT RAINIER NATIONAL PARK           91

22  Mount Fremont Lookout                  93
23  Emmons Glacier                         97
24  Grove of the Patriarchs               101
25  Silver Falls                          104
26  Bench and Snow Lakes                  107
27  Nisqually Vista                       111
28  Skyline Trail                         115
29  Comet Falls                           119
30  Trail of the Shadows                  122
31  Rampart Ridge                         125
32  Westside Road                         128
33  Carbon River Road                     132
34  Naches Peak Loop                      135
35  Pinnacle Saddle                       139
36  Mazama Ridge                          142

## MOUNT ST. HELENS NATIONAL VOLCANIC MONUMENT   147

37  Harmony Falls                         149
38  Norway Pass                           152
39  Smith Creek Trail                     155

| 40 | Windy Ridge | 158 |
| 41 | Hummocks Trail | 161 |
| 42 | Coldwater Lake Trail | 164 |
| 43 | Boundary Trail | 167 |
| 44 | Ape Caves | 170 |
| 45 | Lava Canyon | 174 |
| 46 | Ape Canyon Trail | 178 |

## NEWBERRY NATIONAL VOLCANIC MONUMENT 183

| 47 | Benham Falls Trail | 185 |
| 48 | Lava Cast Forest | 189 |
| 49 | Paulina Falls | 192 |
| 50 | Paulina Creek Trail | 195 |
| 51 | Little Crater Trail | 198 |
| 52 | Paulina Lakeshore Loop | 201 |
| 53 | Silica and Big Obsidian Flow Trails | 204 |
| 54 | Newberry Crater Trail | 207 |

## JOHN DAY FOSSIL BEDS NATIONAL MONUMENT 213

| 55 | Blue Basin Overlook Trail | 215 |
| 56 | Geologic Time–Clarno Arch Trail | 218 |

## CRATER LAKE NATIONAL PARK 223

| 57 | Pacific Crest Trail North | 225 |
| 58 | Annie Spring–Pacific Crest Trail | 228 |

| 59 | Godfrey Glen | 231 |
| 60 | Lady of the Woods and Castle Crest Wildflower Loops | 234 |
| 61 | Garfield Peak Trail | 237 |
| 62 | Discovery Point Trail | 240 |
| 63 | Watchman Peak | 243 |
| 64 | Crater Rim Trail | 246 |
| 65 | Pacific Crest Trail–Red Cone Spring | 249 |
| 66 | Pacific Crest Trail– Pumice Desert | 252 |
| 67 | Cleetwood Cove | 256 |
| 68 | Mount Scott | 259 |
| 69 | Crater Peak | 262 |
| 70 | Sun Notch | 265 |
| 71 | Plaikni Falls | 268 |

## OREGON CAVES NATIONAL MONUMENT 273

| 72 | Oregon Cave Tour | 275 |
| 73 | Big Tree | 278 |

## CASCADE-SISKIYOU NATIONAL MONUMENT 283

| 74 | Pacific Crest Trail–Pilot Rock | 285 |
| 75 | Pacific Crest Trail–Hyatt Meadows | 288 |

| *Index* | | *292* |

# HIKES AT A GLANCE

## STROLL IN THE PARK

| NO. | HIKE NAME | RATING | BEST SEASON | KIDS | DOGS |
|---|---|---|---|---|---|
| 21 | Pacific Ocean Beaches | 🥾🥾🥾🥾🥾 | Summer | ✓ | ✓ |
| 30 | Trail of the Shadows | 🥾🥾🥾🥾 | Summer, fall | ✓ | |
| 48 | Lava Cast Forest | 🥾🥾🥾 | Summer, fall | ✓ | ✓ |
| 59 | Godfrey Glen | 🥾🥾 | Summer, fall | ✓ | ✓ |
| 70 | Sun Notch | 🥾🥾 | Summer, fall | | |

## EASY WALK

| NO. | HIKE NAME | RATING | BEST SEASON | KIDS | DOGS |
|---|---|---|---|---|---|
| 1 | River Loop Trail | 🥾🥾 | Fall | ✓ | ✓ |
| 4 | Rainy Lake | 🥾🥾🥾🥾🥾 | Summer, fall | ✓ | ✓ |
| 6 | Iceberg Point | 🥾🥾🥾🥾 | Spring, fall | | |
| 8 | North Fork, Skokomish River | 🥾🥾 | Spring | ✓ | |
| 9 | Shady Lane Trail | 🥾🥾 | Spring | | |
| 12 | Lower Big Quilcene Trail | 🥾🥾 | Spring | ✓ | ✓ |
| 16 | Dungeness Spit | 🥾🥾🥾🥾 | Winter | | |
| 19 | Elwha Loop | 🥾🥾🥾🥾 | Summer, fall | ✓ | |
| 24 | Grove of the Patriarchs | 🥾🥾🥾🥾 | Spring, summer | ✓ | |
| 25 | Silver Falls | 🥾🥾 | Spring, summer | ✓ | |
| 27 | Nisqually Vista | 🥾🥾🥾 | Summer, fall | ✓ | |
| 33 | Carbon River Road | 🥾 | Spring, fall | ✓ | ✓ |
| 42 | Coldwater Lake Trail | 🥾🥾🥾 | Summer, fall | ✓ | |
| 47 | Benham Falls Trail | 🥾🥾🥾🥾 | Summer, fall | ✓ | ✓ |
| 49 | Paulina Falls | 🥾🥾🥾 | Summer, fall | ✓ | ✓ |
| 54 | Newberry Crater Trail | 🥾🥾 | Summer, fall | | ✓ |
| 57 | Pacific Crest Trail North | 🥾🥾 | Summer, fall | | ✓ |
| 58 | Annie Spring–Pacific Crest Trail | 🥾🥾🥾 | Summer, fall | | |
| 60 | Lady of the Woods and Castle Crest Wildflower Loops | 🥾🥾🥾🥾 | Summer, fall | | ✓ |
| 71 | Plaikni Falls | 🥾🥾🥾🥾 | Summer, fall | ✓ | |

## MODERATE WORKOUT

| NO. | HIKE NAME | RATING | BEST SEASON | KIDS | DOGS |
|---|---|---|---|---|---|
| 2 | Thunder Knob | 🚶🚶🚶 | Spring, fall | ✔ | ✔ |
| 4 | Ann Lake | 🚶🚶🚶🚶🚶 | Summer, fall | ✔ | ✔ |
| 7 | South Fork, Skokomish River | 🚶🚶 | Spring | ✔ | ✔ |
| 11 | Dosewallips Road | 🚶🚶🚶 | Spring | ✔ | ✔ |
| 13 | Camp Handy | 🚶🚶🚶🚶 | Spring | ✔ | ✔ |
| 14 | Royal Lake Trail | 🚶🚶🚶🚶 | Summer, fall | | |
| 15 | Lower Gray Wolf Trail | 🚶🚶🚶 | Spring | ✔ | ✔ |
| 17 | Hurricane Hill | 🚶🚶🚶🚶🚶 | Summer, fall | | |
| 18 | Elk Mountain | 🚶🚶🚶🚶 | Summer, fall | | |
| 19 | Elwha Loop | 🚶🚶🚶🚶 | Summer, fall | ✔ | |
| 20 | Spruce Railroad Trail | 🚶🚶🚶 | Fall | ✔ | |
| 21 | Pacific Ocean Beaches | 🚶🚶🚶🚶🚶 | Summer | ✔ | ✔ |
| 23 | Emmons Glacier | 🚶🚶🚶 | Summer, fall | ✔ | |
| 32 | Westside Road | 🚶🚶 | Spring, fall | ✔ | ✔ |
| 34 | Naches Peak Loop | 🚶🚶🚶🚶🚶 | Summer, fall | | ✔ |
| 36 | Mazama Ridge | 🚶🚶🚶 | Summer, fall | | |
| 40 | Windy Ridge | 🚶🚶🚶🚶🚶 | Fall | | ✔ |
| 41 | Hummocks Trail | 🚶🚶 | Summer, fall | ✔ | |
| 43 | Boundary Trail | 🚶🚶🚶🚶 | Summer, fall | | |
| 44 | Ape Caves | 🚶🚶🚶🚶 | Summer | | |
| 45 | Lava Canyon | 🚶🚶🚶 | Summer, fall | | |
| 46 | Ape Canyon Trail | 🚶🚶🚶🚶 | Fall | | ✔ |
| 51 | Little Crater Trail | 🚶🚶🚶🚶🚶 | Summer, fall | | ✔ |
| 52 | Paulina Lakeshore Loop | 🚶🚶🚶 | Summer, fall | ✔ | ✔ |
| 53 | Silica and Big Obsidian Flow Trails | 🚶🚶🚶🚶🚶 | Summer, fall | ✔ | |
| 56 | Geologic Time–Clarno Arch Trail | 🚶🚶🚶🚶 | Spring, fall | | ✔ |
| 62 | Discovery Point Trail | 🚶🚶🚶 | Summer, fall | | |
| 64 | Crater Rim Trail | 🚶🚶🚶 | Summer, fall | | |
| 65 | Pacific Crest Trail—Red Cone Spring | 🚶🚶 | Summer, fall | | ✔ |
| 69 | Crater Peak | 🚶🚶🚶 | Summer, fall | | |

## PREPARE TO PERSPIRE

| NO. | HIKE NAME | RATING | BEST SEASON | KIDS | DOGS |
|---|---|---|---|---|---|
| 3 | East Bank Trail | 🚶🚶🚶 | Spring, fall | | ✔ |
| 10 | Big Hump | 🚶🚶 | Spring | | ✔ |

| 22 | Mount Fremont Lookout | 🚶🚶🚶🚶 | Summer, fall | | |
| 29 | Comet Falls | 🚶🚶🚶 | Summer, fall | | |
| 31 | Rampart Ridge | 🚶🚶 | Spring, fall | | |
| 35 | Pinnacle Saddle | 🚶🚶🚶 | Summer | | |
| 37 | Harmony Falls | 🚶🚶🚶🚶 | Summer, fall | ✔ | |
| 38 | Norway Pass | 🚶🚶🚶🚶🚶 | Summer, fall | ✔ | |
| 39 | Smith Creek Trail | 🚶🚶 | Fall | | ✔ |
| 44 | Ape Caves | 🚶🚶🚶🚶 | Summer | | |
| 50 | Paulina Creek Trail | 🚶🚶🚶 | Summer, fall | | ✔ |
| 55 | Blue Basin Overlook Trail | 🚶🚶🚶🚶🚶 | Summer, fall | | ✔ |
| 63 | Watchman Peak | 🚶🚶🚶🚶🚶 | Summer, fall | | |
| 66 | Pacific Crest Trail—Pumice Desert | 🚶🚶 | Summer, fall | | ✔ |
| 67 | Cleetwood Cove | 🚶🚶🚶🚶 | Summer, fall | | |
| 72 | Oregon Cave Tour | 🚶🚶🚶🚶🚶 | Summer, fall | | |
| 73 | Big Tree | 🚶🚶🚶 | Summer, fall | | |
| 74 | Pacific Crest Trail—Pilot Rock | 🚶🚶🚶 | Summer, fall | | ✔ |
| 75 | Pacific Crest Trail—Hyatt Meadows | 🚶 | Summer, fall | | ✔ |

## KNEE-PUNISHING

| NO. | HIKE NAME | RATING | BEST SEASON | KIDS | DOGS |
| --- | --- | --- | --- | --- | --- |
| 5 | Cutthroat Pass | 🚶🚶🚶🚶🚶 | Late summer, fall | | ✔ |
| 14 | Royal Lake Trail | 🚶🚶🚶🚶 | Summer, fall | | |
| 26 | Bench and Snow Lakes | 🚶🚶🚶 | Summer, fall | | |
| 28 | Skyline Trail | 🚶🚶🚶🚶🚶 | Summer, fall | | |
| 61 | Garfield Peak Trail | 🚶🚶🚶🚶 | Summer, fall | | |
| 68 | Mount Scott | 🚶🚶🚶🚶🚶 | Summer, fall | | |

# ACKNOWLEDGMENTS

This is the first of my half dozen guidebooks that my wife, Marlene, has accompanied me on every hike that follows. See, until her retirement a couple of years ago, she who I call B. B. Hardbody actually had to work for a living. Now her only task is to prod and poke me with her trekking pole to get me along the trail before I seize up and freeze mid-stride, like the Tin Man in *The Wizard of Oz*. That, and to produce all of the maps for this book, furnish good photos when mine sucked, keep me committed to a hiking schedule when the weather was less than fine, and put up with my continual grousing and groaning. I could thank her a thousand times, but it would not be enough.

Friends old and new continue to support and encourage me as, in my seventh decade of walking Northwest trails, I bitch and moan about how pathways have gotten longer and steeper. Chief among them are Jim Drannan, the Gnarly Dude, and Ron C. Judd. I'm grateful to Joe Weigel, who knows Olympic National Park trails better than me, and his wife, Kathy.

Thanks, too, to the National Park and National Forest staffers who reviewed my work and made certain I didn't miss a critical trail junction or send you marching off a cliff. They included Cristina Rose Peterson, lead ranger, Newberry National Volcanic Monument; Denise M. Shultz, chief of interpretation and education, North Cascades National Park Service Complex; Jeff Axel, chief of interpretation and visitor services, John Day Fossil Beds National Monument; Petrina "Crow" Vecchio, volunteer coordinator, VIP Program, Mount Rainier National Park; and Kathy Steichen, chief of interpretation, Education and Volunteers, Olympic National Park.

My editors at Sasquatch Books—Christy Cox, Emma Reh, and Em Gale—caught my really stupid mistakes as well as all of my really smart mistakes. They deserve more than thanks.

Finally, I would like to thank the waiter at the Old Schoolhouse Brewery in Winthrop, Washington, who found my REI credit card and reported it. Some idiot—I am not saying who—left it on the table after (several) post-hike beers.

# INTRODUCTION

Way back in 1972, I took a picture of the sunset from a beach at Kalaloch in Olympic National Park. Yes, there were cameras back then. You loaded them with stuff called film, which you had to develop in a room that was very dark. It is possibly one reason that photographers disliked daylight, like vampires.

Anyway, I was surprised to see my picture the other day in a newspaper that was only a day or two old. Upon closer examination, I determined that it wasn't my photograph at all, but an image taken from the same spot, showing the same old tree gnarled by Pacific winds, and the same creek curving into the ocean. It was as if, in that spot, time stood still.

Time indeed stands still in all the places you'll find in this book, at least as still as Mother Nature allows. Our national parks and monuments are tasked with preserving and conserving the forests, mountains, beaches, and rivers in their charge for future generations. Your children and your children's children will be able to find the same vistas in the same condition you left them years ago. Mother Nature may move a tree or two, or—in at least one case in our lifetime—blow up a mountain. But for the most part, American parks and monuments will continue to look the same.

The people who manage these sacred places in Oregon and Washington may work for various agencies, like the Department of the Interior or the Department of Agriculture. But they share the same goal when it comes to national parks and monuments, even though they may work in different ways to achieve it. They also share the same boss—a discerning and tough taskmaster who demands a paradox: to provide for the enjoyment of the people yet at the same time conserve and preserve for future generations.

Who sets such a seemingly impossible mission? The owners of these wonderful, timeless places, that's who. And who is that?

Why, it's you.

# USING THIS GUIDE

The beginning of each trail description is intended to give quick information that can help you decide whether the specific day hike is one that interests you. Here's what you'll find:

## TRAIL NUMBER AND NAME

Trails are numbered in this guide following the main highway corridors, all beginning with general descriptions from Interstate 5, from north to south. But listen, if you live in Spokane, Washington, or Bend, Oregon, you needn't drive to I-5 to find the trailhead. I suppose it's unnecessary to point that out, but you never know.

Beyond that, I've tried to organize the hikes as you might encounter their trailheads driving along the road or highway. All but two of the national parks and monuments in this guide are east of I-5, so you'll likely be driving that way to the trailhead. The Olympic National Park hikes are organized in a counterclockwise loop around Highway 101, beginning in the southeast.

## OVERALL RATING

I never fail to describe one hike in glowing terms, only to hear from at least one of my three readers that the hike I described was absolutely the worst hike they had ever taken. They tell me the hike I described as "a stroll down cotton candy lane" was, in fact, "like running a gauntlet of demons armed with rotten eggs." All I ask is that you take my suggestions under advisement.

Another problem I have is attempting to be objective in rating the trails. I'm a pushover for hikes above timberline, where the wildflowers wave in gentle summer breezes, where mountains claw the clouds, where cooling snowfields linger through summer. So I may have rated these trails higher than you might rate them.

If you're a hiker who loves walking along rattling rivers or past forested lakes, or padding on rain-forest trails softened by mosses, I'd suggest you add one star to every lowland hike and subtract one star from every alpland hike in this guide.

Finally, objective criteria like trail conditions, trail length, and obstacles such as creek crossings can affect the overall rating. On the other hand, you can forget all that junk and just take my word for it.

## DISTANCE

The distance listed is round-trip, exclusive of any side trips mentioned along the way. If these excursions off the main trail are longer than 0.2 mile or so, I'll mention it in the description of the hike.

In an effort to prove that trails indeed are getting longer as I grow older, I packed a GPS on some trails and carried my trusty Fitbit on others. I learned to my disappointment that trails aren't getting longer—although there are notable exceptions—and that I might have equipped myself better by carrying my own oxygen supply instead of a bloody GPS unit that is allergic to fir and pine forests.

## HIKING TIME

This is an estimate of the time it takes the average hiker to walk the trail round-trip. Since none of us are average hikers, you may feel free to ignore this entry.

For the most part, I calculated the pace on the trail to be between 1.5 and 2 miles per hour. I assumed the pace might slow on trails with significant elevation gain or loss and tried to err on the conservative side. It's my hope that many of you will wonder what sort of trail slug came up with such ridiculously long hiking times.

## ELEVATION GAIN

This is a calculation of the total number of feet you'll have to climb on the trail. Don't assume, as one fool early in his hiking days did (I have since learned better), that all the elevation will be gained on the way to your destination. Some of these trails actually lose elevation on the way and gain it on the return, or alternately gain and lose elevation along the way. It has always been a source of wonder to me that on a round-trip hike, you always gain the same amount of elevation that you lose.

## HIGH POINT

This is the highest point above sea level you'll reach on any given hike. In cases like the ocean beach walks, it is always at the trailhead.

## EFFORT

This was another tough one for me. I've been hiking for so many years it is a task to remember what it was like to take some of these hikes as a novice. My good friend Grizzly Hemingway once turned back from a hike after encountering a footlog that was too high to cross—a log I had forgotten scared the pee out of me the first time I crossed it too.

So again, I tried to be conservative in judging the effort it would take to finish each hike. Where previous guides discussed overall difficulty of the trail, I thought the energy expended to hike out and back might be more meaningful. A hike might be difficult, for example, if you had to walk that footlog, but the rest of the trail could be flat as a pancake griddle, requiring no more effort than a stroll in the park. Thus you'll find the following categories:

A **Stroll in the Park** will serve up few, if any, hills to climb and is generally between 1 and 3 miles long round-trip, a hike suitable for families with small children.

On a hike rated as an **Easy Walk**, you might expect to find longer, but still gently graded, hills and trails around 2 to 4 miles long round-trip.

A hike described as a **Moderate Workout** would be one with longer grades and elevation changes greater than about 500 feet from beginning to high point, and between 3 and 5 miles long round-trip.

A hike rated as **Prepare to Perspire** is one that will make your deodorant fail you, no matter your excellent physical condition. It will have sustained steep climbs of at least 1 mile, with elevation gain and loss greater than 1,000 feet, and is about 4 to 6 miles long round-trip.

A **Knee-Punishing** hike is one that will challenge your physical abilities beyond what you might expect you can accomplish, one that will send you packing to the anti-inflammatory shelf in your medicine stash upon your return.

## BEST SEASON

Here is my suggestion for the season (or seasons) I think you'd most enjoy this hike, as well as whether the path is accessible throughout the year.

## PERMITS/CONTACT

This entry will tell you whether you need a daily or annual pass or permit and who to contact for information. Hikers who are fortunate enough to have been on earth 62 years or longer qualify for an America the Beautiful Senior Pass that, at $10 for life, gets you onto just about any federally managed trail and gives you half-price camping at national forest and park campgrounds.

## MAPS

I've tried to include the USGS quadrangle maps for every hike in the guide, plus Green Trails maps where available. I've not listed, but recommend, Geo-Graphics maps for several Oregon hiking regions.

## TRAIL NOTES

Here are some regulations specific to each hike you'll most likely want to know: whether leashed dogs can accompany you; whether you'll encounter mountain bikes, horses, or ATVs on the trail; whether your children might like this hike. If there are circumstances about the hike you might like to know, such as whether you'll fry if you hike the trail in summer, I'll mention it here.

## THE HIKE

This is an attempt to convey the feel of the trail in a sentence or two, including the type of trail and whether there's a one-way hiking option.

## GETTING THERE

Here's where you'll either find out how to get to the trailhead or, if I've screwed up, become hopelessly lost. You'll learn the elevation at the trailhead and—assuming my GPS didn't sniff any firs or pines—the coordinates for the trailhead.

As I mentioned, all the hikes are organized according to the major highway corridors you'll follow to get to the national forest, monument, or park roads leading to the trailhead. I've tried to indicate starting points along those corridors, such as cities or towns, or major highway junctions.

## THE TRAIL

Here's where you'll get the blow-by-blow, mile-by-mile description of the trail. I've tried to stick to information your feet will find useful and apologize if, every now and then, I look up to recognize an awesome view or rhapsodize about something absolutely without redeeming social or cultural value. I'm guessing you'll recognize these features without much coaching.

## GOING FARTHER

This is an important category in this guide, because many of you might find some of these hikes too easy, while others will be ready to turn around before they reach my recommended spot. For that reason, I've tried to include a suggestion for extending most hikes from the same trailhead, or from a nearby trailhead that can be accessed before your heart rate decreases or your joints stiffen.

# BE CAREFUL

It is all too easy on a warm, sunny day on the trail to forget all of the stuff you ought to be carrying in your pack. Day hikers, especially, are likely to leave that extra fleece sweater or that waterproof, breathable parka in the trunk. Some folks even forget that First Essential—a hiking partner.

Never hike alone.

Virtually all the time, day hikers who forget one or two of the basic rules for safe wilderness travel return to the trailhead smiling and healthy. No trail cop is going to cite you for negligent hiking if you have only nine of the Ten Essentials, or if you hit the trail without registering or telling someone where you're going.

I dislike preaching safety—if you looked in my pack on a good-weather day hike, you might find my extra clothing consists of a spare do-rag and my map clearly shows the hike I took last week. Perhaps the only weighty argument anyone can make to persuade another day hiker to follow the rules for safe travel in the out-of-doors is to remind them of the annual avoidable tragedies that occur because hikers ignore those rules.

## THE TEN ESSENTIALS

First—no matter the distance or difficulty of the hike—please carry these Ten Essentials in your pack. With no apologies to those credit card slogan writers: don't leave home without them.

- 𝆊 A topographic map of the area.

- 𝆊 A compass, and the ability to use it in conjunction with the map. While excellent aids to navigation, portable GPS units are no substitute for a compass that does not require batteries or satellite reception.

- 𝆊 Extra clothing, which should consist of a top and bottom insulating layer and a waterproof, windproof layer. A hat or cap is absolutely essential; mountaineers will tell you that when your feet are cold, put on your hat. It works.

- 𝆊 Extra food. To avoid grazing on my extra food, I try to pick something I would eat only if I were starving. Stuff like freeze-dried turnips or breakfast bars that taste like pressed sawdust fire starters. In fact, some of my extra food can be used as emergency fire starters.

 ⚐ A flashlight with extra batteries and bulbs. I carry a headlamp because it allows me to swat at the moths that fly into the light without dropping the bloody flashlight. Many of these lights have spare bulbs built in. Lithium batteries, though more expensive, make excellent spares because their shelf life is longer than yours.

 ⚐ A first-aid kit. You can buy these already assembled, and they are excellent. Consider one thing, however: the type of injury that is likely to incapacitate a day hiker is likely to be different from one suffered by a backpacker. If your first-aid kit doesn't include wraps for sprains, add an ankle support, at the very least. Blister treatment for day hikers is another essential.

 ⚐ Matches in a waterproof case. Although butane lighters are often carried as a substitute, both altitude and temperature can affect their performance.

 ⚐ A fire starter. Candles work well, along with a variety of lightweight commercial fire starters.

 ⚐ A pocketknife. In addition to the all-important corkscrew, my Swiss Army knife has 623 blades, including a tiny chain saw.

 ⚐ Sunglasses and sunscreen.

In addition to these items, most day hikers never hit the trail without toting some toilet paper in a plastic bag and perhaps some type of bug repellent on summer hikes. A loud emergency whistle is a lightweight addition. Binoculars may help find your route if you become lost and are worth the weight simply for watching wildlife.

## WEATHER

Every region in Oregon and Washington demands we pay attention to a different facet of the weather. A dry change of clothing in the pack or car is always a good idea because rain can sneak up on you. In the arid lands of John Day or Newberry Crater, an extra liter of water would be a grand idea.

No matter where you're hiking, learn to read the clouds and wind and learn the general rules that may keep you safer or more comfortable. Winds from the southwest often bring storms. Northerlies often herald better weather. Afternoons in the high country are more likely to be stormy. I like to think of Mother Nature as a schizoid who is most often a friendly, generous old lady who bakes cookies and bread for you, but when you least expect it, puts on a goalie's mask and whacks at you with an icicle or lightning bolt.

So be prepared, Scouts.

## WATER

You'll find plenty of opportunities to refill your water bottle on many of the hikes outlined in this book, especially on the wet west side of the Cascades. Treat all water as if it were contaminated, although this is not as great an issue in Northwest wilderness as it is often suggested by those who might be held liable if you were to contract a waterborne illness. The most worrisome problem with the water might be a little critter called *Giardia lamblia*, which can give you a case of the trots that you'll never forget. The most noticeable symptom of giardiasis is "explosive diarrhea." Need I say more? I think not.

Thankfully, there is an easy way to ensure that the water you take from mountain streams and lakes is safe to drink. When used properly, filter pumps eliminate at least 99.9 percent of *Giardia* and other dangerous organisms from the water. A recent and far more convenient substitute for filter pumps, especially for day hikers, are relatively inexpensive water bottles equipped with their own filters. You simply fill the bottle from the stream (taking extreme care not to contaminate the mouthpiece or drinking cap), drop the filter into place, and screw on the top, and you're ready to drink filtered water. Another system purifies water with ultraviolet light, and perhaps the most effective water treatment is with chemicals such as iodine; the trade-off is processing time.

## WILDLIFE

The first time I saw a black bear, a half mile from the trailhead, I snapped a shaky picture of it and considered shedding my pack on the spot so it would eat my lunch and not bother making lunch of me. Since that time, I have come to regard animals and plants that share the Northwest wilderness to be benign for the most part.

Day hikers certainly needn't fear black bears, but must realize these are wild animals that can cause serious injury if provoked. Research indicates that a black bear attack—though extremely rare—may often be more serious than an attack from a grizzly. Respect a bear's personal space, in short, and never get between a cub and its mother. If you encounter a black bear on the trail, make certain it knows you're there by addressing it in a calm voice (it will probably run off at this point), giving it a wide berth, and counting yourself fortunate for seeing it. Some few bears have learned that humans carry food in their packs, but this is a far greater concern to backpackers, and you'll find warnings or closure signs at the trailhead.

A greater potential danger might be from cougars. Until recently, I've regarded myself lucky to have seen a cougar once in the Cascade Mountains and discovered I was once tracked by an unseen cougar through 5 miles of snow. But there is growing evidence to suggest that day hikers should treat cougar sightings as extremely dangerous encounters with predators who, it appears, may sometimes hunt humans for food. Shortly before setting out to check the trails in an earlier guide, I read Jo Deurbrouck's and Dean Miller's excellent book *Cat Attacks*. It convinced me that—though the odds of being attacked by a cougar are on the order of winning the lottery while being struck by lightning—I should be more aware of the animals to whom the wilderness belongs, particularly the ones that are quite capable of hunting you down and killing you.

Trailhead signs will tell you how to respond if you are confronted by a cougar on the trail. Generally, you must face the animal down. Don't turn your back on it or bend down to get something to throw at it. Shouting may help. Barking like a dog may send the animal off into the woods. But most importantly: maintain eye contact at all times.

Most unsettling is the fact that the majority of cougar attacks upon humans don't occur as a result of the kind of encounter described above. Most people who were attacked by cougars in the past decade—attacks have increased significantly in the past 10 years—were struck from behind and were not aware of the cougar's presence until the attack.

How can a hiker defend against such an attack? Given that the odds of an encounter are extremely remote and an attack less likely still, author Deurbrouck suggests hikers simply be aware of places where cougars are most likely to wait in ambush. She says that while trail-running, she tries to think like a deer, the cougar's main prey. In other words, be watchful of banks above the trail and places where the trail rounds hillside corners. In most cases, cougars attack from ambush, above and behind their prey.

Above all, cougar attacks of the past decade have given greater weight to the unbreakable rule against solo hiking. When attacking, cougars appear to be so focused on their prey that they completely ignore other people. Even when companions open a big can of whup-ass on that kitty, they are most likely to escape a retaliatory attack. Those attacked by cougars can be saved by companions who probably won't suffer injury from the animal—and I'm hoping that is by far and away more than you want or will ever need to know about cougars.

Another Northwest mammal to respect is the mountain goat. Though usually shy, goats in some areas like Olympic National Park have become aggressive. One goat gored a hiker to death several years ago. As with information about bears and cougars, you will find tips on avoiding goats at trailheads.

Less dangerous but more common hazards to day hikers might include stinging and biting pests like yellow jackets—particularly in late summer and early autumn—and blackflies, mosquitoes, and deerflies. Liberal doses of insect repellent can take care of the mosquitoes and deerflies but probably won't keep those nasty yellow jackets away. My technique for protection from yellow jacket stings is to send my hiking partner ahead about 100 feet, and if they get stung as they pass a nest, I wait until things settle down, then bypass the area carefully.

Poison oak and ivy grow in some areas, particularly on the east side of Washington and Oregon, but are easily avoided by learning to identify the plants. A more common plant pest is stinging nettle, which grows along many trails on both the wet and dry sides of the Northwest, but it can be recognized and avoided most of the time.

Snakes are common on the sunny sides of Oregon and Washington; you have only to keep a watch out for them to enjoy a safe, bite-free hike. If only I had taken that advice before I stepped on that snake a couple of years ago while ogling the hills for mountain sheep. Neither the snake nor I stuck around long enough to find out if either of us was poisonous.

Early snowfall on Liberty Bell Mountain from the Washington Pass Overlook.

# NORTH CASCADES NATIONAL PARK

Welcome to the finest example of wilderness in the Lower 48. Though split by a state highway and within 3 hours of Seattle, the 684,000 acres of the North Cascades National Park Complex is as far away from anybody or anything human as you can get in the contiguous United States. Grizzly and black bear roam the park and neighboring Ross Lake and Lake Chelan National Recreation Areas, which form the complex. You may hear the cry of wolves or the call of the common loon, two of the sounds that speak most eloquently of pure wilderness. Nine-thousand-foot peaks scratch at clouds and hug more than 300 glaciers in their arms; salmon and steelhead spawn in rivers that begin as tumbling cataracts that give their name to the crags from which they spring: cascades.

This wildness is both a boon and bane to those who choose to travel by the power of their muscles alone. While the park is hiker heaven to backpackers and Real Mountain Climbers, those who take their trekking adventures one day at a time won't find as many opportunities to get to the places in the North Cascades that see only a few Vibram tracks every year. Such places exist under the sharp rock faces of the Picket Range or on the creased ice of the Redoubt or Challenger Glaciers.

But day hikers can still find solitude and wildland on some of the 400 miles of trails that weave through the park. It's easier here than most national parks, simply because the North Cascades are visited by relatively few people when compared to other parks. About 71,000 people came to the park in 2013, compared to more than 3 million visitors at nearby Olympic National Park. Even adding the 725,000 people who visited Ross Lake National Recreation Area and the 40,000 at Lake Chelan, the total is one-third of the people who traveled to Olympic.

So grab those trekking poles and pick one of the five easier trails outlined in this guide. You'll find everything from a comfortable stroll along a river valley to a tough climb to mountain vistas blind to the works of humankind. At the close of this chapter, you'll find recommendations for day hikes that will test those of you whose knees and other joints aren't as creaky as the rest of us.

# NORTH CASCADES NATIONAL PARK

1   River Loop Trail

2   Thunder Knob

3   East Bank Trail

4   Rainy and Ann Lakes

5   Cutthroat Pass

# 1. River Loop Trail

| | |
|---|---|
| RATING | 👫 |
| DISTANCE | 1.8-mile loop |
| HIKING TIME | 1 hour, 30 minutes |
| ELEVATION GAIN | 120 feet |
| HIGH POINT | 590 feet |
| EFFORT | Easy Walk |
| BEST SEASON | Fall; open year-round |
| PERMITS/CONTACT | None/North Cascades National Park, (360) 845-7200, www.nps.gov/noca |
| MAPS | USGS Mount Triumph; Green Trails Marblemount 47 |
| NOTES | Leashed dogs welcome; good family hike; wheelchair accessible with assistance |

## THE HIKE

Stroll through a forest of evergreens and bright fall colors to the edge of the Skagit River, where in the late summer and early fall of every odd-numbered year, you can watch hundreds of spawning pink salmon. The trail is open year-round.

## GETTING THERE

From I-5, follow the North Cascades Highway 20 east about 53 miles from Sedro-Woolley to Newhalem and milepost 120. Turn right and cross a narrow bridge over the Skagit River, and pass Newhalem Campground to the big parking area in front of the North Cascades National Park Visitor Center. The trail begins behind the center, 590 feet above sea level. GPS coordinates: N48°30'53.2"; W121°16'05.8"

## THE TRAIL

As with a good number of the trails labeled "wheelchair accessible" in this guide, hikers in wheelchairs might want to review the trail description before laying rubber. But unlike some trails so labeled, this one might actually be a good choice for wheelchair hikers—especially those with assistance or who can navigate a dirt surface.

Everyone, whether they hike on rubber soles or wheels, should know this trail is smooth as a cashmere sweater, with a grade that will accommodate

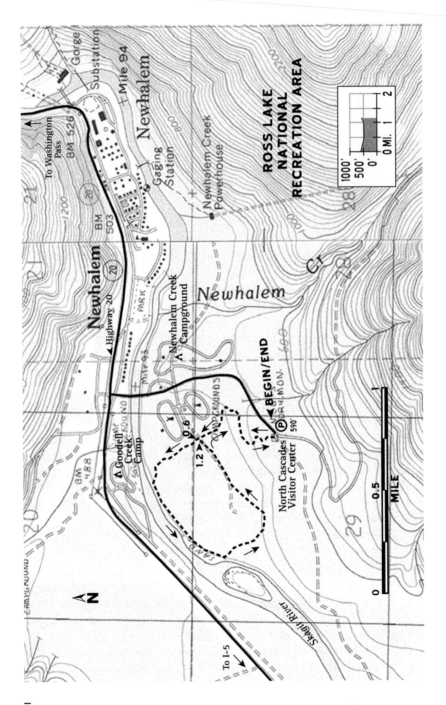

The Skagit River rolls past a gravel bar on the River Loop Trail.

all walking or rolling styles. Since the trail begins with about a quarter mile of gentle downhill, save something for that final, albeit gentle, uphill push back to the trailhead.

From the north side of the exquisite North Cascades Visitor Center, the trail makes a flat beeline toward the rush and shuffle of the Skagit River as it rolls west from Diablo and Ross Lakes toward Puget Sound. After about 100 yards the trail turns at a forested bluff and begins a gentle descending traverse to the northeast and the valley floor. If you're hiking this trail in the fall, you may be tempted (as we were) by both the sight and apricot perfume of chanterelles blooming on the hillside above and below the trail. Remember: you're in a national park, where plucking those fantastic fungi—or any flora—is a no-no.

On the river flats below, the trail turns to the northwest in thick evergreen forest and at **0.6** mile, crosses a junction with trails leading to the Newhalem Campground. Stay left at this well-marked intersection and continue toward the sound of the Skagit River. This mixed forest and river beyond is home and migration motel to as many as 200 species of birds in North Cascades National Park.

After another 0.1 mile, you'll arrive at the riverbank and turn southwest to follow the trail and river downstream for about a quarter mile. Here you'll find a sand and gravel beach along the river that makes

The North Cascades National Park Visitor Center at Newhalem is the River Loop trailhead.

a good spot to watch those spawning humpback salmon in 2015 and uneven years thereafter.

The trail now turns away from the river and curves along an old road-bed to close the loop at the campground trail junction, 1.2 miles from the trailhead. Turn right here and climb back to the visitor center.

## GOING FARTHER

You'll find several short walks that begin at the visitor center, including the To Know a Tree Trail, which links with the River Loop Trail near the river. You'll also find pathways leading to the Trail of the Cedars in Newhalem or up the Lower Newhalem Creek.

# 2. Thunder Knob

| | |
|---|---|
| RATING | 🚶🚶🚶 |
| DISTANCE | 3.8 miles round-trip |
| HIKING TIME | 2 hours, 30 minutes |
| ELEVATION GAIN | 635 feet |
| HIGH POINT | 1,875 feet |
| EFFORT | Moderate Workout |
| BEST SEASON | Spring, fall; open year-round |
| PERMITS/CONTACT | None/North Cascades National Park, (360) 845-7200, www.nps.gov/noca |
| MAPS | National Geographic Trails Illustrated North Cascades National Park |
| NOTES | Leashed dogs welcome; good family hike |

## THE HIKE

Switch back and climb a moderate grade past several viewpoints to the Big Kahuna of viewpoints at the 1,875-foot summit of Thunder Knob, which is dwarfed by the 8,000-foot peaks surrounding it. Look down into the deep, teal waters of Diablo Lake. The trail is open year-round.

## GETTING THERE

Follow the North Cascades Highway 20 from I-5 and Sedro-Woolley to the Colonial Creek Campground, about 10 miles east of Newhalem past milepost 130. The trail starts beyond the north campground loops, and trailhead parking is along the north side of the highway, 1,240 feet above sea level. GPS coordinates: N48°41′41.2″; W121°05′58.0″

## THE TRAIL

By the time you read this, you may be able to cross a new footlog over Colonial Creek at the beginning of this hike. This ornery watercourse might relish ripping a new channel in North Cascades gravel and boulder every decade or so. The last "new" bridge was only seven years old before it was replaced—an ill-timed project for me and my wife, B. B. Hardbody. We arrived to hike the trail on the day that massive old footlog was hauled from the creek with a cable come-along by three men who, it seemed to me, all looked like youthful Arnold Schwarzeneggers.

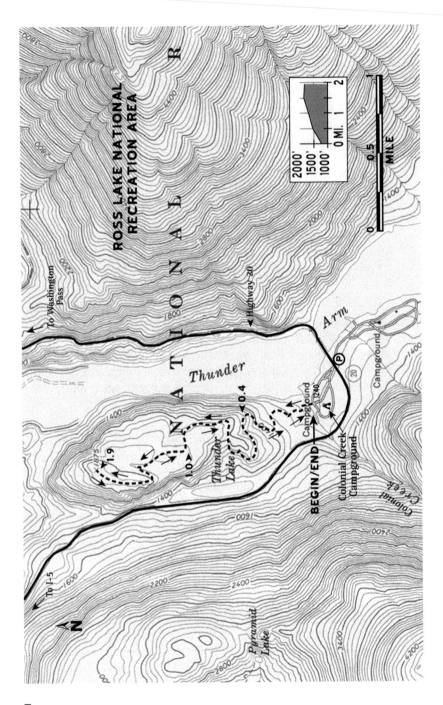

A trail crew hauled the log bridge, left, from Colonial Creek on the Thunder Knob trail.

So we wandered downstream to where the stream splits into an alluvial fan to spill into the Thunder Arm of Diablo Lake and splashed across. Once again, we learned that boots lined with Gore-Tex are excellent for keeping water out, at least until it leaks over the top of the boot. At that juncture, they are far better at keeping water in.

The path is well-graded and wide enough, and kept in excellent condition by trail crews. Once across the footlog, follow the path along one of the former Colonial Creek rampages as it climbs gently through a forest dominated by old hemlocks and carpeted by moss. The trail switches back after climbing about 0.2 mile from the trailhead, then climbs to the northeast to the first viewpoint at 0.4 mile. About 160 feet below, through steep forest hillside to the east, is Thunder Arm.

The trail switches back three times before reaching a sloping bench where pine trees have established themselves above the climax forest below. At 1.0 mile from the trailhead and above a steep hillside tumbling 240 feet down to Thunder Lake, you'll find a bench and view of glaciated Colonial Peak. A half mile beyond, the trail descends briefly on the broad ridge to a shallow saucer of marshy ponds before climbing moderately to a junction and path leading left to a view of Diablo Lake. Continue right on the main trail another 100 yards to the end of the trail with a view of 9,066-foot Jack Mountain, which dominates the northeastern skyline.

## GOING FARTHER

For a longer walk, cross the North Cascades Highway 20 to the south campground and hike the Thunder Creek Trail, a gentle walk 2.1 miles one-way. The trail continues for several more gentle miles along the creek.

# 3. East Bank Trail

| | |
|---|---|
| RATING | 🚶🚶🚶 |
| DISTANCE | 6.4 miles round-trip |
| HIKING TIME | 4 hours |
| ELEVATION GAIN | 1,350 feet |
| HIGH POINT | 2,175 feet |
| EFFORT | Prepare to Perspire |
| BEST SEASON | Spring, fall |
| PERMITS/CONTACT | None/North Cascades National Park, (360) 845-7200, www.nps.gov/noca |
| MAPS | USGS Crater Mountain; Green Trails Mount Logan 49 |
| NOTES | Leashed dogs welcome; road closed in winter |

## THE HIKE

Though the grades are gentle enough, the distance of this forested walk to a viewpoint and picnic spot above the Ruby Arm of Ross Lake is far enough that you'll likely work up a sweat. You'll lose elevation on the way to a lake viewpoint turnaround, so expect to work harder on the way back.

## GETTING THERE

From I-5 and Sedro-Woolley, drive 18 miles east of Newhalem on the North Cascades Highway 20. Turn left into the trailhead parking lot about 0.4 mile beyond milepost 138, 1,860 feet above sea level. GPS coordinates: N48°42′29.2″; W120°58′42.5″

## THE TRAIL

Begin by dropping in several switchbacks to an interpretive sign marking a big hole in the ground, reportedly one of the exploratory digs of George Holmes. A former slave who established a gold claim on the stream in 1894, Holmes built his mining gear by hand and mined the area until 1925, when he died at the age of 71. Just beyond, 0.5 mile from the trailhead, cross a wide wood plank bridge over Ruby Creek to a trail junction.

The trail to the right climbs upstream on the Canyon Creek Trail for 1.1 miles to a washed-out bridge. You'll turn left and begin a very gradual

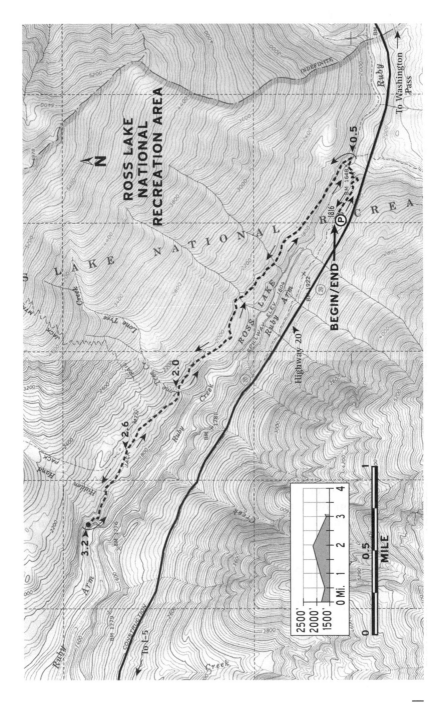

A bridge crosses Ruby Creek on the East Bank Trail.

downstream hike through forested hillside above the creek. Another half mile from the trailhead, you may note that the splashing of the creek has been silenced and the more likely sound you'll hear is that made by traffic climbing the North Cascades Highway, south across the canyon of the Ruby Arm of Ross Lake. Traffic noise could be muffled briefly by two creek crossings about 1.2 and 1.3 miles from the trailhead.

At 2.0 miles, you'll cross Lone Tree Creek and continue traversing along the hillside above the Ruby Arm. At 2.8 miles, find a three-way junction with trails that climb in steep switchbacks up the lower slopes of Jack Mountain, or go straight on the main East Bank Trail. You'll take the leftmost fork of the trail on a spur that leads in 0.4 mile to campsites and just beyond, to a viewpoint of Ross Lake below. This is your turn-around spot.

## GOING FARTHER

For a longer walk, return to the trail junction and follow the East Bank Trail over Hidden Hand Pass another 2 or 3 miles above the shore of Ross Lake. This trail leads past a number of designated campsites for more than 25 miles along the lake.

# 4. Rainy and Ann Lakes

| | |
|---|---|
| RATING | 🚶🚶🚶🚶🚶 |
| DISTANCE | 2.0 miles round-trip/3.6 miles round-trip |
| HIKING TIME | 1 hour/3 hours |
| ELEVATION GAIN | 80 feet/670 feet |
| HIGH POINT | 4,790 feet/5,475 feet |
| EFFORT | Easy Walk/Moderate Workout |
| BEST SEASON | Summer, fall |
| PERMITS/CONTACT | Northwest Forest Pass required/ Okanogan-Wenatchee National Forest, (509) 996-4003, www.fs.usda.gov/okawen |
| MAPS | USGS Washington Pass; Green Trails Mount Logan 49 |
| NOTES | Leashed dogs welcome; good family hikes; Rainy Lake Trail is paved and wheelchair accessible; road closed in winter |

## THE HIKES

If you have time for only two easy hikes in the North Cascades, make them to Rainy and Ann Lakes. You'll walk alpine forests and high mountain meadows, see wildflowers of every color and description, and grab selfies with some of the most scenic mountains in all the Cascades as your background.

## GETTING THERE

From I-5 and Sedro-Woolley, follow the North Cascades Highway 20 for 158 miles to Rainy Pass and turn right on the Rainy Pass Picnic Area road, which leads to a big parking lot and the trailheads to Rainy and Ann Lakes. If you're driving from Winthrop, follow Highway 20 west over Washington Pass to Rainy Pass and the parking area, 4,800 feet above sea level. GPS coordinates: N48º30'58.5"; W120º44'23.2"

## THE TRAILS

These trails begin within 100 feet of each other but head in opposite directions. Hikers seeking the easiest way can take the wheelchair-friendly paved path to Rainy Lake. Heavy winter snows and cold weather have lumped the asphalt in a few spots, but if there's a single trail in this

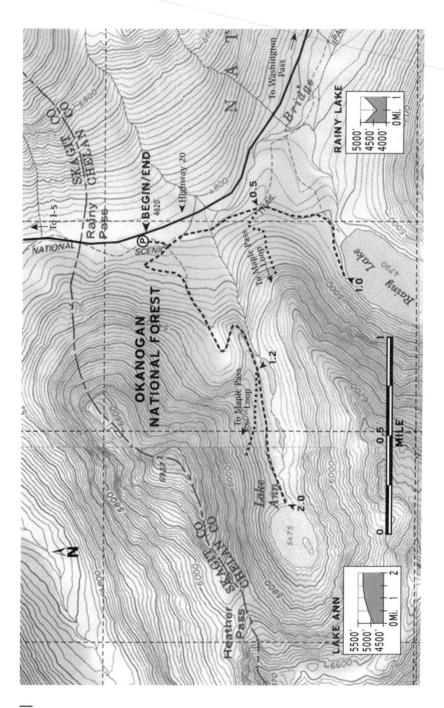

Rainy Lake on a rainy day.

guide that is truly wheelchair accessible (though perhaps not by ADA standards), this is it. Hiking both trails would add up to a 5.6-mile walk.

For Rainy Lake, follow the trail into the alpine forest to the southeast as it parallels the North Cascades Highway 20 toward Washington Pass. This excellent pathway is wide enough to allow two hikers to walk abreast, with occasional pullouts for rest stops where wheelchairs might pass each other. It descends very gradually before climbing at the same gradual grade to a junction with a steep trail descending from Maple Pass, 0.5 mile from the trailhead. Keep left and continue on the pavement.

Beyond, the trail—still in view-blocking alpine forest—begins a wide turn to the southwest, where you'll see marshy meadows and the gully of the Rainy Lake outlet. The way climbs a bit and the view through the evergreens opens some to show the unnamed 6,698-foot peak to the south of the lake. A few minutes later and 1.0 mile from the trailhead, you'll arrive at a paved viewpoint overlooking the lake, nestled in a bowl and decorated with a waterfall from a hidden glacier and tiny lake, 2,000 feet above to the west.

Return the way you came. But only after blowing every pixel in your smartphone.

For Lake Ann, take the trail just west of the Rainy Lake Trail. It begins a long, gentle climb to a switchback above the parking area and then starts a steeper climb west into an alpine forest that soon yields peeka-boo views of the peaks forming Heather and Maple Passes above. A mile from the trailhead, the path takes a broad switchback to climb over a wide forested ridge, and then descends slightly to a junction with the Heather Pass Trail. Continue to the left and pass above a marshy tarn, 1.2 miles from the trailhead.

The trail climbs along the lazy Lake Ann outlet stream and can be muddy and slippery in the early summer months. This area also provides ideal breeding grounds for mosquitoes and other nasty bugs throughout the summer, which is why it is always more pleasant after the first frost of fall. At 1.8 miles, you'll find the scenic east end of Lake Ann. If you seek more adventure, scramble along the south shore to the west end of the lake, where you'll find a tiny island—the remnants of a massive ava-lanche from Maple Pass above. Retrace your tracks back to the trailhead.

## GOING FARTHER

You can make a 7.2-mile loop hike by turning right off the Lake Ann Trail at 1.2 miles and climbing to Heather Pass, then traversing the alpine bowl above Lake Ann before climbing again to Maple Pass, 6,850 feet above sea level. In all, you'll climb 2,150 feet before beginning a 2.5-mile descent to the aforementioned junction with the Rainy Lake Trail.

# 5. Cutthroat Pass

| | |
|---|---|
| RATING | 🚶🚶🚶🚶🚶 |
| DISTANCE | 10.0 miles round-trip |
| HIKING TIME | 7 hours |
| ELEVATION GAIN | 2,050 feet |
| HIGH POINT | 6,820 feet |
| EFFORT | Knee-Punishing |
| BEST SEASON | Late summer, fall |
| PERMITS/CONTACT | Northwest Forest Pass required/ Okanogan-Wenatchee National Forest, (509) 996-4003, www.fs.usda.gov/okawen |
| MAPS | USGS Washington Pass; Green Trails Washington Pass 50 |
| NOTES | Leashed dogs and mountain bikes welcome; road closed in winter |

## THE HIKE

This is among the longest and most difficult hikes in this guide, but if you take your time, practice your "rest step," and enjoy the alleged spectacular view at the top, you won't have time to think about all those aching muscles and sore knees. Visit in summer for wildflowers or wait until the larches turn golden in the fall.

## GETTING THERE

From I-5 and Sedro-Woolley, follow the North Cascades Highway 20 for 158 miles to Rainy Pass and turn left just across the road from the Rainy Pass Picnic Area at the Pacific Crest Trail access sign, which leads to a big parking lot and the trailhead. If you're driving from Winthrop, follow Highway 20 west over Washington Pass to Rainy Pass and the trailhead on the right, 4,800 feet above sea level. GPS coordinates: N48°30′53.2″; W120°44′14.1″

## THE TRAIL

Here's your first chance in this guide to hike part of the 2,650-mile Pacific Crest Trail. This wilderness path stretches from Mexico to Canada and, as of 2014, had been walked end-to-end by Seattle hardbody

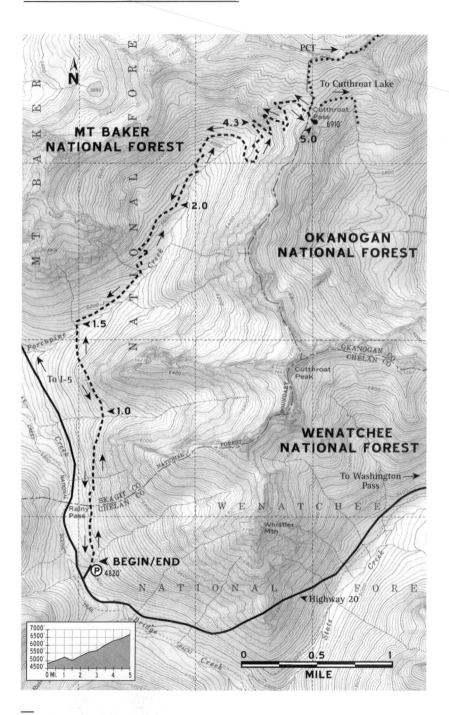

A waterfall along the Cutthroat Pass Trail.

Joe McConaughy in 53 days, 6 hours, and 37 minutes. You needn't hurry—you only have to climb 5 miles on the PCT, then return for a well-earned rest and ice-cold beverage at the trailhead.

The best part of this trail is that it does most of its climbing in the shade of an evergreen alpine forest and is moderately graded for the first 3.5 miles before it gets serious about climbing. It is in this last 1.5 miles to the summit of the pass that I practice the ageless mountaineering technique known as the rest step. It's simple: as you stride forward on the right foot, pause for an instant on your trailing left foot before advancing it. Surprisingly, this briefest of pauses after each step will allow you to walk much farther than you might imagine without fatigue. My wife, B. B. Hardbody, says that when I practice the rest step, I do a lot of resting and very little stepping. But what does she know?

Begin by climbing on a gentle grade through the forest as the traffic noise of the North Cascades Highway gradually fades below. You'll cross a couple of small creeks and an avalanche chute that I have been told provides a view of Fisher Peak to the west. Because on my hike the fog was thicker than Santa's beard, and it was raining hard enough to drown a trout, I could only see as far as my next muddy rest step.

You'll cross a stream with a pretty little waterfall at 1.0 mile, then hike another half mile to noisy Porcupine Creek. Cross the creek on boulders and turn upstream, climbing a bit steeper now. The path climbs directly up the slope above a shallow gully for about a mile in broad, round switchbacks before entering alpine meadows 2.8 miles from the trailhead.

This is a good spot to settle into serious rest step practice, because the trail begins a series of steep switchbacks to gain a traverse around the side of a steep mountain bowl. About the time you catch your breath, 4.3 miles from the trailhead, you'll find a final set of steep switchbacks decorated with granite boulders and alpine larches—those high-mountain trees that resemble evergreens until fall, when their needles turn golden and shiver to the ground.

Reach the summit 5.0 miles from the trailhead. The Pacific Coast Trail turns north here, while the Cutthroat Pass Trail drops steeply to Cutthroat Lake and the North Cascades Highway. The view from the summit is spectacular (I'm told), with views of Silver Star Mountain 8,876 feet high to the south and the Methow Valley toward the sunrise.

## GOING FARTHER

If you've two cars or can arrange for a pickup at the Cutthroat Lake trailhead, you can continue over the pass, dropping in steep switchbacks to a junction with the Cutthroat Lake Trail and following it to the trailhead, 8 miles east of Washington Pass on the North Cascades Highway and 1 mile up the Cutthroat Lake Road. Total distance is 11.2 miles.

## MORE NORTH CASCADES NATIONAL PARK HIKES

🚶 **Thornton Lake,** 10.4 miles round-trip, Prepare to Perspire. Trailhead located 5 miles on rough road from mile 117 on the North Cascades Highway 20.

🚶 **Sourdough Mountain,** 10.4 miles round-trip, Knee-Punishing. Trailhead in Diablo off the North Cascades Highway 20. Turn at mile 126.

🚶 **Pyramid Lake,** 4.2 miles round-trip, Prepare to Perspire. Trailhead near mile 127, North Cascades Highway 20.

🚶 **Easy Pass,** 7.4 miles round-trip, Knee-Punishing. Trailhead at mile 151, North Cascades Highway 20.

🚶 **Bridge Creek,** 7.0 miles round-trip, Prepare to Perspire. Trailhead south of the North Cascades Highway 20, 2 miles east of Rainy Pass, at mile 159.

🚶 **Blue Lake,** 4.4 miles round-trip, Moderate Workout. Trailhead at mile 161, North Cascades Highway 20.

The view from Iceberg Point (#6) curiously lacks any icebergs.

# SAN JUAN ISLANDS NATIONAL MONUMENT

Welcome to the newest national monument in Washington State, designated in 2013 and encompassing more than 950 acres of Bureau of Land Management property in the San Juans. With more than 450 islands and rocks, the San Juan archipelago is a popular boating destination for sailors everywhere along the West Coast and British Columbia.

The monument and the hike that follows lie under the rain shadow of the Olympic Mountains, serving up relatively dry weather compared to Vancouver Island or the Washington coast. Mount Constitution, the highest point in the San Juan Islands at 2,400 feet, is within the monument boundaries but part of Moran State Park, a huge camping park with more than 30 miles of hiking trails.

When it was created by President Barack Obama, the boundaries of the monument encompassed all the San Juans, but management by the Bureau of Land Management was reserved only to the lands it oversees. These lands are scattered over a number of islands and include small parcels that may be difficult to reach except by water, but a number of historical sites and geologically interesting areas can be visited by pedestrians. One such area is Iceberg Point on Lopez Island.

# SAN JUAN ISLANDS NATIONAL MONUMENT

6    Iceberg Point

# 6. Iceberg Point

| | |
|---|---|
| RATING | 🚶🚶🚶🚶 |
| DISTANCE | 3.4 miles, round trip |
| HIKING TIME | 2 hours |
| ELEVATION GAIN | 100 feet |
| HIGH POINT | 110 feet |
| EFFORT | Easy Walk |
| BEST SEASON | Spring, fall |
| PERMITS/CONTACT | None/San Juan Islands National Monument, (360) 468-3754, www.sanjuanislandsnca.org |
| MAPS | USGS Richardson |
| NOTES | Portion of trail passes through private property |

## THE HIKE
Walk along a salmonberry lane to expansive mountain and marine views, where orcas might be seen in early summer and fall.

## GETTING THERE
From I-5 in Burlington, follow Highway 20 west to Anacortes and take the ferry to Lopez Island. From the Lopez Island ferry terminal, follow Ferry Road 2.1 miles to Center Road and turn left. Drive about 5.6 miles on Center Road, turning left to Mud Bay Road. Follow Mud Bay Road to the right and drive 2.6 miles to Mackaye Harbor Road. Turn right onto Mackaye Harbor Road and drive 1.8 miles to a parking lot and trailhead at Agate Beach County Park, 41 feet above sea level. GPS coordinates: N48°25′43″; W122°52′38″

## THE TRAIL
From the county park, walk north along the gravel road to a gated dirt road on the right, 0.3 mile from the trailhead. This portion of the walk is on private property; please stay on the trail.

If it's still there, you'll spy a saw mounted high on a utility pole pointing to the trail and Iceberg Point. Follow the road for about 500 feet to a second junction and take the path to the left along an old roadbed lined with salmonberry bushes.

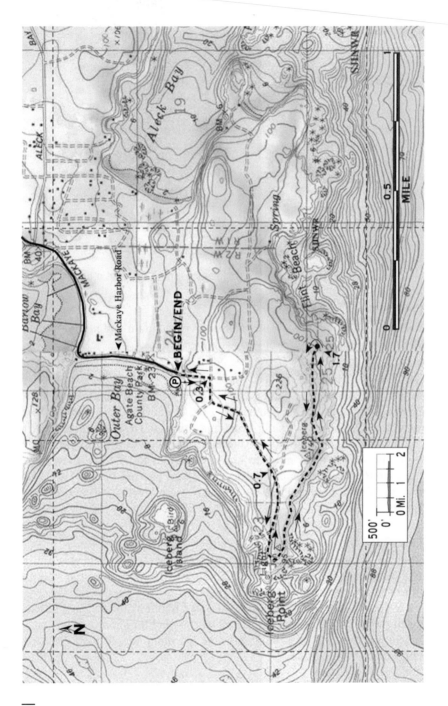

Ospreys keep a lookout for food around Iceberg Point.

After walking **0.7** mile from the trailhead, you'll emerge onto a rocky bluff overlooking Haro Strait, San Juan Island, and Rosario Strait, where orcas can often be seen just offshore during early summer and fall. A number of boot-beaten paths lead along the bluffs toward Iceberg Point to the west and along the edge of the bluff to the east.

You'll enjoy splendid views to the east and south of Mount Baker and the North Cascades, to the west toward Vancouver Island, and southwest to the Olympic Mountains. In short, there's something to see in just about any direction you look.

After exploring the several trails that lead west to Iceberg Point, turn to the east to find a trail along the edge of the bluff towards Flint Beach. You can follow this path to your turnaround point, **1.7** miles from the trailhead.

## MORE SAN JUAN ISLANDS NATIONAL MONUMENT HIKES

🚶 **Mountain Lake,** Moran State Park, Orcas Island, 4.0-mile loop, Moderate Workout. Trailhead at Mountain Lake Campground.

🚶 **Mount Constitution,** Moran State Park, Orcas Island, 7.2 miles round-trip, Knee-Punishing. Trailhead at Cascade Lake day-use area.

The saw points the way up the trail.

Tarn above Royal Lake (#14).

# OLYMPIC NATIONAL PARK

No other national park in the Northwest—or Lower 48—offers as much diversity for both hikers and tourists as Olympic National Park. Hikers can enjoy more than 600 miles of trails, which is about six times the road mileage within the park. Nearly all of those trail miles are located within the designated wilderness area in Olympic, which encompasses more than 90 percent of the park.

That wilderness includes 73 miles of Pacific Ocean coastline that looks very much the same as it did when European explorers first saw it more than two centuries ago. The interior wilderness of the park wasn't explored until 1889—a scant two decades before Robert Peary visited the North Pole. US Highway 101 circles the park, but few roads penetrate the wild emerald interior, which is both good news and bad news for the day hiker.

The bad news really isn't all that bad: some of the wilderness trails outlined here begin or traverse Olympic National Forest, which supports five designated wilderness areas. So the good news is that it doesn't matter whether you're hiking in forest or national park unless you'd like to take Fido along, in which case you must limit your walks to the forest. Even so, the park allows leashed dogs on a couple of beach walks outlined here.

You'll hear a lot about the rainfall on the Olympic Peninsula, and if you plan to hike here, it's always good to pack an umbrella or rain gear. But thanks to those splendid snow-capped Olympic Mountains, you'll be much drier by taking your Olympic hikes on the north and east sides of the park.

There, the amount of rainfall is dramatically reduced by the rainshadow. The mountains form a barrier to rain-soaked clouds from the southwest, where most of the precipitation falls. Mount Olympus, the summit of the Olympic Peninsula, records more than 200 inches of rain every year. But folks in Sequim (Sequimites? Sequimians?), only 30 miles to the northeast, only see about 17 inches of rain annually. So if it's raining along the coast, try some of the hikes south of that community or along the northern parts of Hood Canal.

The Olympic hikes in this guide begin along Highway 101 at the south end of Hood Canal and continue counterclockwise, following the highway around the Olympic Peninsula. Directions are provided from I-5; skip to the nearest community off Highway 101 if you're already in the area.

# OLYMPIC NATIONAL PARK

7  South Fork,
   Skokomish River

8  North Fork,
   Skokomish River

9  Shady Lane Trail

10 Big Hump

11 Dosewallips Road

12 Lower Big Quilcene Trail

13 Camp Handy

14 Royal Lake Trail

15 Lower Gray Wolf Trail

16 Dungeness Spit

17 Hurricane Hill

18 Elk Mountain

19 Elwha Loop

20 Spruce Railroad Trail

21 Pacific Ocean Beaches

# 7. South Fork, Skokomish River

| | |
|---|---|
| RATING | 🚶🚶 |
| DISTANCE | 6.0 miles round-trip |
| HIKING TIME | 3 hours, 30 minutes |
| ELEVATION GAIN | 350 feet |
| HIGH POINT | 850 feet |
| EFFORT | Moderate Workout |
| BEST SEASON | Spring; open year-round |
| PERMITS/CONTACT | Parking pass required/ |
| | Hoodsport Information Station, |
| | (360) 877-5254, www.fs.fed.us/r6/olympic |
| MAPS | USGS Mount Tebo; Green Trails Mount Tebo |
| NOTES | Leashed dogs and mountain bikes welcome |

## THE HIKE

Although this walk begins with a short, steep climb followed by an equally steep descent, you'll get plenty of time to catch your breath on the flat river-bottom trail that follows.

## GETTING THERE

From I-5 in Olympia, take exit 104 and follow Highway 101 north past Shelton for 7 miles to the Skokomish Valley Road, milepost 340, and turn left. Follow the Skokomish Valley Road for 5 miles to a Y intersection and keep right on Forest Road 23. This mostly paved road climbs 9 miles to a junction with Forest Road 2353, where you'll turn right and go downhill to the Skokomish River Bridge. Cross the bridge and turn left to the trailhead, about 0.1 mile upstream from the bridge, 580 feet above sea level. GPS coordinates: N47°25'08"; W123°19'45"

## THE TRAIL

If you've been in hibernation all winter and choose this mostly easy walk for a spring tune-up, prepare to take the first 0.4 mile at a snail's pace. The first 0.2 mile is so steep that you can almost spit on the trailhead parking area below, which I would not advise as there may be other hikers below you, prone and suffering.

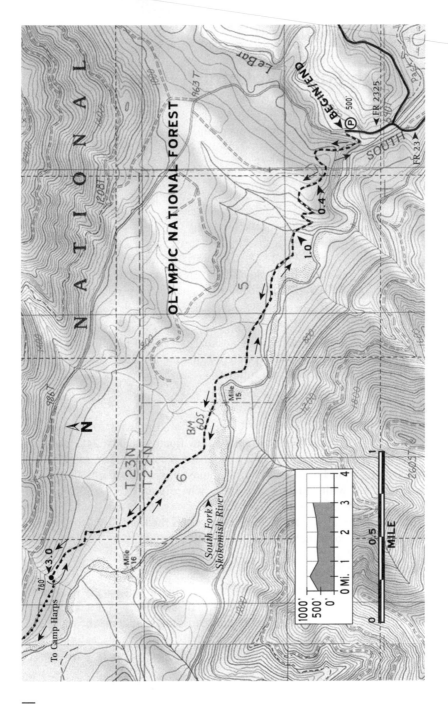

Early spring along the South Fork of the Skokomish.

But once past the first 150 vertical feet, the trail flattens a bit and climbs past a trail junction at **0.4** mile. The right fork leads to the LeBar Horse Camp; you'll stay left and climb more gently to a second trail junction, staying left again, and at **0.6** mile, reach the crest of a ridge overlooking the South Fork of the Skokomish River. You'll round the ridge and begin descending in switchbacks through a massive ancient forest alight in spring from the glow of hundreds of trillium blossoms.

Cross a creek at **1.0** mile and find the alder and maple forest of the river valley, where the trail first passes a riverside camp at **1.2** miles before meandering away from the river and into the forest. If you're hiking with youngsters, the riverside camp makes a good turnaround spot.

Farther on, the trail continues along mostly flat valley floor under moss-draped maple and alder under the occasional shade of a massive ancient cedar. Small creeks cross the trail along the way before you arrive at the site of the 1890s Rufus LeBar homestead, **2.0** miles from the trailhead. This is a good picnic area and another turnaround spot for younger (or perhaps older) hikers.

Beyond, the trail once again wanders away from the river, but never so far that it can't be heard. You'll climb a gentle grade and descend to the river flats, cross a wide rocky outwash, and arrive at a bridge crossing a side creek, **3.0** miles from the trailhead. This is a good spot for a picnic and to turn back. For a riverfront seat, follow the rocky outwash down to the river.

## GOING FARTHER

You can walk another 2.0 miles on the trail, climbing over a side ridge and passing several creek crossings to a junction with a trail connecting to the road above, to the right, **4.2** miles from the trailhead. Turn left, pass Camp Comfort on the left, and climb to a bluff overlooking the river upstream, **5.0** miles from the trailhead.

# 8. North Fork, Skokomish River

| | |
|---|---|
| RATING | 🚶🚶 |
| DISTANCE | 2.0-mile loop |
| HIKING TIME | 1 hour, 30 minutes |
| ELEVATION GAIN | 100 feet |
| HIGH POINT | 1,000 feet |
| EFFORT | Easy Walk |
| BEST SEASON | Spring; open year-round |
| PERMITS/CONTACT | Olympic National Park entrance fee required/ Hoodsport Information Station, (360) 877-5254, www.nps.gov/olym |
| MAPS | USGS Mount Steel; Custom Correct Mount Skokomish–Lake Cushman; Green Trails Mount Steel |
| NOTES | Dogs and bikes prohibited; good family hike |

## THE HIKE

This is a most enjoyable springtime walk along two banks of a wild river, where you may have the company of a resident elk herd or share the path with deer.

## GETTING THERE

From I-5 in Olympia, take exit 104 and follow Highway 101 north past Shelton to Hoodsport. Turn left on the Lake Cushman Road and follow it 9 miles to Forest Road 24. Turn left on FR 24 and drive 6 miles around Lake Cushman to the Staircase Ranger Station. Turn right before reaching the ranger station into a wide dirt parking area to find the trailhead at the west end, 825 feet above sea level. GPS coordinates: N47°30′57″; W123°19′141″

## THE TRAIL

This is a gently graded trail that leads through ancient lowland forest where the understory isn't as thick as it is in the rain forest to the west. You can see farther into the woods as you climb above the North Fork of the Skokomish River, where you'll want to keep an eye out for the herd of Roosevelt elk that hangs out in the river valley.

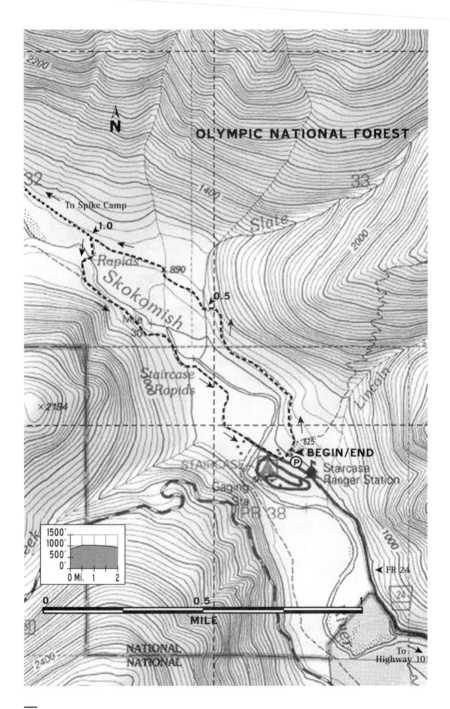

A concrete bridge spans the North Fork of the Skokomish at Staircase.

Begin by climbing the steepest hill you'll encounter on the entire hike, made even more steep because the old road that was once the trail washed out above the ranger station, and the route was moved into the forest to the north. In about 0.1 mile, you'll climb past the washout, which affords an excellent view upriver. Walk another 0.1 mile in forest before regaining the old road on the other side of the washout and continue climbing more gently to a high point above Slate Creek. Stay right at a junction with a nature trail that circles a forested bench upstream from the ranger station.

The trail drops down to Slate Creek and crosses it on a footlog, following a flat river plain in forest above the river. Trees here are massive, and some of the cedars have been around since Columbus landed on the New World. The trail crosses a second creek and traverses the forest for 1.0 mile to a junction with the Staircase Loop Trail.

Turn left and drop down to the river, where you'll find a long suspension bridge across the North Fork. The bridge replaced an old fiberglass span that lasted only one year before it was crushed by heavy snows, and the new span makes a nice spot to settle and watch the river roll to Lake Cushman.

On the other side of the river, you'll climb past a huge overhanging boulder to a junction with the Four Stream Trail, **1.1** miles from the trailhead. Turn left here, and walk downstream past the Staircase Rapids and Dead Horse Hill, named after a pack animal in the O'Neil exploring party that reportedly went to the great hay barn in the sky while climbing the trail you are descending. That was way back in 1890, when Lt. Joseph O'Neil and his party blazed the trail you are hiking.

At **1.7** miles from the trailhead, you'll reach the bottom of Dead Horse Hill and stroll along forest flats past a trail on your right leading to the remains of one giant cedar tree. Just beyond, turn past a couple of park buildings to a paved bridge over the river and walk past the ranger station to the trailhead.

## GOING FARTHER

For a longer hike, you can continue past the loop trail junction another 2.6 miles one-way to Spike Camp and the junction with the Flapjack Lakes trailhead. Return the way you came or cross the river at the loop trail junction. The North Fork Trail continues past the trail junction another 6.0 miles to Nine Stream and beyond, over First Divide. Another alternative would be to turn right at the Four Stream Trail junction and follow it another mile to its official end at Four Stream.

# 9. Shady Lane Trail

| | |
|---|---|
| RATING | 🚶🚶 |
| DISTANCE | 3.0-mile loop |
| HIKING TIME | 2 hours |
| ELEVATION GAIN | 120 feet |
| HIGH POINT | 840 feet |
| EFFORT | Easy Walk |
| BEST SEASON | Spring; open year-round |
| PERMITS/CONTACT | Olympic National Park entrance fee required/ Hoodsport Information Station, (360) 877-5254, www.nps.gov/olym |
| MAPS | USGS Mount Steel; Custom Correct Mount Skokomish–Lake Cushman; Green Trails Mount Steel |
| NOTES | Dogs and bikes prohibited on park section; short wheelchair-accessible loop at trailhead |

## THE HIKE

Here's a nice walk along a historic trail to the edge of Olympic National Park, where elk can often be seen on the river flats below, and where you can return on a road or turn back for a forest walk.

## GETTING THERE

From I-5 in Olympia, take exit 104 and follow Highway 101 north past Shelton to Hoodsport. Turn left on the Lake Cushman Road and follow it 9 miles to Forest Road 24. Turn left on FR 24 and drive 6 miles around Lake Cushman to the Staircase Ranger Station. Turn right before reaching the ranger station into a wide dirt parking area to find the trailhead at the west end, 825 feet above sea level. GPS coordinates: N47°30′57″; W123°19′141″

## THE TRAIL

Like the North Fork Trail (hike #8 in this book), the Shady Lane Trail makes an excellent hike for those camped at the park's Staircase Campground. From the campground or the trailhead, cross the paved bridge over the North Fork of the Skokomish River and turn left on the Shady Lane Trail. A portion of this trail is supposed to be wheelchair accessible,

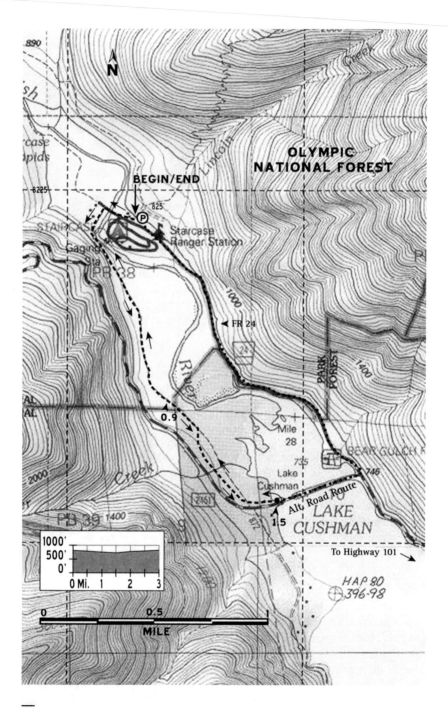

Hikers can cross the bridge at Bear Gulch, shown here, or turn back the way they came on the Shady Lane Trail.

but when I attempted it years ago while trying to find out what wheelchair hiking was all about, I failed miserably and came close to rolling off into the river.

The trail crosses river flats past a couple of Olympic National Park buildings before climbing across rock cliffs above the river past a hole in the rock that seems to fascinate children enough that proceeding farther could lead to trauma. Telling them they may see an elk herd farther on could help, so walk downstream across the river from the campground and above river flat forests of alder and maple.

This wide plain is one of the favorite spots of a resident elk herd in the spring, and a good place to stray off the trail to the river's edge. It was once the site of a Seattle Mountaineers' outing camp and is believed to have been one of the spots Lt. Joseph O'Neil camped when his exploring party blazed the trail in the early 1890s.

Farther on, **0.9** mile from the trailhead, you'll arrive at the boundary of Olympic National Park and Forest. Look for a trail that branches and climbs to the right and in a few hundred feet emerges on Forest Road 2457. Turn left and descend the road to the west end of Lake Cushman and a causeway that crosses the lake to Forest Road 24 and the road past Bear Gulch back to the Staircase trailhead.

The causeway is **1.5** miles from the trailhead, and if you prefer quiet forest walking to hiking the road back to the trailhead, turn around at the causeway and return the way you came. Either way, from the causeway the hike is 3.0 miles.

# 10. Big Hump

| | |
|---|---|
| RATING | 🚶🚶 |
| DISTANCE | 7.2 miles round-trip |
| HIKING TIME | 4 hours, 30 minutes |
| ELEVATION GAIN | 1,300 feet |
| HIGH POINT | 1,750 feet |
| EFFORT | Prepare to Perspire |
| BEST SEASON | Spring; open year-round |
| PERMITS/CONTACT | Parking pass required/Hood Canal Ranger Station, (360) 765-2200, www.fs.fed.us/r6/olympic |
| MAPS USGS | Mount Jupiter; Custom Correct The Brothers–Mount Anderson; Green Trails The Brothers |
| NOTES | Leashed dogs welcome |

## THE HIKE

This is the longest, probably toughest workout you'll get in the Olympic Peninsula portion of this guide. Besides a great view from the turnaround point, your reward might be in knowing you can finish a tough hike like this while still breathing.

## GETTING THERE

From I-5 in Olympia, take exit 104 and follow Highway 101 north past Shelton for 37 miles to the Duckabush River Road, Forest Road 2510, at milepost 310. Turn left and follow it 6 miles to Forest Road 2510-060 and turn right to the parking area, 420 feet above sea level. GPS coordinates: N47°41′06″; W123°02′23″

## THE TRAIL

Although this hike is in forest the entire distance, you'll get peekaboo views to the steep hills across the river, and at the top of the notorious Big Hump, break out onto moss-covered rock with a view down the Duckabush River valley to Hood Canal and to St. Peter's Dome, that 4,475-foot-high rock formation to the southwest. The 1,300-foot climb to the top of the Hump may not be along the steepest trail you've hiked, but it could be one of the longest.

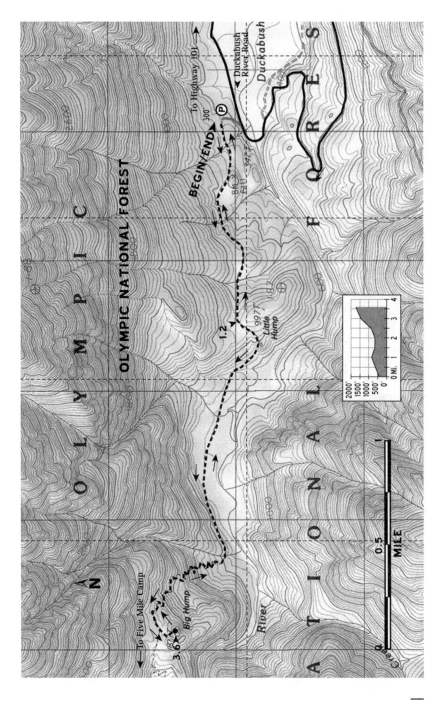

Hikers look down on the cloud-filled Duckabush valley from Big Hump.

The trail begins with a steady, even grade that once was a roadbed to the top of the Little Hump, a barely noticeable 990-foot-high ridge crest in the forest to the left of the trail. You'll probably notice it more on your return, since you've got to climb about 250 vertical feet back over it.

After dropping over the Little Hump, 1.1 miles from the trailhead, you'll walk in quiet forest away from the Duckabush River. You'll cross a stream and hike another mile to the base of the Big Hump, where the path 2.4 miles from the trailhead turns abruptly and begins climbing around the first of about 38 switchbacks. The trail is evenly graded and the distance between turns is about the same, which may make the climb longer than it actually is. Take your time and pause when you need to catch your breath, and you'll be at the top before you know it.

The trail crests a broad notch behind the actual 1,877-foot-high summit of the Big Hump, to the left, 3.6 miles from the trailhead. A way trail leads to the open rock of the summit, and other rock perches provide viewpoints just downhill of the top of the rock. These make a good spot for a rest, a lunch, or a gulp of water, and high fives (or chest bumps, if you've got the strength) before turning around.

## GOING FARTHER

It's difficult to imagine why you'd want to, but you can hike another 2.0 miles one-way to Five Mile Camp on the Duckabush River, keeping in mind that the trail drops almost as much elevation as it gained on the way up to Big Hump. Beyond Five Mile, the trail follows the river for more than 15 miles, making it one of the most popular river backpacks on the Olympic Peninsula.

# 11. Dosewallips Road

| | |
|---:|:---|
| RATING | 🚶🚶🚶 |
| DISTANCE | 5.6 miles round-trip |
| HIKING TIME | 3 hours |
| ELEVATION GAIN | 650 feet |
| HIGH POINT | 1,255 feet |
| EFFORT | Moderate Workout |
| BEST SEASON | Spring; open year-round |
| PERMITS/CONTACT | None/Hood Canal Ranger Station, (360) 765-2200, www.fs.fed.us/r6/olympic |
| MAPS | USGS The Brothers, Tyler Peak; Custom Correct Buckhorn Wilderness; Green Trails The Brothers, Tyler Peak |
| NOTES | Leashed dogs and mountain bikes welcome to park boundary; excellent family hike |

## THE HIKE

It would be difficult to lose your way on this hike because it follows a road that was closed when the river gobbled up a quarter mile chunk of it. The road's loss is your gain: easy walking in wild river forest.

## GETTING THERE

From I-5, take the Seattle-Bremerton, Seattle-Bainbridge, or Edmonds-Kingston ferries to highways connecting to Highway 101, then follow Highway 101 to Brinnon and the Dosewallips Road.

From Brinnon, turn west on the Dosewallips Road and follow it about 10 miles to parking alongside the road at the spot where the road was swallowed up by the river in 2002, 600 feet above sea level. GPS coordinates: N47º44′12″; W123º04′45″

## THE TRAIL

Just east of the washout, you'll find a trail switching back into the forest—the steepest part of this hike. You'll climb above the massive washout to a forested plateau and follow it for 0.2 mile before switching back, again steeply, to the old road. Turn right and follow the old road as it parallels the river upstream.

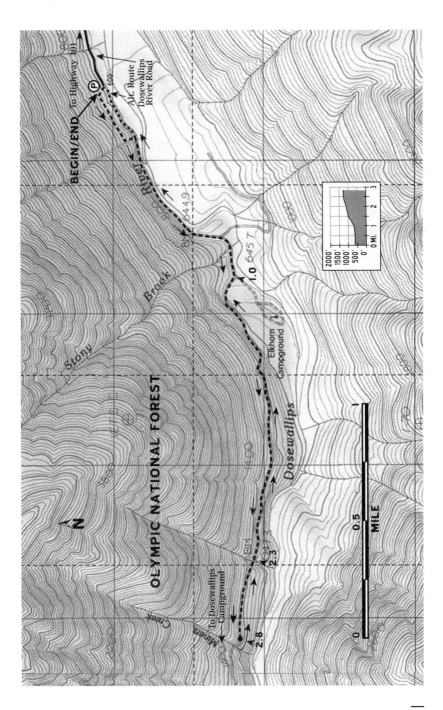

The washed-out Dosewallips Road, shown here, makes a good day hike.

At **0.8** mile, you'll find a junction with an old logging road that crossed the river on a solid concrete bridge. Stay right and continue on the road as it climbs to a second junction with Elkhorn Campground, which the Forest Service closed after the road washed out. The campground is still an excellent spot for a picnic and a turnaround spot for families with young children. Round-trip distance from the campground is 2.2 miles.

Beyond the campground, the road begins to climb on a moderate grade along a hillside decorated with second-growth timber. The river below disappears into a forested canyon as the road climbs over a bench and crosses an unnamed creek, **2.3** miles from the trailhead. Walk another half mile to Miners Creek, where a nice bridge that sometimes crosses the creek, sometimes not, is a good spot for lunch and to turn back.

## GOING FARTHER

The Dosewallips Road travels another 2.7 miles to its end at the old Dosewallips Campground in Olympic National Park. You'll cross from Olympic National Forest into the park just before a trail junction with the notorious Lake Constance Trail, 0.9 mile from Miners Creek.

The road drops steeply down to scenic Dosewallips Falls, 0.6 mile past the Lake Constance trail junction, before climbing even more steeply beside the falls. It then traverses above the river before dropping down to the old riverside campground, **5.8** miles from the trailhead.

# 12. Lower Big Quilcene Trail

|  |  |
|---|---|
| RATING | 🚶🚶 |
| DISTANCE | 5.2 miles round-trip |
| HIKING TIME | 3 hours |
| ELEVATION GAIN | 200 feet |
| HIGH POINT | 1,525 feet |
| EFFORT | Easy Walk |
| BEST SEASON | Spring; open year-round |
| PERMITS/CONTACT | Parking pass required/Hood Canal Ranger Station, (360) 765-2200, www.fs.fed.us/r6/olympic |
| MAPS | USGS Tyler Peak; Custom Correct Buckhorn Wilderness; Green Trails Tyler Peak |
| NOTES | Leashed dogs and mountain bikes welcome; good family hike |

## THE HIKE

This forested walk leads along an old road grade logged long ago to the site of an old hiking shelter beside the Big Quilcene River. Besides hiking, it's a good way to get muddy on a mountain bike in the spring.

## GETTING THERE

From I-5, take the Seattle-Bremerton, Seattle-Bainbridge, or Edmonds-Kingston ferries to highways connecting to Highway 101, then follow Highway 101 to Quilcene.

From Quilcene, drive south on Highway 101 for 1.4 miles to the Penny Creek Road and bear right. Follow Penny Creek Road a short distance to the Big Quilcene River Road, Forest Road 27, and follow it for 3.3 miles to Forest Road 27-080 and turn left. Follow FR 27-080 downhill for 0.4 mile to the trailhead, 1,340 feet above sea level. GPS coordinates: N47°47′01″; W122°57′56″

## THE TRAIL

This hike begins with a gentle downgrade along an old roadbed cut into the hillside through a second-growth forest that is beginning to look like old-growth once again. You'll find occasional openings in the fir canopy

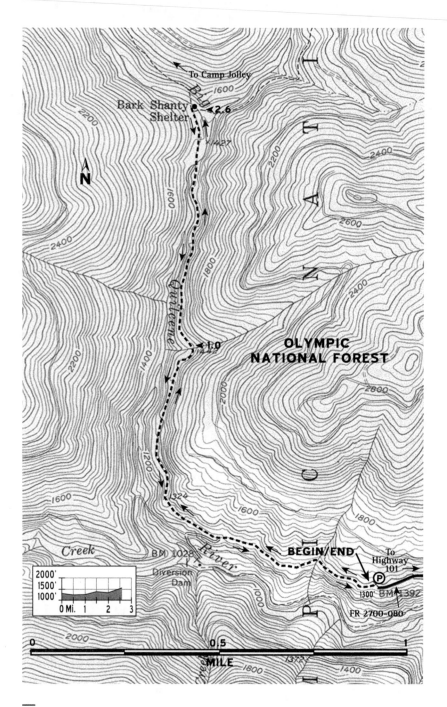

The Big Quilcene River begins in meadows like this.

to look down to the Big Quilcene River below and across to the forested slopes of Mount Crag.

The trail, Forest Trail 833, stays about a 100 feet above the river for more than a mile, crossing a tributary creek at **1.0** mile, the site of several washouts over the past decade. The path then turns north and levels off briefly to traverse the hillside, then begins descending again toward the river. It crosses the river on a plank bridge, **2.5** miles from the trailhead, and climbs to a wide bench above the river, the site of an old shelter called the Bark Shanty, **2.6** miles from the trailhead. This is a good turnaround point, with a wide, open shelf above the river.

## GOING FARTHER

You can follow the trail for another 2.4 miles one-way to Camp Jolley, and continue another mile to an upper trailhead on Forest Road 2750. Hikers (and bicyclists) with two cars can arrange for a key exchange and a one-way trip totaling 6.2 miles.

# 13. Camp Handy

| | |
|---|---|
| RATING | 𝀵𝀵𝀵𝀵 |
| DISTANCE | 6.6 miles round-trip |
| HIKING TIME | 3 hours, 30 minutes |
| ELEVATION GAIN | 600 feet |
| HIGH POINT | 3,120 feet |
| EFFORT | Moderate Workout |
| BEST SEASON | Spring; open three seasons |
| PERMITS/CONTACT | Parking pass required/Hood Canal Ranger Station, (360) 765-2200, www.fs.fed.us/r6/olympic |
| MAPS | USGS Tyler Peak; Custom Correct Buckhorn Wilderness; Green Trails Tyler Peak |
| NOTES | Leashed dogs welcome; good family hike |

## THE HIKE

Walk through forest beside a river that's in a rush to get to the Strait of Juan de Fuca to lounge in a beautiful subalpine meadow you might share with wild critters.

## GETTING THERE

From I-5, it's most convenient to take the Seattle-Bremerton, Seattle-Bainbridge, or Edmonds-Kingston ferries to highways connecting to Highway 101 near Discovery Bay at the junction of Highways 104 and 101.

From the junction, follow Highway 101 north and west from Discovery Bay for 16 miles to the Louella Road, just south of Sequim Bay State Park entrance. Turn left on the Louella Road and drive 1 mile to the Palo Alto Road intersection. Turn left on the Palo Alto Road and drive 4.6 miles, where it becomes Forest Road 28. Follow FR 28 for another 1.1 miles to Forest Road 2880 and bear right on FR 2880. Cross the Dungeness River and drive 1.7 miles to a junction with Forest Road 2870.

Stay left on FR 2870 and drive 2.6 miles to a junction with a road leading to the Gold Creek trailhead. Stay right and drive another 6 miles on FR 2870 to the trailhead. This road makes an excellent mountain drive, climbing almost 3,100 feet above sea level, with views across the Dungeness River canyon and above the road to Tyler and Maynard Peaks.

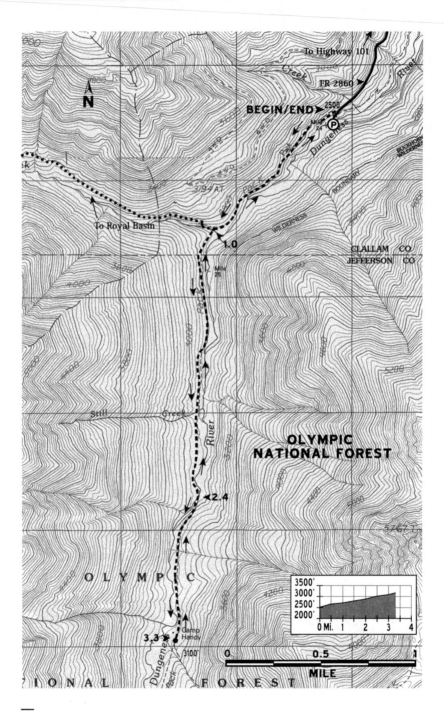

Trillium decorate the forest in early spring on the way to Camp Handy.

The trailhead is 2,500 feet above sea level. GPS coordinates: N47°52′41″; W123°08′13″

## THE TRAIL

Here's one of my favorite hikes in the Olympics. It begins at an elevation that lets you climb into subalpine country without working so hard your legs turn to Greek yogurt. It's within the Olympic Mountain's rain shadow, which means it could be sunny here while Mother Nature launders the west side of the Olympics. In the event some of that water spills across the mountains, you'll find shelter in the forest or in a real wooden three-sided shelter at Camp Handy.

Start by climbing a short switchback from the trailhead that lifts you above the Dungeness River and transports you along a high bank into a mature evergreen forest. Past the first switchback, the trail climbs gently and meanders toward the river flats. You'll round a forested hill above the river and may see signs of a way trail leading up the hill to the right, the remains of a shortcut trail that once led to a closed road above.

At **1.0** mile, you'll arrive at a trail junction where the path comes close to the river. The trail to the right leads to Royal Lake (hike #14 in this guide); you'll turn left and cross a big log bridge. The two watercourses crashing together at this point are Royal Creek on the right and the infant Dungeness River on the left.

After crossing Royal Creek, you'll climb around a hillside where you may see a number of game trails heading off into the woods in different directions. They all lead toward a small mineral lick above the trail, 1.5 miles from the trailhead. Beyond, the trail steepens a bit, then drops back to the river to cross it on a bridge at 2.4 miles.

You'll climb over a forested hill on a slightly steeper trail before traversing through the forest around a wide ridge. At 3.3 miles, look down to the right to find the Camp Handy shelter, which looks out onto a wide meadow with a view of the 6,900-foot-high mountain ridge that separates you from the Royal Basin.

## GOING FARTHER

The meadows at Camp Handy extend upriver for almost 1.5 miles, and you walk along grassy flats and alpine evergreens. Picnic spots abound beside the river. If you're there in the spring, keep a lookout for black bear in the meadows, and families with small children should know that Camp Handy is the decades-old site of a rare cougar attack in the Olympics.

Another alternative for more exercise is to continue up the trail for 3.0 miles one-way to Boulder Shelter, with its fine alpine view of the peaks above Royal Lake and the Gray Wolf Ridge.

# 14. Royal Lake Trail

| | |
|---|---|
| RATING | ♀♀♀♀ |
| DISTANCE | 6.2–14.0 miles round-trip |
| HIKING TIME | 4–8 hours |
| ELEVATION GAIN | 950–2,650 feet |
| HIGH POINT | 3,550–5,100 feet |
| EFFORT | Moderate Workout–Knee Punishing |
| BEST SEASON | Summer, fall |
| PERMITS/CONTACT | Parking pass required/Hood Canal Ranger Station, (360) 765-2200, www.fs.fed.us/r6/olympic; Olympic National Park Wilderness Information Center, (360) 565-3100, www.nps.gov/olym |
| MAPS | USGS Tyler Peak; Custom Correct Buckhorn Wilderness; Green Trails Tyler Peak |
| NOTES | Dogs prohibited on Olympic National Park trail portions |

## THE HIKE

Take this long trek for stunning vistas of the Gray Wolf Ridge and 7,788-foot Mount Deception, second-highest peak in the Olympic Mountains, to an alpine lake and meadow that is among the most beautiful spots in Olympic National Park.

## GETTING THERE

From I-5, it's most convenient to take the Seattle-Bremerton, Seattle-Bainbridge, or Edmonds-Kingston ferries to highways connecting to Highway 101 near Discovery Bay at the junction of Highways 104 and 101.

From the junction, follow Highway 101 north and west from Discovery Bay for 16 miles to the Louella Road, just south of Sequim Bay State Park entrance. Turn left on the Louella Road and drive 1 mile to the Palo Alto Road intersection. Turn left on the Palo Alto Road and drive 4.6 miles, where it becomes Forest Road 28. Follow FR 28 for another 1.1 miles to Forest Road 2880 and bear right on FR 2880. Cross the Dungeness River and drive 1.7 miles to a junction with Forest Road 2870.

Stay left on FR 2870 and drive 2.6 miles to a junction with a road leading to the Gold Creek trailhead. Stay right and drive another 6 miles on FR 2870 to the trailhead. This road makes an excellent mountain drive,

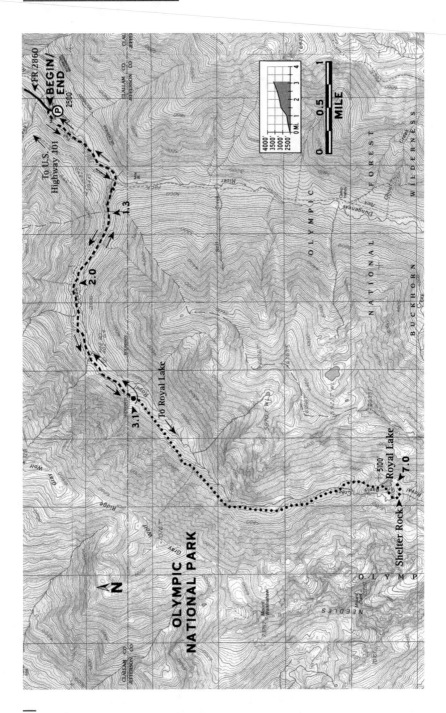

climbing almost 3,100 feet above sea level, with views across the Dungeness River canyon and above the road to Tyler and Maynard Peaks. The trailhead is 2,500 feet above sea level. GPS coordinates: N47°52'41"; W123°08'13"

## THE TRAIL

Royal Lake and its splendid alpine basin is a popular backpacking destination and is one of those wilderness gems that Olympic National Park is protecting with a permit system for overnight stays. There are no restrictions on day hikers, however. You'll share the first mile of this trail with hikers headed toward Camp Handy (hike #13 in this guide), but keep right on the Royal Basin Trail at the bridge crossing the creek.

This is one of those hikes where the destination doesn't matter as much as the journey. Don't skip this walk if the entire 7.0 one-way miles seems a bit too far, because even the first 2.0 miles will yield spectacular views to the Gray Wolf Ridge above and into the Royal Basin and at its head, Mount Deception. Beyond the Camp Handy trail junction, you'll switch back to gain a bit of elevation above churning Royal Creek, then traverse along the lower slopes of Gray Wolf Ridge, on your right. Across the creek, the 6,000-foot ridge that separates Royal Creek and the Dungeness River begins to rise from the forest.

At 1.3 miles, you'll cross into Olympic National Park, where dogs are prohibited from the trails. Although the grade is mostly uphill, the trail is gentle and never gulps large amounts of altitude until the final mile.

Perhaps the best spot to turn around if you don't plan to hike the entire distance would be at a creek crossing and open slide area with wide views upstream, 3.1 miles from the trailhead. The creek tumbles from the rock cliffs of 7,218-foot Gray Wolf Peak directly above. You'll have climbed 950 vertical feet at this spot.

Farther on, the trail continues to traverse the slopes and viewpoints become more numerous as the pathway alternately crosses rocky chutes, slide alder, and creeks bordered by yellow cedar. The next good picnic and turnaround spot might be where the trail turns south above noisy, low falls on Royal Creek below, 4.8 miles from the trailhead. This spot is 4,500 feet above sea level.

If you want to continue, you'll begin a slightly steeper climb before switching back, 5.6 miles from the trailhead, and traversing the hillside to cross Royal Creek, 6.0 miles from the trailhead. Cross the creek and climb around a ridge decorated with alpine evergreens and heather to where the trail traverses across a steep hillside into the Royal Basin. At the head of the basin is Shelter Rock, 6.8 miles from the trailhead, which you'll recognize because it is the only giant boulder you can stand under to stay dry in a rainstorm. You can follow the trail to the left and climb up to Royal Lake at **7.0** miles.

## GOING FARTHER

As difficult as it may be to believe, some strong hikers continue past Shelter Rock, following a Royal Creek tributary on a way trail to Upper Royal Basin. This beautiful alpine meadow, with its own tiny lakes underneath the ice and rock of Mount Deception, is about a mile beyond the lower basin and another 600 vertical feet above.

# 15. Lower Gray Wolf Trail

| | |
|---|---|
| RATING | 🚶🚶🚶 |
| DISTANCE | 4.2 miles round-trip |
| HIKING TIME | 2 hours, 30 minutes |
| ELEVATION GAIN | 300 feet |
| HIGH POINT | 1,380 feet |
| EFFORT | Moderate Workout |
| BEST SEASON | Spring; open year-round |
| PERMITS/CONTACT | Parking pass required/Hood Canal Ranger Station, (360) 765-2200, www.fs.fed.us/r6/olympic |
| MAPS | USGS Tyler Peak; Custom Correct Buckhorn Wilderness; Green Trails Tyler Peak |
| NOTES | Leashed dogs welcome; good family hike |

## THE HIKE

Walk through a second-growth forest to one of the clearest rivers on the Olympic Peninsula, where a number of riverside picnic spots can be found.

## GETTING THERE

From I-5, it's most convenient to take the Seattle-Bremerton, Seattle-Bainbridge, or Edmonds-Kingston ferries to highways connecting to Highway 101 near Discovery Bay at the junction of Highways 104 and 101.

From the junction, follow Highway 101 north and west from Discovery Bay for 16 miles to the Louella Road, just south of Sequim Bay State Park entrance. Turn left on the Louella Road and drive 1 mile to the Palo Alto Road intersection. Turn left on the Palo Alto Road and drive 4.6 miles, where it becomes Forest Road 28. Follow FR 28 for another 1.1 miles to Forest Road 2880 and bear right on FR 2880. Cross the Dungeness River and drive 1.7 miles to a junction with Forest Road 2870. Bear right here and descend to a crossing of the Gray Wolf River, following FR 2870 for another 1.7 miles to the trailhead on the left, 1,400 feet above sea level. GPS coordinates: N47°58'01"; W123°07'38"

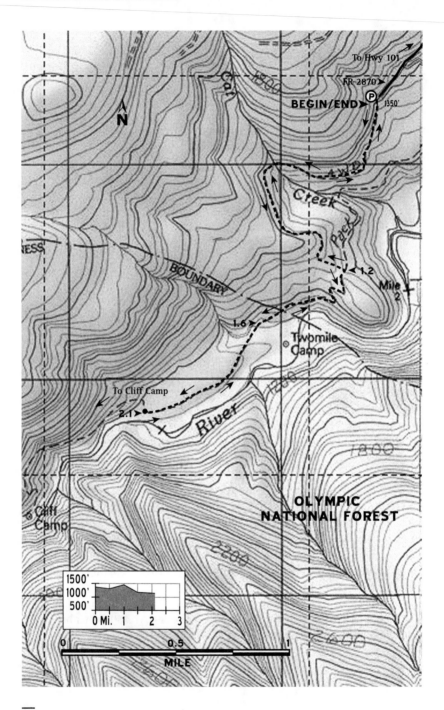

## THE TRAIL

This hike begins on an old logging road in what some might call dog hair forest—thin-trunked, close-packed fir and hemlock all fighting with one another to reach the sunlight. The road traverses a hillside and soon becomes a single path heading on a gentle grade downhill, with occasional views through the trees to the river gorge below and the Buckhorn Wilderness across the canyon.

After walking a half mile, you'll find a loop trail that drops steeply downhill to the left, and you'll keep right to cross Cat Creek **0.6** mile from the trailhead. The forest is older here and the pathway is likely to be a bit less muddy than the first section. Round the Cat Creek canyon and drop to a forested saddle to rejoin the loop trail at **1.1** miles. From here, the trail drops in steep switchbacks down to a flat bench above the river. Two Mile Camp, a riverside rest stop and old campsite, is off the trail to the left, **1.6** miles from the trailhead.

The flat section of trail beyond serves up some of the best riverside picnicking in the eastern Olympics. With the help of a "rain shadow" umbrella, you and your pâté de foie gras are more likely to have sunshine for company. After about a half mile, the trail turns away from the river and climbs a forested bank. This spot, **2.1** miles from the trailhead, is a good place to turn around.

## GOING FARTHER

You can hike another 1.5 miles along the river to a narrow gorge where a high footbridge once crossed the river for a round-trip hike of 7.2 miles. The trail traverses a steep hillside above the river to Cliff Camp, **2.6** miles from the trailhead, then descends to a bench along the river canyon, crossing Twin and Sutherland Creeks before reaching the end of the trail.

# 16. Dungeness Spit

| | |
|---|---|
| RATING | 🚶🚶🚶🚶 |
| DISTANCE | 6.4 miles round-trip |
| HIKING TIME | 3 hours, 30 minutes |
| ELEVATION GAIN | 110 feet |
| HIGH POINT | 120 feet |
| EFFORT | Easy Walk |
| BEST SEASON | Winter; open year-round |
| PERMITS/CONTACT | Trail fee required/Dungeness National Wildlife Refuge, (360) 457-8451, www.fws.gov/refuge/dungeness |
| MAPS | USGS Dungeness |
| NOTES | Dogs prohibited; wheelchair accessible first 0.5 mile; spit closed 30 minutes before sunset |

## THE HIKE

Here's an easy walk along a sandy spit you'll share with wildlife ranging from hundreds of bird species and marine creatures. Watch ships from all nations pass the Strait of Juan de Fuca, or US Navy aircraft carriers or Trident submarines headed to or from the Pacific.

## GETTING THERE

From I-5, it's most convenient to take the Seattle-Bremerton, Seattle-Bainbridge, or Edmonds-Kingston ferries to highways connecting to Highway 101 near Discovery Bay at the junction of Highways 104 and 101.

From the junction, follow Highway 101 north and west past Sequim via the 101 bypass (or follow the old highway through town). Cross the Dungeness River and drive 5 miles to the Kitchen-Dick Road. Turn right and drive 3.3 miles to a right turn on Lotzgesell Road. Follow Lotzgesell Road for 0.2 mile to the Dungeness National Wildlife Refuge entrance on the left at Voice of America Road.

Follow the main refuge road a mile through the refuge and Dungeness Campground to a wide parking area at the trailhead, 120 feet above sea level. GPS coordinates: N48°08′29″; W123°11′25″

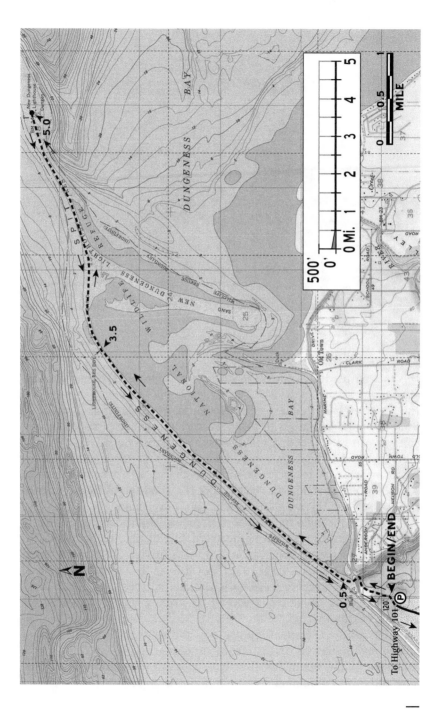

The Dungeness Spit stretches for more than 5 miles along the Strait of Juan de Fuca.

## THE TRAIL

This is a terrific beach walk, especially if you haven't the time or inclination to drive out to the wild Pacific beaches of Olympic National Park. The Strait of Juan de Fuca serves up flocks of marine and shore birds, seals share the beaches with hikers, a constant parade of ships pass by, and you can gaze at snowy mountains in three directions.

Begin by walking a graveled road, suitable for those who do their hiking in wheelchairs (perhaps with assistance), to a wooden platform 0.5 mile from the trailhead. The big deck is a good spot for surveying the 5-mile-long spit below and turning around wheelchairs.

From here, the wide trail drops steeply down to the sandy spit, where hikers are asked to stay on the northern side of the beach. The southern side is reserved for wildlife, which you can view from several platforms along the spit. A ridge of driftwood lines the top of the spit, and walking is easiest where the sand is wet and compacted. On rare occasions, high tides create but a narrow strip along the sand, making for difficult walking.

Thanks to the Olympic Mountains to the south, which block major rainstorms, Dungeness Spit is one of the sunniest spots on the Olympic Peninsula. While mountains a scant 30 miles to the southwest get more than 200 inches of rainfall a year, the spit gets around 17.

For a pleasant walk, plan to hike to the Dungeness Lighthouse Reservation boundary, 3.1 miles from the trailhead. The spit here makes a broad curve to the east and offers great views up and down the strait, north to Vancouver Island, northeast to snowy Mount Baker, and south to Olympic Mountain peaks.

## GOING FARTHER

For a longer hike, continue another 1.9 miles to the New Dungeness Lighthouse, where volunteers keep watch on the historic working lighthouse. While there, you'll likely find out about the opportunity to be a volunteer lighthouse keeper and spend a week on the spit. For information, visit www.newdungenesslighthouse.com.

# 17. Hurricane Hill

| | |
|---|---|
| RATING | 🏃🏃🏃🏃🏃 |
| DISTANCE | 3.2 miles round-trip |
| HIKING TIME | 2 hours, 30 minutes |
| ELEVATION GAIN | 700 feet |
| HIGH POINT | 5,757 feet |
| EFFORT | Moderate Workout |
| BEST SEASON | Summer, fall; open winter weekends |
| PERMITS/CONTACT | Olympic National Park entrance fee/ Olympic National Park Wilderness Information Center, (360) 565-3100; Olympic National Park Visitor Center, (360) 565-3130, www.nps.gov/olym |
| MAPS | USGS Mount Angeles, Hurricane Hill; Custom Correct Hurricane Ridge; Green Trails Mount Angeles, Mount Olympus |
| NOTES | Dogs and bikes prohibited on trails; wheelchair accessible with assistance |

## THE HIKE

This is the stunning alpine showcase of Olympic National Park. You drive to flower-filled meadows above timberline to marvel at mountains scattered across three compass points, all as wild as they were centuries ago.

## GETTING THERE

From I-5, it's most convenient to take the Seattle-Bremerton, Seattle-Bainbridge, or Edmonds-Kingston ferries to highways connecting to Highway 101 near Discovery Bay at the junction of Highways 104 and 101.

From the junction, follow Highway 101 north and west to Port Angeles and turn left on Race Street. Follow Race Street past the Olympic National Park Visitor Center and turn right on the Hurricane Ridge Road for 5.7 miles to Heart O'the Hills, where you'll pay an entrance fee.

Continue up the Hurricane Ridge Road for 11.8 miles to the Hurricane Ridge Visitor Center and drive through the large parking area past the visitor center to a narrow, paved road that drops along a ridge past a picnic area and up to a parking loop at the trailhead, 1.5 miles from the center, 5,075 feet above sea level. Parking here is limited; if there is no

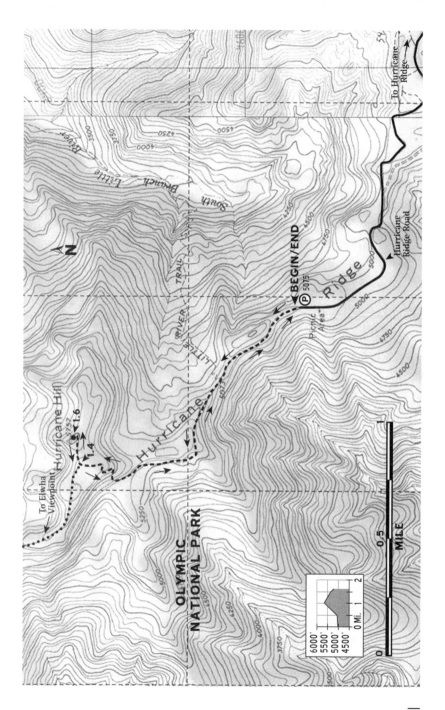

A surprise summer frost decorates trees at Hurricane Hill.

space, drop off your passengers and drive about 0.5 mile back downhill to the larger parking area on the right. Upper parking loop GPS coordinates: N47°58′37″; W123°31′04″

## THE TRAIL
The path to Hurricane Hill is paved to within a quarter mile of the summit, although severe winter frosts have taken their toll on parts of the trail. This isn't likely to be a problem for hikers, but those in wheelchairs will definitely need assistance on some of the steep grades and narrower sections.

Still, on foot or wheels, this is the must-do trail of the high Olympics, even if you only get as far as the picnic area a few hundred feet from the parking lot.

You won't see a single sign of human meddling on the glorious landscape if you look west, south, or east as you walk the trail or stand on the summit of Hurricane Hill. Here was the site of a World War II aircraft spotter's cabin, occupied at least one winter by Herb and Lois Crisler, who filmed one of the first Disney nature movies, *The Olympic Elk*. Looking north, you'll see the Strait of Juan de Fuca and Vancouver Island.

The trail initially drops on a gentle grade to a wide saddle with views to the north, then angles on a steeper grade along an open hillside underneath an unnamed 5,260-foot peak. You'll round a corner into an even steeper bowl where winter snowshoe hikers and cross-country skiers find the warning sign "Steep and Icy." You probably won't find the ice, but the steep is still in abundance. In the summer, scan the wide slopes below for bears searching the meadows for food.

At **0.5** mile, arrive at a junction with the Little River Trail, which climbs steeply from below to join the Hurricane Hill Trail to the left. The trail here crosses a saddle and begins a steep climb along a mostly open hillside to an alpine forest, where it rounds a ridge that may hold snow into midsummer. If you're not already tired of wildflowers, look in the shaded areas for avalanche lilies, and listen for the shrieks of marmots on the open slopes of Hurricane Hill ahead.

You'll emerge from the forest to an open saddle with views across a valley to the southeast to Hurricane Ridge and Mount Angeles and look down upon the Elwha and Lillian River valleys. Long Ridge stretches above the Elwha and points south and west to Mount Carrie, the Bailey Range, and Mount Olympus. The trail begins a steep climb along a ridge, switching back a couple of times to the end of the pavement, **1.2** miles from the trailhead. Climb to a flat saddle below the summit and find a trail leading to the left along the ridge at **1.4** miles. Stay right and continue climbing another 0.2 mile to the summit of Hurricane Hill, 5,757 feet above sea level.

## GOING FARTHER

For a longer walk, follow the trail to the junction 0.2 mile below the summit and turn right. This trail follows a high ridge for around 1.8 miles to a viewpoint overlooking the Elwha River valley, where you may be able to see the remnants of the Glines Canyon Dam and a parking area on the Olympic Hot Springs Road. The viewpoint is a good turnaround spot, making a round-trip hike of 6.8 miles. Beyond the viewpoint, the trail drops very steeply to the Elwha River Ranger Station, 4,400 feet below.

# 18. Elk Mountain

| | |
|---|---|
| RATING | 🚶🚶🚶🚶 |
| DISTANCE | 4.2 miles round-trip |
| HIKING TIME | 3 hours |
| ELEVATION GAIN | 600 feet |
| HIGH POINT | 6,600 feet |
| EFFORT | Moderate Workout |
| BEST SEASON | Summer, fall |
| PERMITS/CONTACT | Olympic National Park entrance fee/ Olympic National Park Wilderness Information Center, (360) 565-3100; Olympic National Park Visitor Center, (360) 565-3130, www.nps.gov/olym |
| MAPS | USGS Mount Angeles; Custom Correct Gray Wolf-Dosewallips; Green Trails Mount Angeles |
| NOTES | Dogs and bikes prohibited on trails; carry water; road closed in winter |

## THE HIKE

You'll climb along the highest trail in Olympic National Park through wildflower meadows with views in every direction including north to Canada and southwest to the glaciers and summit of the Olympic Peninsula, 7,980-foot Mount Olympus.

## GETTING THERE

From I-5, it's most convenient to take the Seattle-Bremerton, Seattle-Bainbridge, or Edmonds-Kingston ferries to highways connecting to Highway 101 near Discovery Bay at the junction of Highways 104 and 101.

From the junction, follow Highway 101 north and west to Port Angeles and turn left on Race Street. Follow Race Street past the Olympic National Park Visitor Center and turn right on the Hurricane Ridge Road for 5.7 miles to Heart O'the Hills, where you'll pay an entrance fee.

Continue up the Hurricane Ridge Road for 11.8 miles to the big parking area at Hurricane Ridge Visitor Center, where you should stop for water if you're not carrying any. As you enter the parking area, look to the left, where a dirt and gravel road drops steeply along a hillside below the main road. This is the Obstruction Point Road, a narrow, winding route

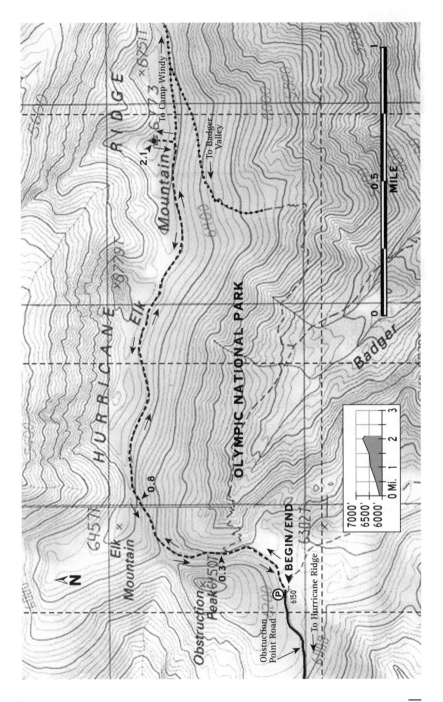

The Obstruction Point Road to the Elk Mountain trailhead isn't usually opened until mid-July.

with turnouts that should be avoided by drivers who are uncomfortable on mountain roads—but it is also one of the most spectacular roads in the entire state. Take a hard left and follow it 7.6 miles to a big parking area underneath 6,450-foot Obstruction Point, 6,101 feet above sea level. GPS coordinates: N47°55′06″; W123°22′55″

## THE TRAIL

This alpine path would easily rate five teeny hikers if the Obstruction Point Road weren't so intimidating for some drivers not used to high, narrow dirt and gravel roadways. The hike is exclusively above timberline, with views in every direction. Olympic marmots, a species unique to the Peninsula, populate the meadows where wildflowers of every color decorate the hillsides.

Two trails begin at the parking area; you'll take the one that begins at the very east end of the parking area and drops down to round the cliffs of Obstruction Point, on your left. This moderately steep trail is carved from the mountainside and crosses a steep snowfield that often lingers through midsummer. Park rangers sometimes thread a rope handline above the route, which is usually dug into the snow. This snowy section is short and often ends at a trail junction climbing steeply up out of Badger Valley, 0.3 mile from the trailhead.

Stay left at the junction and begin a steep climb to a flat saddle below 6,764-foot Elk Mountain. This section of trail is along small, sharp rocks called scree, which may elicit "screems" from those who take one step up and slide a half step back. It's a short climb, however, and **0.8** mile from the trailhead, you'll reach the saddle.

From here, the trail turns east and meanders along flat meadows and south-facing ridges where long and low ridges to the north offer viewpoints to Vancouver Island and the Strait of Juan de Fuca. To the south, look into the Badger Valley and across Grand Pass, and west to the Bailey Range and Mount Olympus. After hiking **2.1** miles from the trailhead, you'll arrive at the turnaround point, a junction with the Badger Valley Trail.

## GOING FARTHER

You can follow the trail to the left, which drops to Camp Windy and passes Maiden Peak before climbing to Deer Park, 5.4 miles from the trail junction. This is a good one-way hike of 7.5 miles for those who have cars parked at Obstruction Point and Deer Park, and exchange car keys at the halfway point at Camp Windy.

Another option is to turn right, and follow the Badger Valley Trail as it drops very steeply 1,200 vertical feet in 1.4 miles to a junction with the Badger Valley cutoff. Turn right and climb just as steeply in 1.0 mile to the junction under Obstruction Point, **0.3** mile from the trailhead. This would make a very strenuous 4.9-mile loop.

# 19. Elwha Loop

| | |
|---|---|
| RATING | 🏃🏃🏃🏃 |
| DISTANCE | 4.8–6.7 miles |
| HIKING TIME | 3–4 hours |
| ELEVATION GAIN | 400 feet |
| HIGH POINT | 1,170 feet |
| EFFORT | Easy Walk–Moderate Workout |
| BEST SEASON | Summer, fall; open year-round |
| PERMITS/CONTACT | Olympic National Park entrance fee/ Olympic National Park Wilderness Information Center, (360) 565-3100; Olympic National Park Visitor Center, (360) 565-3130, www.nps.gov/olym |
| MAPS | USGS Hurricane Hill; Custom Correct Elwha Valley; Green Trails Mount Olympus |
| NOTES | Dogs and bikes prohibited on trails; good family hike |

## THE HIKE

Both long and short loop trails take you down to the Elwha River, now flowing freely from its high mountain snow source to its mouth on the Strait of Juan de Fuca, thanks to the removal of two dams built a century ago.

## GETTING THERE

From I-5, it's most convenient to take the Seattle-Bremerton, Seattle-Bainbridge, or Edmonds-Kingston ferries to highways connecting to Highway 101 near Discovery Bay at the junction of Highways 104 and 101.

From the junction, follow Highway 101 north and west 8.7 miles past Port Angeles to the Olympic Hot Springs Road, just before crossing the Elwha River. If you wish to bypass downtown Port Angeles, turn left on Race Street and follow it to Lauridsen Boulevard. Turn right and follow Lauridsen to its junction with Highway 101 and turn left.

Turn left onto the Olympic Hot Springs Road off Highway 101, just before crossing the Elwha River, and follow Olympic Hot Springs Road for 4.7 miles to a junction with the Whiskey Bend Road, stopping to pay the Olympic National Park entrance fee. Turn left on the Whiskey Bend

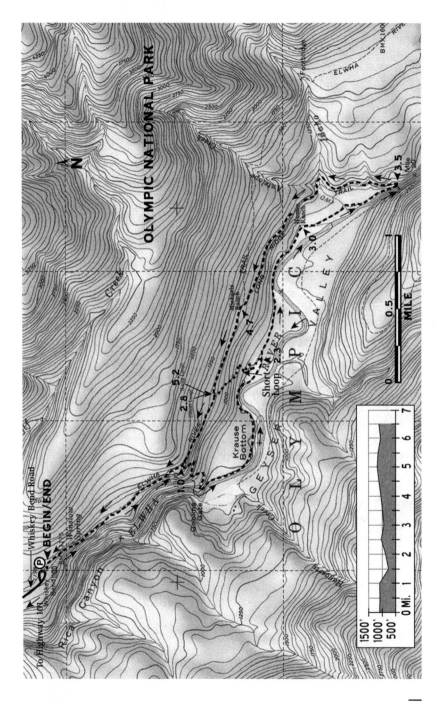

Michael's Cabin, along the Elwha River Trail, was once home to a cougar hunter.

Road, a narrow, winding dirt and gravel route that passes the remnants of the Glines Canyon Dam and ends in a wide parking area 5.0 miles from the Olympic Hot Springs Road junction, 1,170 feet above sea level. GPS coordinates: N47°58′06″; W123°34′59″

Note: In early 2015, a slide closed the Whiskey Bend Road and hikers may have to add 4 miles to their walk if repairs haven't yet been made. Call the center photo numbers provided for current road conditions.

## THE TRAIL

This hike follows the route blazed by the first white explorers up the Elwha River valley and out the Quinault River. The party, sponsored by the Seattle Press, spent the winter of 1889 and summer of 1890 traversing the Olympic wilderness. Pieces of Olympic history can be found all along the route, from the silted bottom of Lake Mills when the Glines Canyon Dam was removed in 2013 to Humes Ranch, settled around 115 years ago by Will Humes.

Begin by following the trail 0.5 mile to an overlook of the Elwha River and flats on the other side where elk are frequently seen. It's a short, steep drop down to the overlook. Stay left and continue along the hillside forested with madrona and other evergreens to a junction with a trail leading to Krause Bottom, **1.0** mile from the trailhead. Turn right and drop in steep switchbacks to a trail junction. To the right is a short, steep trail leading to Goblins Gate, a rocky cliff and rapids named by the Seattle Press Exploring Party.

Turn left at this junction, **1.3** miles from the trailhead, and wander through forest along flats above the river for a mile to another junction with a trail that climbs up to the main Elwha Trail, **2.3** miles from the trailhead. Turn left and climb to the Elwha Trail for the shorter 4.8-mile loop, joining the Elwha Trail in 0.5 mile and turning left to hike 1.4 miles to the trailhead.

Stay right for the longer loop, and walk along increasingly open forest to the clearing 0.7 mile from the trail junction that marks the historic Humes Ranch. You'll pass the cabin Grant and Will Humes called home, then drop to wide, flat fields along the Elwha River, which are popular with backpackers. Cross the fields to a river bend where the Elwha took a bite out of the old trail and dogwood trees blossom in the spring, then climb to a junction with the Dodger Point Trail, **3.5** miles from the trailhead and a short distance downhill to the suspension bridge crossing the Elwha River.

Turn left at this junction and begin a gentle climb through the forest to rejoin the main Elwha River Trail at **4.8** miles. This is the site of Michael's Cabin, occupied a century ago by "Cougar Mike," who as you might guess from the name, did not hunt marmots. Stay left at the trail junction and continue on the main trail. You'll pass the two trail junctions leading down to the river at **5.3** and **5.7** miles, staying to the right and reaching the trailhead at **6.7** miles.

## GOING FARTHER

If you'd like more exercise, turn right at Michael's Cabin and climb another 2.5 miles to the Lillian River crossing, returning the way you came. This would add 5.0 miles, out and back, to your hike.

# 20. Spruce Railroad Trail

| | |
|---|---|
| RATING | 🚶🚶🚶 |
| DISTANCE | 8.2 miles round-trip |
| HIKING TIME | 4 hours, 30 minutes |
| ELEVATION GAIN | 100 feet |
| HIGH POINT | 630 feet |
| EFFORT | Moderate Workout |
| BEST SEASON | Fall; open year-round |
| PERMITS/CONTACT | None/Olympic National Park Wilderness Information Center, (360) 565-3100; Olympic National Park Visitor Center, (360) 565-3130, www.nps.gov/olym |
| MAPS | USGS Lake Crescent; Custom Correct Lake Crescent–Happy Lake Ridge; Green Trails Lake Crescent |
| NOTES | Mountain bikes welcome; dogs prohibited on trail; good family hike |

## THE HIKE

Though fairly long, this walk is mostly level and gently graded because it follows a historic railroad bed along the shores of beautiful Lake Crescent.

## GETTING THERE

From I-5, it's most convenient to take the Seattle-Bremerton, Seattle-Bainbridge, or Edmonds-Kingston ferries to highways connecting to Highway 101 near Discovery Bay at the junction of Highways 104 and 101.

From the junction, follow Highway 101 north and west through Port Angeles. If you wish to bypass the downtown area, turn left on Race Street and drive to Lauridsen Boulevard. Turn right at Lauridsen and drive to its intersection with Highway 101 on the west end of town. Continue on Highway 101 for 16 miles to the East Beach Road and turn right.

Follow the East Beach Road for 3.3 miles, passing the Log Cabin Resort on the left, to Boundary Creek Road and bear left, crossing the Lyre River and following the signs to the Spruce Railroad Trail in another mile. The trailhead is 600 feet above sea level. GPS coordinates: N48°05′31″; W123°48′05″

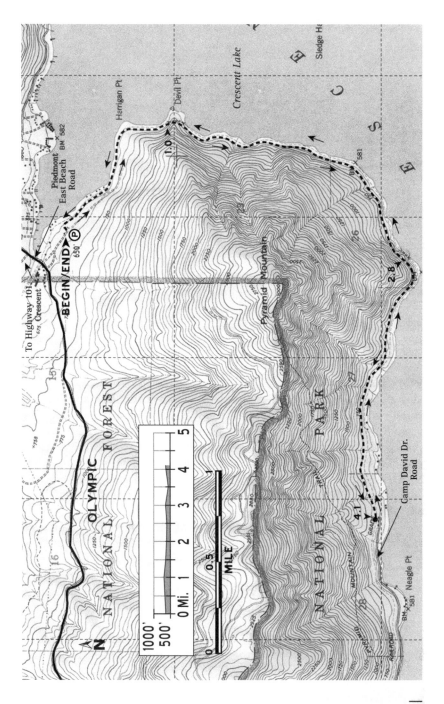

The Spruce Railroad Trail crosses the Devil's Punchbowl.

## THE TRAIL

This trail is popular in the summer with both hikers and single-track bike riders, and with good reason. You'll walk along a mostly flat trail in a shaded forest of evergreens and around hillsides looking down on sparkling Lake Crescent, a 9-mile-long jewel whose waters are so clear you can see Crescenti cutthroat and Beardslee rainbow trout swimming 20 feet under the surface. You don't need a license for catch-and-release-only fishing from shore, a real treat for the kids or grandkids (or those who feel like them).

Begin by following a renovated section of the trail, which is a model of what the entire route will look like in the future. For the first quarter mile, you'll walk a universally accessible 8-foot pathway with a gravel shoulder before dropping down to the old railroad grade. This new trail will eventually be paved for 9.5 miles, pass through two old tunnels now closed for safety, and serve muscle-powered travelers on bikes, boots, wheelchairs, and horses.

Built near the end of World War I to carry the lightweight spruce prized for aircraft plywood to the mills, the railroad served for almost 40 years before it was abandoned in the early 1950s. Today, it's a great way to tour the less-populated side of the lake. After leaving the new section, you'll round Devil Point, 1.0 mile from the trailhead. Look right into the woods for a peek at the first railroad tunnel, while the trail drops to water's edge around the point.

Beyond, you'll cross a metal bridge over the Devil's Punchbowl, a popular swimming hole for youngsters looking to scramble through the poison oak that grows nearby. The bridge might also make the best place to try to catch (and release!) one of those trout.

The trail continues along the lake for another three miles, passing a second railroad tunnel 2.8 miles from the trailhead. The only difficulties hikers might encounter are where the trail cuts through hillside above the lake, making for muddy walking in the spring or fall. It ends 4.1 miles from the trailhead at the Camp David Jr. Road, an alternate spot to begin your hike or a parking area for those who plan a key-exchange hike.

# 21. Pacific Ocean Beaches

| | |
|---|---|
| RATING | 🚶🚶🚶🚶🚶 |
| DISTANCE | 1.0–5.0 miles round-trip |
| HIKING TIME | 1–3 hours |
| ELEVATION GAIN | 100 feet or fewer |
| HIGH POINT | 120 feet |
| EFFORT | Stroll in the Park–Moderate Workout |
| BEST SEASON | Summer; open year-round |
| PERMITS/CONTACT | None/Olympic National Park Wilderness Information Center, (360) 565-3100; Olympic National Park Visitor Center, (360) 565-3130, www.nps.gov/olym |
| MAPS | USGS La Push, Destruction Island; Custom Correct South Olympic Coast; Green Trails La Push |
| NOTES | Leashed dogs welcome at La Push and Kalaloch Beach; excellent family hike |

## THE HIKE
Choose any or all of these eight beach walks for exploring the wild Pacific coastline in Olympic National Park.

## GETTING THERE
From I-5, it's most convenient to take the Seattle-Bremerton, Seattle-Bainbridge, or Edmonds-Kingston ferries to highways connecting to Highway 101 near Discovery Bay at the junction of Highways 104 and 101.

From the junction, follow Highway 101 north and west through Port Angeles to Forks. If you wish to bypass the downtown area, turn left on Race Street and drive to Lauridsen Boulevard. Turn right at Lauridsen and drive to its intersection with Highway 101 on the west end of town.

For Rialto Beach, turn west on the La Push–Mora Road, Highway 110 just outside of Forks, and follow signs to Mora and Rialto Beaches, turning right at Three Rivers Resort. Drive past Mora Campground to Rialto Beach parking area. GPS coordinates: N47°55'11"; W124°38'18"

For Ruby and Kalaloch (say "clay lock") Beaches, continue on Highway 101 through Forks for 35 miles to the Ruby Beach trailhead on the right. GPS coordinates: N47°42'33"; W124°24'51"

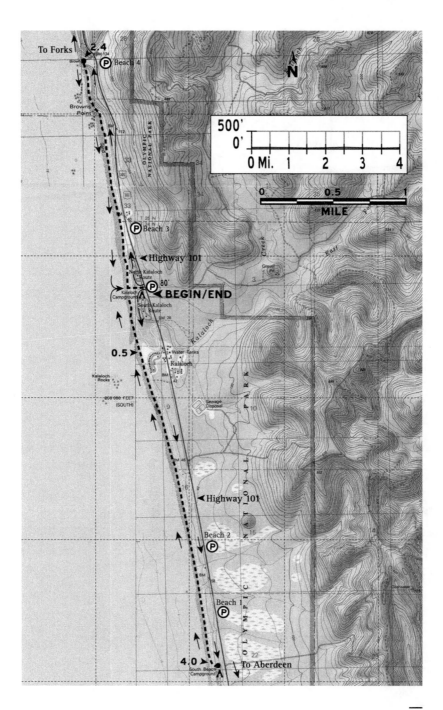

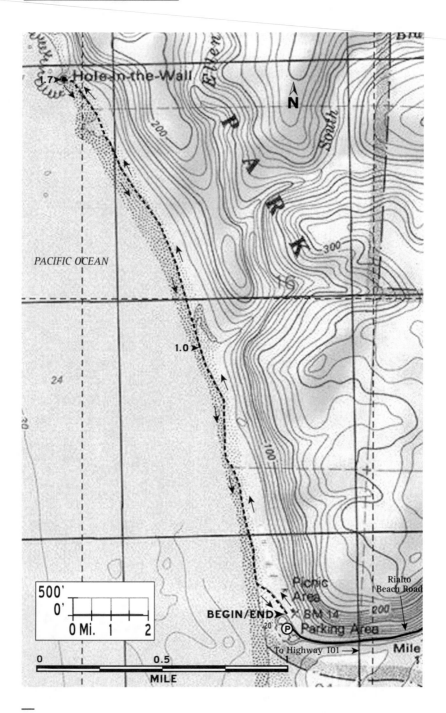

Kalaloch beaches are numbered from north to south beginning with Beach 5, with trailhead parking lots or pullouts along the 11-mile ocean stretch of Highway 101 between Ruby and South Beaches.

## THE TRAIL

Perhaps the most entertaining hike for families is the 3.4-mile walk, out and back, along Rialto Beach to Hole-in-the-Wall, a tunnel carved by the surf that is passable at low tide. Leashed dogs are permitted on the beach as far as Ellen Creek, 1.0 mile from the trailhead. At 1.7 miles, you'll see the rock spanning Hole-in-the-Wall and walk under if it's low tide. If not, the trail climbs a sometimes muddy path over the headland (look for the orange and black target marking the trail) but your beach-walking is finished for a couple of miles.

Ruby Beach, south on Highway 101, is the first of seven beach walks along Highway 101. Those looking for relative solitude might choose Beach 5 or 4; beaches at Kalaloch Lodge are likely the most popular. The longest beach walk, which might include wading several shallow creeks, is the 5.2-mile trek, out and back, from the Kalaloch Lodge to South Beach.

Beach 4 and the rocky pools in front of Kalaloch Lodge might be the best walks for seeing starfish and other tide-pool critters. Beach 1 features a walk through a gnarled spruce forest shaped by coastal winds and weather.

## MORE OLYMPIC NATIONAL PARK HIKES

🏃 The most popular day hike on the ocean might be the 9.3-mile plank trail and beach hike at **Cape Alava**, at the extreme northwest tip of Olympic National Park. Nearby is beautiful Shi Shi Beach and Point of the Arches, an 8-mile walk round-trip, Easy Walk.

🏃 Closer to Rialto Beach at La Push are **Second Beach** and the less-frequented **Third Beach**, Easy Walks of 4.2 and 3.6 miles, respectively. Backpackers can take hikes of 30 miles or more along pristine Pacific beaches.

Silver Falls (#25) from the overlook.

# MOUNT RAINIER NATIONAL PARK

The fifth oldest national park in the United States, Mount Rainier smiles down on half the state with two faces. Above, ice and snow stretch 14,410 feet into the sky while more than 2 vertical miles below, rivers feed forests of fir and cedar that were here before Europeans landed on the shores of America.

Rainier was established in 1899, and its biggest challenge is meeting the mandate of all national parks: to conserve the scenery, history, and wildlife, leaving them unimpaired for the enjoyment of future generations. That is no small task for a park that welcomes more than 1.5 million visitors every year and overlooks tidelands filled with more than 4.2 million people. Yet there are times when day hikers can find themselves alone on a mountain trail watching marmots dance, or in a forest glade trying to see the top of a tree an entire football field above.

You can hike more than 260 miles of trails at Mount Rainier, and most of those pathways host those who take their walks one day at a time. Roads in the park lead to spots a mile above sea level and the trails radiating from places like Paradise and Sunrise stretch to viewpoints where you can actually look down upon glaciers. Along the way, you might spot wildlife that doesn't live anywhere but on this island in the clouds. Mountain goats graze the hillsides of Sourdough Ridge at Sunrise, while pikas pile tiny haystacks for the winter.

In late July and August, short, easy trails can take you to fields of wildflowers so thick you can't see the ground beneath. They push up from under seasonal snowfields that attract diehards riding skis or snowboards and along the edges of prancing creeks bubbling from the remnants of winter.

It should be noted that the season of silence is a fine time to visit Rainier. You can drive from what is most likely a snow-free town to a place like Paradise, where as much as 93 feet of white stuff has been recorded in a single season.

Finally, the earlier you can get to a trailhead at Rainier, the more likely you won't be disappointed on crowded days when you can't find a parking space or get some elbow room on your chosen path. Following are some of the easier day hikes at Rainier, along with some walks that will take your breath away—both for the scenery and the altitude.

# MOUNT RAINIER
# NATIONAL PARK

22  Mount Fremont Lookout

23  Emmons Glacier

24  Grove of the Patriarchs

25  Silver Falls

26  Bench and Snow Lakes

27  Nisqually Vista

28  Skyline Trail

29  Comet Falls

30  Trail of the Shadows

31  Rampart Ridge

32  Westside Road

33  Carbon River Road

34  Naches Peak Loop

35  Pinnacle Saddle

36  Mazama Ridge

# 22. Mount Fremont Lookout

|  |  |
|---|---|
| **RATING** | 🛉🛉🛉🛉 |
| **DISTANCE** | 5.6 miles round-trip |
| **HIKING TIME** | 3 hours, 30 minutes |
| **ELEVATION GAIN** | 900 feet |
| **HIGH POINT** | 7,181 feet |
| **EFFORT** | Prepare to Perspire |
| **BEST SEASON** | Summer, fall |
| **PERMITS/CONTACT** | Entrance fee/Sunrise Visitor Center, (360) 663-2425, www.nps.gov/mora |
| **MAPS** | USGS Sunrise; Green Trails Mount Rainier East 270 |
| **NOTES** | Dogs are bikes prohibited; road closed in winter |

## THE HIKE

You'll probably have company on this climb to a historic fire lookout with a stunning view of the north face of the mountain Native Americans called Tahoma. Mount Rainier day hikers have long accepted the fact that awe-inspiring scenery trumps solitude every time.

## GETTING THERE

From I-5, follow Highways 18 and 164 to Enumclaw, then take Highway 410 about 43 miles to the White River Entrance of Mount Rainier National Park, where you'll be asked to pay a fee. Beyond the entrance, stay right at the junction with the road leading to White River Campground and drive 14 miles to the end of the road at the large Sunrise parking area, 6,400 feet above sea level. GPS coordinates: N46°54′52.9″; W121°38′19.3″

## THE TRAIL

If there's one thing that thins the crowds of hikers on this path—or any of the many Sunrise or Paradise trails—it's the fact that the drive to the trailhead is almost as spectacular as views from the trail. But you came here to wear more cartilage off those old knee joints, so climb out of the car and begin climbing up the paved trail toward Sourdough Ridge. At **0.2** mile, the trail forks and the pavement ends. Take the left fork and

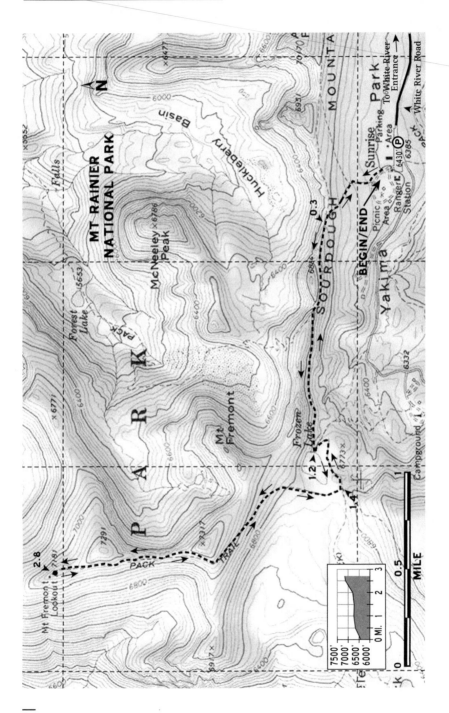

Frozen Lake from the Mount Fremont Lookout trail.

continue climbing for another 0.1 mile to the summit of the ridge and a junction with the Sourdough Ridge Trail.

Turn left here and climb what is likely the steepest part of the trail to the crest of the ridge. It's only about 100 feet or so, and once you reach the top, the views to the north and west will give you an excuse to catch your breath. From this point, the trail alternately climbs and drops more gently through thin alpine forest and ridgeline saddles with views into the Huckleberry Basin to the north. At 1.0 mile from the trailhead, you'll strike a junction with a trail that drops steeply to Forest Lake; keep left.

Next, cross a wide talus slope where park trail crews have built an intricate rock wall to keep gravity from sucking the trail downhill to the marmot villages around Shadow Lake and the beautiful former Sunrise Campground. At 1.2 miles, descend to a junction with a trail leading down to the lake, and keep right to climb around a hill hiding Frozen Lake. You'll find a three-way trail junction and a view of Frozen Lake 1.4 miles from the trailhead.

Take the right fork of the trail to the lookout, which circles the lake—the water supply for Sunrise—and climbs across a wide meadow where you might hear marmots whistle, or perhaps pikas peeping "knee" from the rocks. The trail begins a long uphill traverse across the steep south slope of Mount Fremont, whose summit you'd expect would host the Mount Fremont Lookout. You'd be wrong.

Instead, the trail rounds a rocky 7,317-foot-high peak to the west of Mount Fremont, 2.0 miles from the trailhead, and begins a long traverse along a narrow ridge to the lookout, now visible from the trail for the first time. The trail actually descends slightly as you look out across Berkeley Park to the cliffs of the Willis Wall and ice of Carbon Glacier on Rainier.

At 2.8 miles, you'll arrive at the lookout and can clamber up the steps to a deck with views in every direction. Rainier grabs most of your pixels to the south, but you can look east and north along the Cascade crest and down to the Puget Sound basin, then west to the Olympic Mountains. Crowds? What crowds?

# 23. Emmons Glacier

| | |
|---|---|
| RATING | 🚶🚶🚶 |
| DISTANCE | 3.4 miles round-trip |
| HIKING TIME | 2 hours, 30 minutes |
| ELEVATION GAIN | 850 feet |
| HIGH POINT | 5,190 feet |
| EFFORT | Moderate Workout |
| BEST SEASON | Summer, fall |
| PERMITS/CONTACT | Entrance fee/Sunrise Visitor Center, (360) 663-2425, www.nps.gov/mora |
| MAPS | USGS Sunrise; Green Trails Mount Rainier East 270 |
| NOTES | Dogs are bikes prohibited; good family hike; road closed in winter |

## THE HIKE

It may be hard to convince the kids and grandkids that all that rock you see below the trail is actually covering a giant river of ice, but all you have to do to persuade them is point up to that massive wall of white above, creased with crevasses and occasionally cracking and popping loudly like an ancient pair of giant knees.

## GETTING THERE

From I-5, follow Highways 18 and 164 to Enumclam, then take Highway 410 about 43 miles to the White River Entrance of Mount Rainier National Park, where you'll be asked to pay a fee. Beyond the entrance, turn left at the road leading to White River Campground and drive to the large day-use parking area below the campground, 4,350 feet above sea level. The trailhead is located at the west end of campground Loop D. Parking GPS area coordinates: N46º54′08″; W121º38′31″

## THE TRAIL

That nasty old Emmons Glacier is a massive pain in the you-know-what for those of us who write hiking guides. Just about the time we tell you about the trail, along comes a flood or some other disaster that wipes out a wildland pathway. Thus it was that in 2006, a flood pretty much wiped clean the Emmons Moraine Trail and all the words that described it in

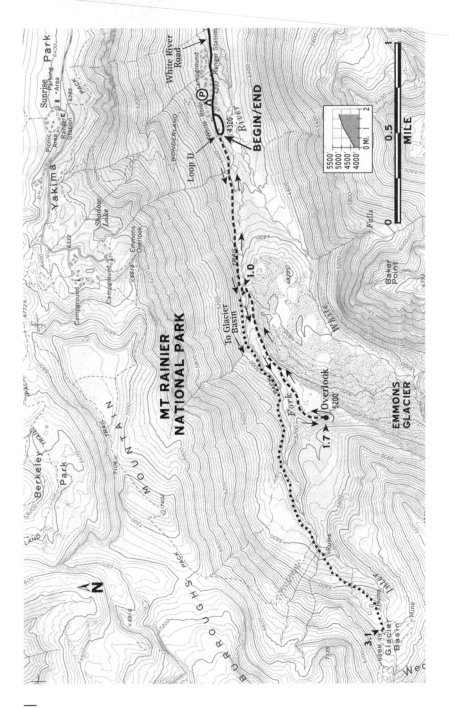

The Emmons Glacier sweeps from Liberty Cap to Rainier under Little Tahoma Peak, left. Inter Glacier is the pyramid-shape peak, center.

various guidebooks. Thanks to Mount Rainier trail crews and more than 400 volunteers who spent the better part of two seasons rebuilding the trail, a few years later we can now hike back to this scenic overlook of the glacier whose surface area is the largest in the Lower 48.

The trail shares bootprints for the first mile with Real Mountain Climbers and hikers headed for Glacier Basin, Inter Glacier, and the summit of Mount Rainier, passing through a subalpine forest and crossing several creeks. The climb is nicely graded and moderately steep for the first **0.9** mile since the new trail was rerouted to higher ground. The trail winds around some humongous boulders, ancient gifts from the retreating glacier and Burroughs Mountain, above you to the north.

At **1.0** mile, you'll arrive at a trail junction and follow the left fork, where a sign points to the Emmons Moraine Trail. Cross a footlog that spans the Inter Fork of the White River, which may discourage younger children or those with balance problems to continue. There's a handrail to steady your way. Once across, you'll climb around a riverbank to look out on the toe of the Emmons Glacier where you might see bright turquoise ponds on the ice surface.

The trail climbs along the crest of the moraine above the glacier, which is blanketed from rockfall and debris from slides. You'll see the birth of the White River, which spits from the snout of the glacier near the end of the maintained trail, 1.5 miles from the trailhead. You can scramble another 0.2 mile or so along the moraine, which is steep, unstable, and perhaps scary for younger children.

## GOING FARTHER

For a longer hike and steeper climb into high mountain meadows and the beginning of the climb of Rainier via the Emmons Glacier, return to the trail junction and turn left. It's 3.1 miles one-way to Glacier Basin and about another mile to the toe of the Inter Glacier, where climbers usually rope up and climb over Steamboat Prow before descending to Camp Schurman.

# 24. Grove of the Patriarchs

| | |
|---|---|
| RATING | 🏃🏃🏃🏃 |
| DISTANCE | 1.25 miles round-trip |
| HIKING TIME | 1 hour |
| ELEVATION GAIN | 80 feet |
| HIGH POINT | 2,200 feet |
| EFFORT | Easy Walk |
| BEST SEASON | Spring, summer; open year-round |
| PERMITS/CONTACT | Entrance fee/Ohanapecosh Visitor Center, (360) 569-6046, www.nps.gov/mora |
| MAPS | USGS Chinook Pass; Green Trails Mount Rainier East 270 |
| NOTES | Dogs and bikes prohibited; good family hike |

## THE HIKE

This short walk is the best example of the other face of Mount Rainier National Park: instead of alpine splendor, an ancient forest forms a green cathedral that inspires awe from all who walk inside. Some of these venerable cedar, fir, and hemlock sprouted before Columbus arrived in America.

## GETTING THERE

Follow Highway 12 for 72 miles east of I-5 through Morton and Packwood (watch out for elk!) to the junction with Highway 123. Turn left and follow Highway 123 to the Stevens Canyon Entrance to Mount Rainier National Park, where you'll pay a fee. From the Seattle or Tacoma area, you can drive to Enumclaw, then follow Highway 410 to Cayuse Pass and take Highway 123 to the Stevens Canyon Entrance. Follow the road to a large and sometimes full parking area on the left—the best reason to arrive early. GPS coordinates: N46°45′26″; W121°33′28″

## THE TRAIL

The best part of this hike for kids might be the bouncy suspension bridge across the Ohanapecosh River, 0.4 mile from the trailhead. They won't be able to play long on the bridge, however, because there's often a line of old folks like me waiting to cross. It's just another reason to plan to

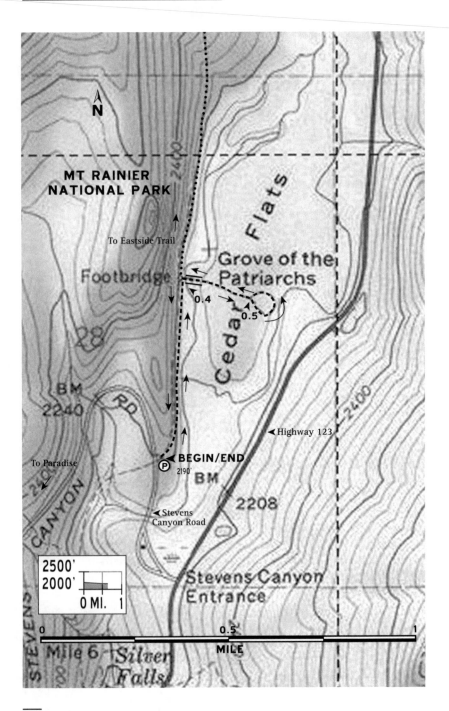

N

MT RAINIER
NATIONAL PARK

To Eastside Trail

Footbridge

Grove of the
Patriarchs

Cedar Flats

0.4

0.5

28

BM
2240

RD

Highway 123

2400

To Paradise

BEGIN/END
2190'

BM
2208

Stevens
Canyon Road

CANYON

Stevens Canyon
Entrance

2500'
2000'
0 MI.  1

STEVENS

0                           0.5                          1

MILE

Mile 6  Silver
Falls

A suspension bridge crosses the Ohanapecosh River to the Grove of the Patriarchs.

arrive early in the morning for this walk; things get pretty busy on this trail around noontime.

The walk to the bridge is a gentle one above the river, passing under several fallen tree giants that won't look so big on your return, once you've seen those Patriarchs. You'll arrive at a junction with the Eastside Trail at the suspension bridge and turn right across the bridge. Handrails are located on both sides and a sign suggests only one person at a time use the span.

Once across, you'll pass the first of the Patriarchs, a huge red cedar on the left. Just beyond, you can climb onto a plank boardwalk that makes walking much easier and saves the forest understory from a whole bunch of trampling feet. The boardwalk circles the grove in about 0.3 mile, and if you were unable to tell the difference between a cedar and Douglas fir before, you'll be able to give a lecture on the subject when you return. When you reach the end of the loop, turn back to the bridge and trail.

## GOING FARTHER

The Eastside Trail on the north side of the suspension bridge climbs all the way to Cayuse Pass. That's a bit of a trek for a day hike, but if you'd like more exercise, wander up the trail a mile or two under a green umbrella forest along the Ohanapecosh River valley. The Eastside Trail is much quieter and lonely for boots, once past the Grove bridge.

# 25. Silver Falls

| | |
|---|---|
| RATING | 🏃🏃 |
| DISTANCE | 2.6 miles round-trip |
| HIKING TIME | 1 hour, 30 minutes |
| ELEVATION GAIN | 330 feet |
| HIGH POINT | 2,100 feet |
| EFFORT | Easy Walk |
| BEST SEASON | Spring, summer; open year-round |
| PERMITS/CONTACT | Entrance fee/Ohanapecosh Visitor Center, (360) 569-6046, www.nps.gov/mora |
| MAPS | USGS Chinook Pass; Green Trails Mount Rainier East 270 |
| NOTES | Dogs and bikes prohibited; good family hike |

## THE HIKE

The tumbling Ohanapecosh River serves up one of the easiest hikes to a Mount Rainier National Park waterfall, and it's a beauty. Walk the river canyon upstream through an old forest, then switch back down to a viewpoint bridge.

## GETTING THERE

Follow Highway 12 for 72 miles east of I-5 through Morton and Pack-wood (watch out for elk!) to the junction with Highway 123. Turn left and follow Highway 123 to the entrance to Ohanapecosh Campground. Turn left into the campground and park at the day-use area on the right by circling the first campground loop, 1,900 feet above sea level. If the lot is full, as it sometimes is on summer days, try the Ohanapecosh Ranger Station. From the Seattle or Tacoma area, you can drive to Enumclaw, then follow Highway 410 to Cayuse Pass and take Highway 123 to the campground entrance. The trail begins on either side of the bridge across the river; the hike described here is for the trail on the west side of the river. GPS coordinates: N46°42′12″; W121°33′58″

## THE TRAIL

Walk across the bridge and turn right on the trail that climbs into the forest below one of the many Ohanapecosh Campground loops. The trail

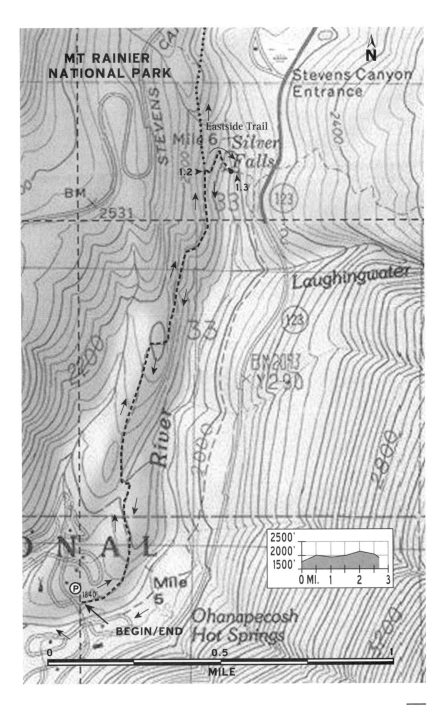

climbs on a moderate grade to a broad evergreen ridge above the river on your right, then levels slightly as it follow the crest of the ridge for about a half mile to the high point, 2,100 feet above sea level.

From here, you begin a gradual half mile descent to a junction with a trail that climbs toward the Stevens Canyon Entrance and becomes the Eastside Trail, 1.2 miles from the trailhead. Turn right at the junction and descend 0.2 mile in a steep switchback to a bridge crossing the river. The falls—in case you haven't noticed—are upstream. You can return the same way or cross the bridge and follow the trail to the right downstream to the campground, passing a junction with the Laughingwater Creek Trail on the left.

## GOING FARTHER

You can make a longer hike to the Grove of the Patriarchs (hike #24 in this guide) by turning around at the falls and climbing back to the trail junction at 1.2 miles, then turning right to follow the trail to the Stevens Canyon Entrance, about 0.3 mile, and the Grove trail, 0.4 mile beyond. For more mileage, continue along the Eastside Trail as far as you wish.

# 26. Bench and Snow Lakes

| | |
|---|---|
| RATING | 𝍠𝍠𝍠 |
| DISTANCE | 2.6 miles round-trip |
| HIKING TIME | 3 hours |
| ELEVATION GAIN | 700 feet |
| HIGH POINT | 4,760 feet |
| EFFORT | Knee-Punishing |
| BEST SEASON | Summer, fall |
| PERMITS/CONTACT | Entrance fee required/Paradise Visitor Center, (360) 569-6036, www.nps.gov/mora |
| MAPS | USGS Mount Rainier East; Green Trails Paradise 270 S |
| NOTES | Dogs and bikes prohibited; road closed in winter |

## THE HIKE

Here's a short but brutal climb up and down (and up again) that is worth its weight in sweat and ibuprofen when you reach the viewpoint from Snow Lake, a high alpine tarn set in a steep-walled cirque that cradles snow well into summer.

## GETTING THERE

From I-5 in Tacoma, take the Highway 7 exit 133 and follow Highway 7 south to Elbe and Highway 706. Follow Highway 706 east through Ashford to the Nisqually Entrance of Mount Rainier National Park, where you'll be asked to pay an entry fee. Continue past Longmire to the Stevens Canyon–Reflection Lakes Road and turn right. Follow this road 2.8 miles past Reflection and Louise Lakes to a wide parking lot on the right, 4,560 feet above sea level. GPS coordinates: N46o46′08″; W121o42′30″

If you wish to bypass most of urban Tacoma, Parkland, and part of Spanaway, continue north on I-5 to the Highway 512 exit 127 and follow the highway to the first exit, Steele Street. Turn left on Steele and follow the Spanaway Loop Road back to Highway 7 on the southern outskirts of Spanaway, and turn right to join the route described above.

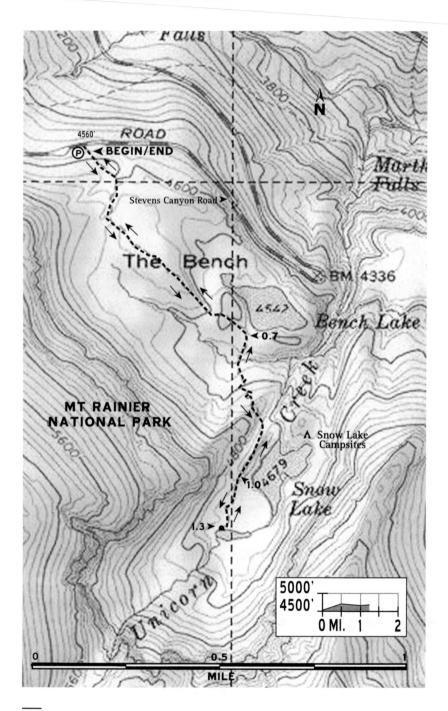

Bench Lake.

## THE TRAIL

If this short trail weren't so bloody steep in places, it would be a great walk for everyone. But some of the water-bar steps both up and down seem designed for giants, and unless you've already got metal joints in your knees, you can shorten the time before you need them by hiking to Snow Lake. Nonetheless, the lucky healthy-jointed among us will find the hike rewarding as one of the best ways to climb to an alpine vista of that incredible snowy volcano just a few miles to the north.

You'll enjoy this hike most in the early hours of an autumn morning, when the smallish trailhead parking lot isn't yet full and the crowds of summer may have dwindled somewhat. Another reason for waiting until the first frost is that many of the bugs that pester summer hikers have frozen their little suck tubes or mandibles off.

Begin with a straightforward 160-vertical-foot, quarter-mile climb to a plateau decorated by alpine fir and silver snags before leveling off a bit, then dropping a bit onto a marshy meadow called the Bench. You may wish, at this point, that it were a piece of furniture and not a geographic feature.

At **0.3** mile, the trail drops almost as steeply as it climbed, then promptly regains that altitude to offer a glimpse of Bench Lake through the mountain ash and brush to the left, **0.6** mile from the trailhead. It's a pretty little lake, but surrounded by brush and Alaska cedar and not nearly as hospitable as Snow Lake, ahead.

The trail turns away to the south and at **0.7** mile, reaches a junction with a way trail to Bench Lake. Keep right and begin another assault on the steep ridge ahead, climbing more than 200 vertical feet before rounding the ridge and descending to a trail leading to campsites to the left at **1.2** miles. Stay right, and follow the trail another 0.1 mile to a small tarn above Snow Lake, **1.3** miles from the trailhead, 4,700 feet above sea level.

After a well-earned rest and tall cool beverage, turn around and limp back to the trailhead. Going farther is not an option.

# 27. Nisqually Vista

| | |
|---|---|
| RATING | 🚶🚶🚶 |
| DISTANCE | 1.4-mile loop |
| HIKING TIME | 1 hour, 30 minutes |
| ELEVATION GAIN | 200 feet |
| HIGH POINT | 5,420 feet |
| EFFORT | Easy Walk |
| BEST SEASON | Summer, fall |
| PERMITS/CONTACT | Entrance fee required/Paradise Visitor Center, (360) 569-6036, www.nps.gov/mora |
| MAPS | USGS Mount Rainier East; Green Trails Paradise 270 S |
| NOTES | Dogs and bikes prohibited; great family hike; excellent novice ski/snowshoe walk in winter |

## THE HIKE

Walk on a paved path through wildflower fields that would inspire poets and send photographers into a crazed frenzy on this gentle hike to a steep-walled canyon overlooking the remains of the retreating Nisqually Glacier.

## GETTING THERE

From I-5 in Tacoma, take the Highway 7 exit 133 and follow Highway 7 south to Elbe and Highway 706. Follow Highway 706 east through Ashford to the Nisqually Entrance of Mount Rainier National Park, where you'll be asked to pay an entry fee. Continue past Longmire and Narada Falls, keeping left at the Stevens Canyon–Reflection Lakes Road to the giant parking lot east of the Henry M. Jackson Visitor Center at Paradise. Walk west past the visitor center to find the trailhead, 5,420 feet above sea level. Parking area GPS coordinates: N46°47′07″; W121°42′30″

If you wish to bypass most of urban Tacoma, Parkland, and part of Spanaway, continue north on I-5 to the Highway 512 exit 127 and follow the highway to the first exit, Steele Street. Turn left on Steele and follow the Spanaway Loop Road back to Highway 7 on the southern outskirts of Spanaway, and turn right to join the route described above.

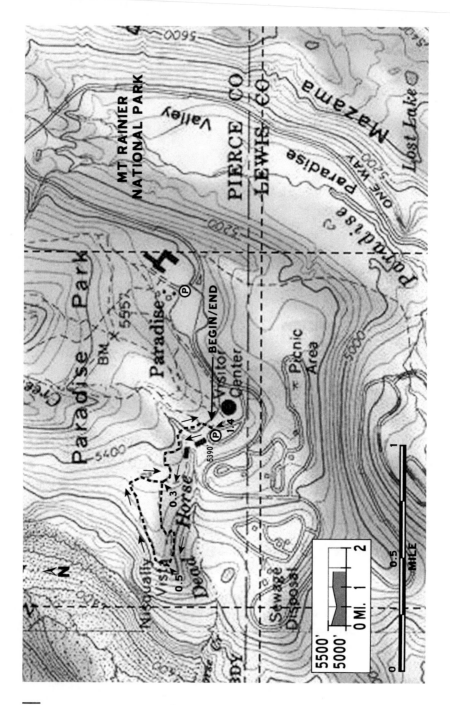

Lower Nisqually Glacier from the Nisqually Vista trail.

## THE TRAIL

In the interest of keeping whatever is left of my credibility as a guide-book author, I must confess that I have never walked on this trail. I have been on this path many times, however, on cross-country skis. And I can tell you from experience that the wildflowers are infinitely showier when they are not covered by 10 feet of snow.

You'll climb along a gentle slope for miles through wildflower gardens where the purple of lupine might dominate. Look for avalanche lily in the shade of alpine trees, Columbia tiger lilies, Sitka columbine, rosy spiraea, and a whole bunch of flowers I lump under the name "colorful ask-me-not."

At **0.3** mile, find a junction with your return trail and turn left to follow a steep hillside above Dead Horse Creek before turning north to round a forest ridge with a long meadow to the east and a sharp ridge dropping off to the west. The trail climbs gradually along the ridge to the glacier overlook, where you can look down on the rubble deposited by the ice river as it retreated. The ragged snout of the glacier might be visible upstream; not too many decades ago, it reached almost to the Nisqually bridge you crossed on the road to Paradise.

Back on the trail, continue climbing along the meadow and circle a tarn named Fairy Pool to close the pathway loop, **0.9** mile from the trail-head. The wildflower meadows around Fairy Pool host one of the more rare blossoms of the Northwest mountains, Jeffrey's shooting star.

## GOING FARTHER

The best way to add mileage to your Vibrams after this hike is to follow any one of the myriad trails that radiate from Paradise. Consider some of the best that follow in this guide.

# 28. Skyline Trail

| | |
|---|---|
| RATING | 🚶🚶🚶🚶🚶 |
| DISTANCE | 5.5-mile loop |
| HIKING TIME | 4 hours, 30 minutes |
| ELEVATION GAIN | 1,750 feet |
| HIGH POINT | 6,975 feet |
| EFFORT | Knee-Punishing |
| BEST SEASON | Summer, fall |
| PERMITS/CONTACT | Entrance fee required/Paradise Visitor Center, (360) 569-6036, www.nps.gov/mora |
| MAPS | USGS Mount Rainier East; Green Trails Paradise 270 S |
| NOTES | Dogs and bikes prohibited |

## THE HIKE

This strenuous, beautiful hike is best started early on fall or summer mornings for solitude and to avoid the greater possibility that afternoon clouds will hamper unbeatable, unlimited views. It's the must-do hike at Paradise, even if you need to consume an entire bottle of NSAIDs on your return.

## GETTING THERE

From I-5 in Tacoma, take the Highway 7 exit 133 and follow Highway 7 south to Elbe and Highway 706. Follow Highway 706 east through Ashford to the Nisqually Entrance of Mount Rainier National Park, where you'll be asked to pay an entry fee. Continue past Longmire and Narada Falls, keeping left at the Stevens Canyon–Reflection Lakes Road to the giant parking lot east of the Henry M. Jackson Visitor Center at Paradise. Walk west past the visitor center to find the trailhead, 5,420 feet above sea level. Parking area GPS coordinates: N46°47′07″; W121°42′30″

If you wish to bypass most of urban Tacoma, Parkland, and part of Spanaway, continue north on I-5 to the Highway 512 exit 127 and follow the highway to the first exit, Steele Street. Turn left on Steele and follow the Spanaway Loop Road back to Highway 7 on the southern outskirts of Spanaway, and turn right to join the route described above.

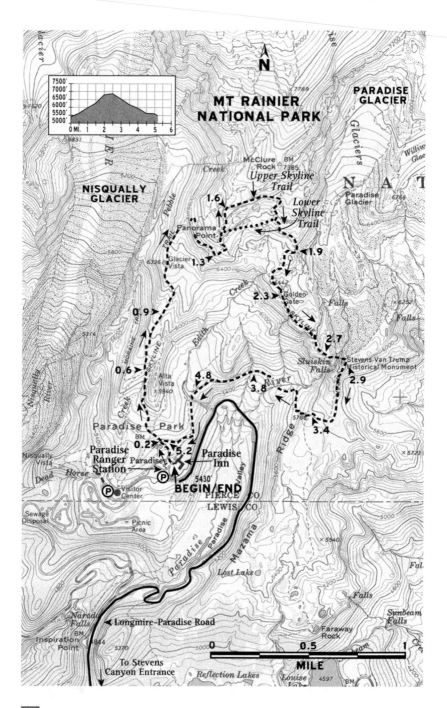

Mount Rainier from the Skyline Trail.

## THE TRAIL

First off, this rugged route isn't for everyone. It's a long, steep climb with rock steps along a few exposed slopes, an approach trail used by Real Mountain Climbers who chug along like human freight trains on their way to camp at 10,000-foot-high Camp Muir. You have been warned.

On the other hand, nobody says you have to complete the entire loop hike. The first 1.2 miles of the trail lead to the Glacier Vista, which looks down upon the still-impressive crevasses and ice of the Nisqually Glacier and up, up to the summit of Rainier and the red lump of Gibraltar Rock. If you can only make it that far, you'll have seen the dancing marmots and hiked a stunning part of the best trail at Paradise.

Begin by climbing the wide steps just west of the Paradise Ranger Station and following the paved trail to signs pointing left to the Skyline Trail. The path is moderately steep and was reconditioned in the fall of 2014, so it should be in excellent shape. Stay left at a junction with a trail leading up and over Alta Vista.

Stay right at the Glacier Vista junction and begin climbing in a wide switchback up a rocky ledge to the south, where you'll look across Paradise to the Tatoosh Range and on clear days, view Mounts St. Helens and Adams. Mount Hood is sometimes visible when there are no clouds to the south. Just past this view, stay right past the rocky trail to Pebble Creek, 1.6 miles from the trailhead, and continue climbing more moderately,

The dancing marmots take a break along the Skyline Trail.

following the signs to Panorama Point. Arrive there 2.0 miles from the trailhead.

Pan Point, as ancient backcountry skiers call it, provides a great view and resting spot before climbing left on the High Skyline Trail at a junction with the Lower Skyline Trail, which crosses an extremely steep snowfield and should be avoided. The high trail switches back and climbs a rocky slope with a cliffside view, 6,975 feet above sea level and the high point of the hike. You should be able to see a trough in the Muir Snowfield above, marking the climbers' route to Camp Muir, which is located on the flat saddle underneath Gibraltar Rock.

Beyond, the trail descends a rocky section that may hold snow well into the summer season and rejoins the Lower Skyline Trail before passing a junction with the old Golden Gate Trail, 3.1 miles from the trailhead. Stay right and continue dropping down the high valley carved by the retreating Paradise Glacier, reaching Sluiskin Falls and the Stevens–Van Trump Historical Monument in 3.7 miles. Keep right, passing a trail to the glacier and descend Mazama Ridge to a junction with the Lakes Trail on the left, 4.3 miles from the trailhead.

Stay right and switch back down Mazama Ridge to cross the wide bowl of the upper Paradise Creek basin, climb a forested glade to a bridge over Edith Creek, 4.8 miles from the trailhead, and close the loop at 5.2 miles.

As we limped down the paved path to the parking lot, we passed an ancient mountaineer headed up the trail. "Did you see the dancing marmots?" he asked my wife, B. B. Hardbody.

Yes, we did.

# 29. Comet Falls

| | |
|---|---|
| RATING | 🚶🚶🚶 |
| DISTANCE | 3.2 miles round-trip |
| HIKING TIME | 3 hours, 30 minutes |
| ELEVATION GAIN | 1,600 feet |
| HIGH POINT | 4,800 feet |
| EFFORT | Prepare to Perspire |
| BEST SEASON | Summer, fall |
| PERMITS/CONTACT | Entrance fee/Longmire Wilderness Information Center, (360) 569-4453, www.nps.gov/mora |
| MAPS | USGS Mount Rainier West; Green Trails Mount Rainier West 269 |
| NOTES | Dogs and bikes prohibited; hard trail for younger kids |

## THE HIKE

Probably the most impressive waterfall in Mount Rainier National Park crashes 320 feet into a basin that is a short but steep climb through the forest.

## GETTING THERE

From I-5 in Tacoma, take the Highway 7 exit 133 and follow Highway 7 south to Elbe and Highway 706. Follow Highway 706 east through Ashford to the Nisqually Entrance of Mount Rainier National Park, where you'll be asked to pay an entry fee. Continue past Longmire 4.5 miles to a wide parking lot and trailhead just below Christine Falls, 3,600 feet above sea level. GPS coordinates: N46°46′45″; W121°46′57″

If you wish to bypass most of urban Tacoma, Parkland, and part of Spanaway, continue north on I-5 to the Highway 512 exit 127 and follow the highway to the first exit, Steele Street. Turn left on Steele and follow the Spanaway Loop Road back to Highway 7 on the southern outskirts of Spanaway, and turn right to join the route described above.

## THE TRAIL

As with many of the trails at Mount Rainier National Park in summer, the earlier you start hiking, the more likely you'll find a parking spot at the trailhead and less human company on the trail. Begin with a no-nonsense

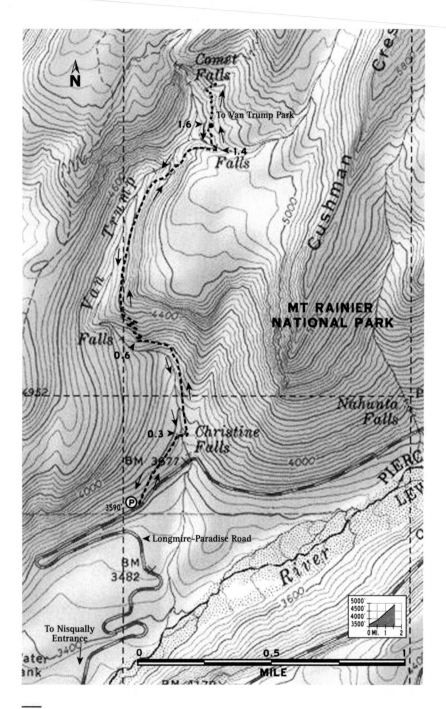

Early snow at Comet Falls.

climb into dense forest up a rock-walled trail to a viewpoint where Van Trump Creek flies over a cliff to form Christine Falls—a better view than from the auto bridge below. Beyond, the trail climbs to a bridge across the creek, **0.3** mile from the trailhead, then turns up the valley to climb at a more gradual pace above the creek.

The creek valley turns westerly **0.6** mile from the trailhead, still in deep forest, and you'll begin climbing a series of steep switchbacks over a ridge. The grade eases a bit after the switchbacks and curves back along the canyon carved by Van Trump Creek. Climb another 0.8 mile to a footlog crossing Falls Creek, to the right, and round a ridge to a junction with a trail leading to the first good viewpoint of Comet Falls, **1.6** miles from the trailhead. Follow this trail left to the viewpoint.

## GOING FARTHER

You can begin a serious switchback climb from the junction for another 0.2 mile to a spur trail leading to the base of the falls, or continue climbing the steep headwall to the top of the falls, where you can climb over a steep ridge into lower Van Trump Park, an alpine meadowland **3.5** miles from the trailhead.

# 30. Trail of the Shadows

| | |
|---|---|
| RATING | 👤👤👤👤 |
| DISTANCE | 0.8-mile loop |
| HIKING TIME | 1 hour |
| ELEVATION GAIN | 40 feet |
| HIGH POINT | 2,780 feet |
| EFFORT | Stroll in the Park |
| BEST SEASON | Summer, fall; open year-round |
| PERMITS/CONTACT | Entrance fee/Longmire Wilderness Information Center, (360) 569-4453, www.nps.gov/mora |
| MAPS | USGS Mount Rainier West; Green Trails Mount Rainier West 269 |
| NOTES | Dogs and bikes prohibited; good family hike |

## THE HIKE

Though the shortest walk outlined in this guide, the Trail of the Shadows shouldn't be missed because it tells as much about the geology of Mount Rainier as it does the history.

## GETTING THERE

From I-5 in Tacoma, take the Highway 7 exit 133 and follow Highway 7 south to Elbe and Highway 706. Follow Highway 706 east through Ashford to the Nisqually Entrance of Mount Rainier National Park, where you'll be asked to pay an entry fee. Continue to Longmire; turn right into the big parking lot just past the Longmire Inn. The trailhead is across the road in front of the inn, 2,770 feet above sea level. Parking area GPS coordinates: N121°48′39″; W46°45′01″

If you wish to bypass most of urban Tacoma, Parkland, and part of Spanaway, continue north on I-5 to the Highway 512 exit 127 and follow the highway to the first exit, Steele Street. Turn left on Steele and follow the Spanaway Loop Road back to Highway 7 on the southern outskirts of Spanaway, and turn right to join the route described above.

## THE TRAIL

What makes this short loop so downright compelling is the fact that it circles one of the reasons pioneer Puget Sound residents visited Mount

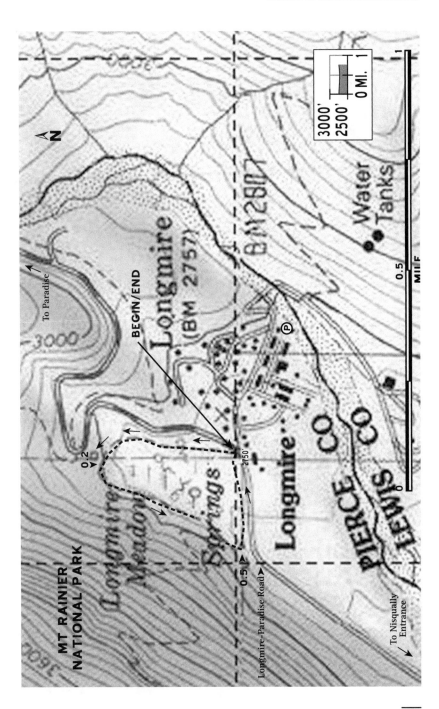

Longmire Meadow from the Trail of the Shadows.

Rainier—and it wasn't to see the showy 14,410-foot-high main attraction that hunkers over Longmire Meadow. It was, instead, to partake of the elixir that flowed from hillside springs around the meadow. Way back in 1883, James Longmire built a trail and cabins in the meadow, where as many as 500 people a year sloshed around in rock-walled tubs filled by the springs. The liquid was supposed to be good for you, but judging from the liquid flowing from one of today's springs, you might be better off bathing in a pond populated by flatulent hippopotamuses.

Walk up the paved pathway to the east to begin the hike, shortly reaching the end of the pavement and following a nicely graded path into the forest. You'll see remnants of the stone structures that gathered spring water for bathing along the trail, and in 0.2 mile, pass the log cabin built by Longmire's son, Elcaine, in 1888. It's the oldest man-made structure in the park.

The trail curves southwest and passes a meadow where an interpretive sign explains the geology of the area, one of the few geothermal springs from that big volcano above. Just beyond, **0.5 mile from where you** started, is the junction with the Rampart Ridge Trail, hike #31 in this guide. Stay left to close the loop.

## GOING FARTHER
The best option is to take the Rampart Ridge Trail, a 4.5-mile climb and descent from Longmire.

# 31. Rampart Ridge

| | |
|---|---|
| RATING | 🚶🚶 |
| DISTANCE | 5.4-mile loop |
| HIKING TIME | 3 hours, 30 minutes |
| ELEVATION GAIN | 1,300 feet |
| HIGH POINT | 4,025 feet |
| EFFORT | Prepare to Perspire |
| BEST SEASON | Spring, fall |
| PERMITS/CONTACT | Entrance fee/Longmire Wilderness Information Center, (360) 569-4453, www.nps.gov/mora |
| MAPS | USGS Mount Rainier West; Green Trails Mount Rainier West 269 |
| NOTES | Dogs and bikes prohibited |

## THE HIKE

The climb around Rampart Ridge is a good spring tune-up for later adventures higher on the mountain.

## GETTING THERE

From I-5 in Tacoma, take the Highway 7 exit 133 and follow Highway 7 south to Elbe and Highway 706. Follow Highway 706 east through Ashford to the Nisqually Entrance of Mount Rainier National Park, where you'll be asked to pay an entry fee. Continue to Longmire; turn right into the big parking lot just past the Longmire Inn. The trailhead is across the road in front of the inn, 2,770 feet above sea level. Parking area GPS coordinates: N121°48′39″; W46°45′01″

If you wish to bypass most of urban Tacoma, Parkland, and part of Spanaway, continue north on I-5 to the Highway 512 exit 127 and follow the highway to the first exit, Steele Street. Turn left on Steele and follow the Spanaway Loop Road back to Highway 7 on the southern outskirts of Spanaway, and turn right to join the route described above.

## THE TRAIL

Start by following the Trail of the Shadows downhill to the left to the junction with the Rampart Ridge Trail, at about **0.1** mile, and turn left. The first half mile of the path is not as steep as what follows, where

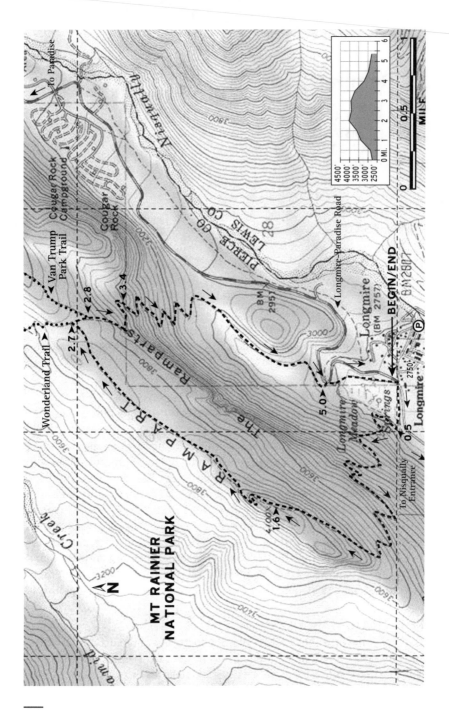

The Rampart Ridge Trail begins along the Trail of the Shadows.

you'll begin a series of steep switchbacks up a forested ridge. You'll climb another 1.5 miles on a steady grade before breaking out at a viewpoint, **1.7** miles from the trailhead.

A short climb beyond, you'll strike a junction with a trail leading right to a view of Rainier, the Longmire valley below, and Eagle Peak across the valley. The trail climbs more gently along the crest of the ridge, with the steep cliffs of the Ramparts off to your right. You'll crest the ridge at 4,025 feet before dropping and climbing to a junction with the Wonderland Trail, **3.0** miles from the trailhead. Turn right and 0.1 mile later, pass a junction with the Van Trump Park trail on the left. Continue descending in steep switchbacks for 2.3 miles to Longmire.

# 32. Westside Road

| | |
|---|---|
| RATING | 🚶🚶 |
| DISTANCE | 7.0 miles round-trip |
| HIKING TIME | 3 hours, 30 minutes |
| ELEVATION GAIN | 670 feet |
| HIGH POINT | 3,550 feet |
| EFFORT | Moderate Workout |
| BEST SEASON | Spring, fall; open year-round |
| PERMITS/CONTACT | Entrance fee/Longmire Wilderness Information Center, (360) 569-4453, www.nps.gov/mora |
| MAPS | USGS Mount Rainier West; Green Trails Mount Rainier West 269 |
| NOTES | Leashed dogs and mountain bikes welcome; good family hike |

## THE HIKE

Quiet and generally less crowded than many hikes around Mount Rainier during the summer months, the walk along the closed Westside Road offers wildlife watchers and casual hikers a gentle journey.

## GETTING THERE

From I-5 in Tacoma, take the Highway 7 exit 133 and follow Highway 7 south to Elbe and Highway 706. Follow Highway 706 east through Ashford to the Nisqually Entrance of Mount Rainier National Park, where you'll be asked to pay an entry fee. Continue about 1.0 mile past the entrance station to the Westside Road, on the left. Turn and follow the Westside Road 3.3 miles to a gate and wide trailhead parking area, 2,875 feet above sea level. GPS coordinates: N46°46′47″; W121°53′06″

If you wish to bypass most of urban Tacoma, Parkland, and part of Spanaway, continue north on I-5 to the Highway 512 exit 127 and follow the highway to the first exit, Steele Street. Turn left on Steele and follow the Spanaway Loop Road back to Highway 7 on the southern outskirts of Spanaway, and turn right to join the route described above.

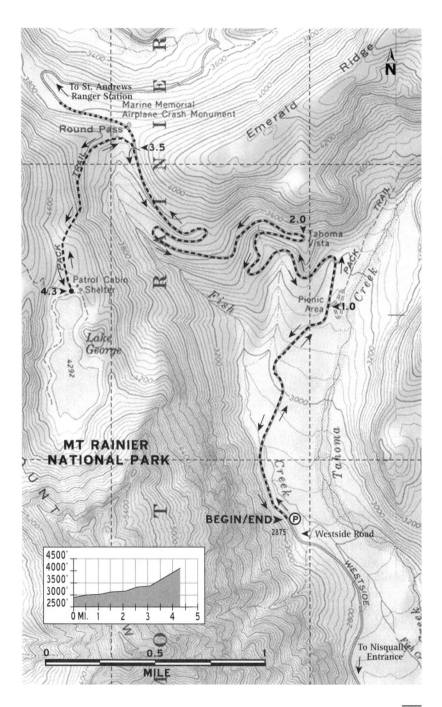

To St. Andrews Ranger Station

Marine Memorial Airplane Crash Monument

Round Pass

◄3.5

RAINIER TRAIL

Emerald Ridge

2.0 Tahoma Vista

PACK TRAIL

PACK

Fish Creek

Patrol Cabin Shelter

4.3►

Picnic Area

◄1.0

Tahoma Creek

Lake George
4292

MT RAINIER NATIONAL PARK

MOUNT

BEGIN/END► Ⓟ
2875 ◄ Westside Road

WESTSIDE

To Nisqually Entrance

4500'
4000'
3500'
3000'
2500'
0 MI. 1 2 3 4 5

0        0.5        1
MILE

Mount Rainier peeks over the Westside Road.

## THE TRAIL

The Westside Road once provided access to distant trailheads leading to alpine meadows and glacier snouts that can only be reached today by long hikes—or bike rides—almost 8 miles up the closed road. Credit or blame that nasty Tahoma Glacier for the road closure, which with very little notice spits huge quantities of mud, water, and glacial debris from its mouth. This slurry races down Tahoma Creek and pretty much buries or crushes everything along the way. Years ago, it wiped out an entire campground and some time later, tore a huge chunk out of the Westside Road.

So you end up walking along what is generally a pretty nice roadway, still used by park rangers in vehicles to access and service the St. Andrews Ranger Station. That's a good thing, because unlike on park trails, your leashed dog can accompany you along the road. It's a great ride for beginning mountain bikers, especially on the way down from Round Pass. And in the winter, when the road is gated at the junction with the Longmire-Paradise Road, you can ski or snowshoe when the white stuff covers the ground below 2,000 feet.

If you're looking for a view of Mount Rainier, you needn't walk much farther than 1.0 mile up the road, where one of the Tahoma Creek's rampages opened the view to the mountain's west face. It's the only good sight of Rainier you'll get on this hike; the switchback a mile farther signed "Tahoma Vista" is overgrown and provides peekaboo views at best.

Once past Tahoma Novista, the road angles around the headwaters of Fish Creek, switches back, and climbs to Round Pass, your turnaround point 3.5 miles from the trailhead. The pass is wide and flat and once was the big parking area and trailhead to Lake George and beyond.

## GOING FARTHER

It's a 1.6-mile moderate climb, out and back, from Round Pass to Lake George, a small lake surrounded by forest under Gobblers Knob. That former lookout site affords an excellent view of Mount Rainier and can be reached in a half mile one-way of serious climbing from Lake George.

A gentler hike would be to follow the Westside Road down to the South Puyallup trailhead, 1.4 miles out and back from Round Pass. From that trailhead, it's 3.3 miles one-way to the St. Andrews Ranger Station.

# 33. Carbon River Road

| | |
|---|---|
| RATING | 🚶 |
| DISTANCE | 6.0 miles round-trip |
| HIKING TIME | 3 hours |
| ELEVATION GAIN | 340 feet |
| HIGH POINT | 2,110 feet |
| EFFORT | Easy Walk |
| BEST SEASON | Spring, fall; open year-round |
| PERMITS/CONTACT | Entrance fee/Carbon River Ranger Station, (360) 829-9639, www.nps.gov/mora |
| MAPS | USGS Carbon River; Green Trails Mount Rainier West 269 |
| NOTES | Leashed dogs and mountain bikes welcome; good family hike |

## THE HIKE
Walk along a gentle road through a big lowland forest beside a rumbling, tumbling glacier-fed river.

## GETTING THERE
From I-5, follow Highways 18 and 164 to Enumclaw, then drive south on Highway 410 to Buckley and bear left onto Highway 165. Follow Highway 165 through Wilkeson and Carbonado. Stay left after crossing the Carbon River on a narrow, high bridge at the junction of the Carbon River Road and the Mowich Lake Road. Drive past the Carbon River Ranger Station to the Mount Rainier National Park Entrance, where the hike begins at the gated road. GPS coordinates: N46°59′42″; W121°54′55″

## THE TRAIL
This is the latest example of the havoc a melting glacier and the big river that is born from it can create on man-made objects such as roads. The Carbon River Road was once a smooth gravel thoroughfare that took vehicles 5 miles along the river to an auto campground at Ipsut Creek and trailheads leading to the toe of the Carbon Glacier and way up the mountain to climbing routes on the steep northern ridges of Rainier.

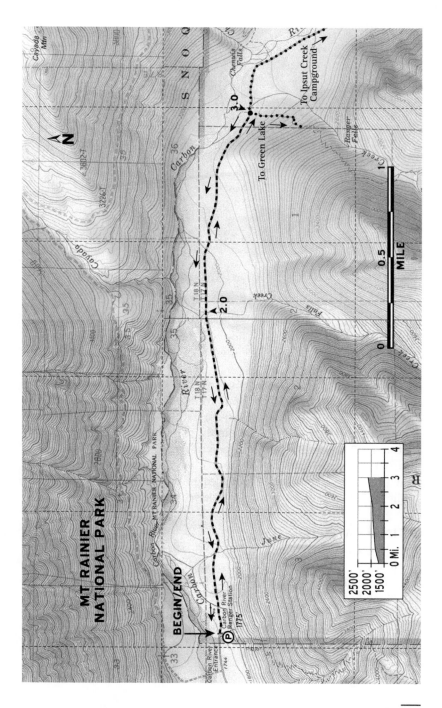

The Carbon River flows below the road.

In 2006, a flood washed out the road for the final time, after several attempts to repair it after previous washouts.

The road's loss is your gain, however, because you can now take an easy walk along the road, listening to the crashing of the river and watching for wildlife in the deep old forest beside you. Save this hike for a rainy or foggy day, because there's very little to see along the way. Early spring might be the best time, with lowland wildflowers like trillium and spring beauty decorating your path. If you visit in the fall, you might see elk or hear their bugling in the forest.

At about **2.0** miles, you'll cross one of the major washouts along the road, which is still passable by park rangers tending to the old auto campground at Ipsut Creek. Your turnaround point is the Green Lake trailhead, **3.0** miles from the park entrance.

## GOING FARTHER
If you want more exercise, climb the 1.8 miles up the moderate trail to Green Lake, a forested tarn set under the cliffs of Rust Ridge and Howard Peak. The trail passes splendid Ranger Falls about halfway up the 1,100-foot climb to the lake.

An easier alternative is to continue on the Carbon Road to Ipsut Creek, 2.0 miles one-way. Besides the campground, you'll find the Carbon River Trail, which leads in about 3 miles one-way to a viewpoint of the Carbon Glacier.

# 34. Naches Peak Loop

| | |
|---|---|
| RATING | 𑁋𑁋𑁋𑁋𑁋 |
| DISTANCE | 4.5-mile loop |
| HIKING TIME | 3 hours |
| ELEVATION GAIN | 700 feet |
| HIGH POINT | 5,900 feet |
| EFFORT | Moderate Workout |
| BEST SEASON | Summer, fall |
| PERMITS/CONTACT | None/Longmire Wilderness Information Center, (360) 569-4453, www.nps.gov/mora |
| MAPS | USGS Chinook Pass, Cougar Lake, White River Park and Norse Peak; Green Trails Chinook Pass 270 and Bumping Lake 271 |
| NOTES | Leashed dogs welcome in US forest section; road closed in winter |

## THE HIKE

Expect company on this hike that provides one of the nicest views of the southeast side of Mount Rainier from scenic Tipsoo Lake. This walk is one of the best in (and out) of the park for wildflowers and golden larch in the fall.

## GETTING THERE

From I-5, follow Highways 18 and 164 to Enumclaw, then take Highway 410 about 3 miles east of its junction with Highway 123 to the Tipsoo Lake Picnic Area on the left, 5,290 feet above sea level. When the state of Washington ceded the Highway 410 corridor to Mount Rainier National Park, the state specified that no fees would be charged for entry or passage along the highway. It's one of the few places in the park that is exempt from entrance fees. GPS coordinates: N46°52′10″; W121°31′10″

## THE TRAIL

Although there are several places to park and begin the walk around Naches Peak, the trailhead at Tipsoo Lake will save you money because the parking areas outside of the park, east of Chinook Pass, require a parking fee. So park here and begin by walking around the north side

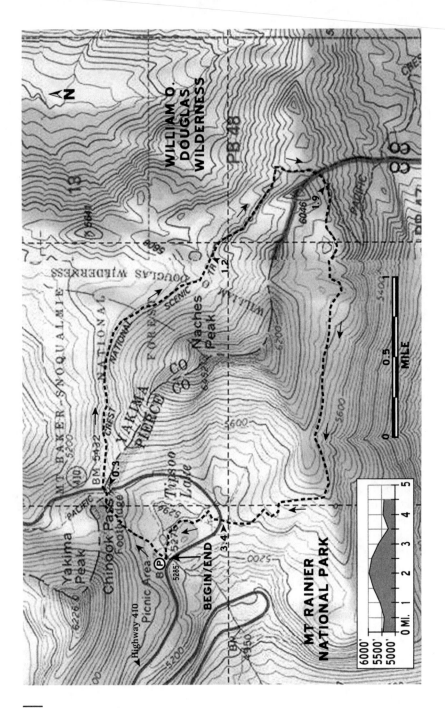

Tipsoo Lake is the trailhead for the Naches Peak Loop.

of this splendid alpine tarn and climbing about 120 vertical feet over a saddle under 6,226-foot Yakima Peak on your left. If you plan to take Fido along on this hike, drive over Chinook Pass and park in the big lot on your left, where the parking fee is required.

Descend to a junction with the Pacific Crest Trail, turn right, and cross the big log bridge over Highway 410—the boundary between the park and Okanogan-Wenatchee National Forest. This trail climbs briefly before traversing into alpine forest and entering the William O. Douglas Wilderness. The trail continues to climb on a gentle grade underneath the east cliffs of Naches Peak, where you've expansive views down the valley of the American River. At 1.1 miles from the trailhead, pass above a tarn that makes an excellent cooling swim on a hot summer day.

Beyond, the route climbs toward a ridge before switching back and cresting the ridge. It curves back toward the west in a broad meadow to a trail junction with the Dewey Lake Trail, 2.2 miles from the trailhead. If you've brought your leashed dog, you must turn back here or follow the Pacific Crest Trail down to Dewey Lake.

Stay right for the loop hike, pass another tarn above the trail, and look south to Mount Adams and the Goat Rocks Wilderness. Just beyond, as the trail curves farther west, you'll walk straight into a great view of Mount Rainier. Try to keep at least one eye on the trail, as it begins to descend along a ridge to a wide bowl overlooking Tipsoo Lake, 3.0 miles from the trailhead. This bowl is an early spring destination for backcountry skiers who climb up a portion of the closed Highway 410 from Cayuse Pass.

The trail finally turns north and begins a steep descent to a round tarn just above the highway, crosses the road, and connects with the Tipsoo Lake Trail around the lake to the picnic area.

## GOING FARTHER

The best way to make a longer hike is to follow the Dewey Lake Trail down to Dewey Lake, about 1.1 miles one-way. Another option is to follow the Sheep Lake Trail just over Chinook Pass for 1.9 one-way miles to the lake, returning via the Naches Peak loop.

# 35. Pinnacle Saddle

| | |
|---|---|
| RATING | 🚶🚶🚶 |
| DISTANCE | 2.6 miles round-trip |
| HIKING TIME | 3 hours |
| ELEVATION GAIN | 1,060 feet |
| HIGH POINT | 5,920 feet |
| EFFORT | Prepare to Perspire |
| BEST SEASON | Summer |
| PERMITS/CONTACT | Entrance fee/Paradise Visitor Center, (360) 569-6036, www.nps.gov/mora |
| MAPS | USGS Mount Rainier East; Green Trails Paradise 270 S |
| NOTES | Dogs or bikes prohibited; road closed in winter |

## THE HIKE

The climb to Pinnacle Saddle is a good, short trail to experience what Real Mountain Climbers might feel on their approach route to climbing Rainier. It's a steep, rocky, somewhat exposed trail where you might feel more comfortable with good hiking poles and sturdy boots.

## GETTING THERE

From I-5 in Tacoma, take the Highway 7 exit 133 and follow Highway 7 south to Elbe and Highway 706. Follow Highway 706 east through Ashford to the Nisqually Entrance of Mount Rainier National Park, where you'll be asked to pay an entry fee. Continue past Longmire to the Stevens Canyon–Reflection Lakes Road and turn right. Follow this road 1.7 miles to the Reflection Lakes parking area. The trailhead is across the road, 4,865 feet above sea level. GPS coordinates: N46º46′06″; W121º43′54″

If you wish to bypass most of urban Tacoma, Parkland, and part of Spanaway, continue north on I-5 to the Highway 512 exit 127 and follow the highway to the first exit, Steele Street. Turn left on Steele and follow the Spanaway Loop Road back to Highway 7 on the southern outskirts of Spanaway, and turn right to join the route described above.

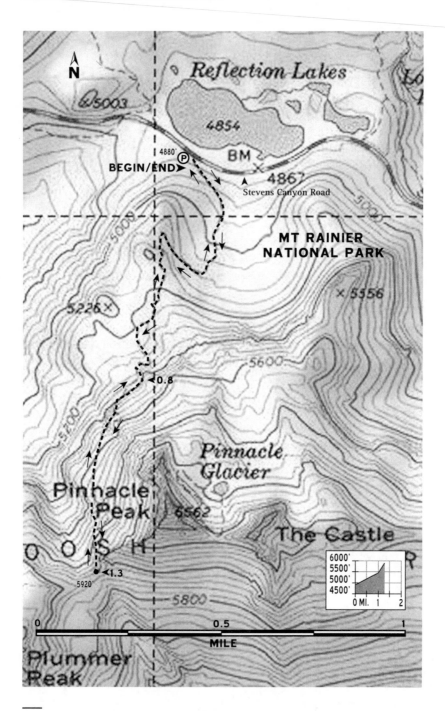

Hikers study the map before setting out on the Pinnacle Peak trail.

## THE TRAIL

This is a no-nonsense climb from the very beginning, climbing first in subalpine forest to gain 260 vertical feet in the first half mile before switching back and climbing a ridge crest between forest and hillside meadows that sometimes turn white as snow with fields of avalanche lilies. The trail continues climbing at a gentler pace for about 0.2 mile before climbing another steep 120-foot pitch.

At the top, the trail turns southerly and begins a long climb along a steep, open rock field where trail crews have done extensive work building walls to keep the trail from slipping downhill. The climb doesn't let up until you've traversed the sidehill to arrive at a narrow, rocky perch between triangular Pinnacle Peak, 350 feet above you on the left, and 6,370-foot-high Plummer Peak, on the right.

The saddle, 1.3 miles from the trailhead, affords a fine view to the south of Mount Adams and the Goat Rocks Wilderness. To the north is that big mountain that gives the park its name.

# 36. Mazama Ridge

| | |
|---|---|
| **RATING** | 👤👤👤 |
| **DISTANCE** | 4.0 miles round-trip |
| **HIKING TIME** | 2 hours, 30 minutes |
| **ELEVATION GAIN** | 800 feet |
| **HIGH POINT** | 5,680 feet |
| **EFFORT** | Moderate Workout |
| **BEST SEASON** | Summer, fall |
| **PERMITS/CONTACT** | Entrance fee/Paradise Visitor Center, (360) 569-6036, www.nps.gov/mora |
| **MAPS** | USGS Mount Rainier East; Green Trails Paradise 270 S |
| **NOTES** | Dogs or bikes prohibited; road closed in winter |

## THE HIKE

Climb to a cliffside view of Louise Lake and the Stevens Canyon, then turn along the broad Mazama Ridge, decorated with wildflower meadows and alpine tarns overlooked by Mount Rainier.

## GETTING THERE

From I-5 in Tacoma, take the Highway 7 exit 133 and follow Highway 7 south to Elbe and Highway 706. Follow Highway 706 east through Ashford to the Nisqually Entrance of Mount Rainier National Park, where you'll be asked to pay an entry fee. Continue past Longmire to the Stevens Canyon–Reflection Lakes Road and turn right. Follow this road 1.7 miles to the Reflection Lakes parking area. The trailhead is located between the Reflection Lakes and Louise Lake, 4,880 feet above sea level. GPS coordinates: N46°46′08″; W121°43′27″

If you wish to bypass most of urban Tacoma, Parkland, and part of Spanaway, continue north on I-5 to the Highway 512 exit 127 and follow the highway to the first exit, Steele Street. Turn left on Steele and follow the Spanaway Loop Road back to Highway 7 on the southern outskirts of Spanaway, and turn right to join the route described above.

## THE TRAIL

This trail drops down to the Reflection Lakes and a marshy meadow where you'll spot Jeffrey's shooting star, marsh marigold, and monkey flower.

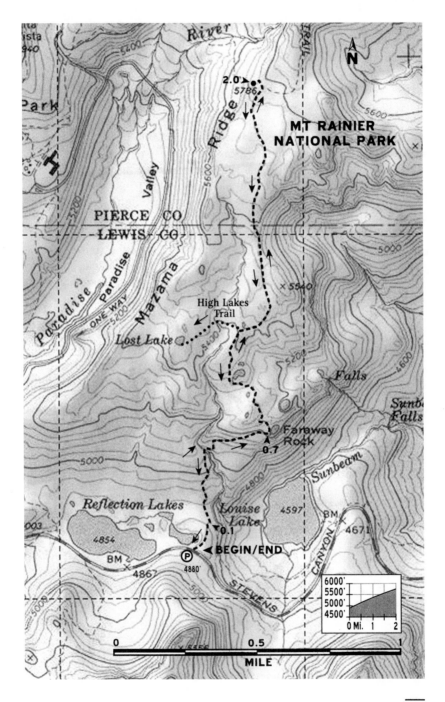

Across the meadow, you'll begin a moderately steep 220-foot climb in subalpine forest and sloping meadows filled with avalanche lilies. Cross a creek at **0.6** mile and switch back twice before climbing on a traverse to a bench and alpine tarn that marks Faraway Rock.

This is a great place to catch your breath and look down the Stevens Canyon valley across Louise Lake. Once you've taken in the view, turn north as the trail begins a gentle climb along the wide ridge, alternating between alpine forest and meadow. Ahead, Mount Rainier towers above.

The trail continues to climb, though never as steep as the first mile, along the ridge crest where you can sometimes look across the Paradise Valley to the Paradise Inn and Paradise Park. At **1.1** miles, pass a 5,540-foot hill on the right, where the ridge narrows slightly and the way steepens briefly.

This short climb ends as Mazama Ridge broadens and heather meadows spread on both sides of the trail. At **2.0** miles, the trail reaches a junction with the Skyline Trail, your turnaround point. The meadows and bowls of Mazama Ridge provide excellent backcountry skiing and snowshoeing for those heading out from Paradise.

## GOING FARTHER

The best way to extend this hike is to turn right and climb the Skyline Trail to the Stevens–Van Trump Historical Monument and Sluiskin Falls, about a half mile one-way. You can continue climbing along the Skyline Trail or turn right at its junction with the trail to the Paradise Glacier, about 1.5 miles one-way.

# MORE MOUNT RAINIER NATIONAL PARK HIKES

🚶 **Glacier View,** 5.8 miles round-trip, Moderate Workout. Trailhead located off Highway 706 east of Ashford on Forest Road 59.

🚶 **Noble Knob,** 7.0 miles round-trip, Moderate Workout. Trailhead located off Highway 410 at the top of Corral Pass on rough, steep Forest Road 7174.

🚶 **Crystal Lakes,** 6.0 miles round-trip, Prepare to Perspire. Trailhead off Highway 410, 4.6 miles east of Crystal Mountain Boulevard.

🚶 **Summerland,** 8.4 miles round-trip, Prepare to Perspire. Trailhead 3 miles past the White River Entrance Station at Fryingpan Creek bridge.

🚶 **Eunice Lake and Tolmie Peak,** 6.2 miles round-trip, Prepare to Perspire. Trailhead at Mowich Lake and the end of Highway 165.

🚶 **Spray Park,** 7.0 miles round-trip, Prepare to Perspire. Trailhead at Mowich Lake and the end of Highway 165.

The upper part of Smith Creek Trail (#39) provides a view of Mount St. Helens.

# MOUNT ST. HELENS NATIONAL VOLCANIC MONUMENT

True story: I was driving furiously to Paradise on Mount Rainier for a springtime ski on May 18, 1980. I was listening to Stravinsky's "The Rite of Spring" and oblivious to pretty much everything but getting to the mountain before the corn snow turned to mush.

Thus it was that I drove into the ash cloud from a volcanic explosion so powerful that pieces of Mount St. Helens landed in Montana. I was speeding—ironically, it seemed to me—through Ashford and initially thought I was driving into a thunderstorm. Seconds later, I realized that the big drops of rain hitting the windshield were actually clumps of the volcano exploding in dark puffs. I turned on the headlights, but they were no match for the midnight ashfall. I turned around and headed back to the sunlight, which was a good move since the skiing at Paradise was ruined for the rest of the season.

Though that eruption was nearly four decades ago, day hiking around Mount St. Helens remains one of the most relevant ways to experience a historic day. Trails take you past the steaming maw of a volcano that is only sleeping by the geologic calendar, along a lake that didn't exist before that explosive day, past the rusting hulk of an auto thrown 60 feet by the blast, along a ridge 6 miles away from the crater where a geologist was killed, past hills up to 600 feet high that were once the guts of the volcano.

The 110,000-acre monument draws about 250,000 visitors each year, which is about one quarter of the number of people who arrived a decade after the eruption. One of the larger groups of people who tour the mountain these days does so aboard mountain bikes; a number of the trails are open to mountain bike travel. These routes are clearly marked so hikers can avoid those pathways if they wish, but the riders you may encounter are courteous and follow the golden rule of trail traffic: bikers yield to hikers and horses; hikers yield to horses.

Remember that the blast zone around St. Helens is still devoid of any forest that is big enough to deflect wind or shelter you from rain, so carry a windbreaker on trails in that area. Another caveat: there's little shade and summer days can get mighty hot, especially for the poor pets left in cars because they are prohibited on trails.

# MOUNT ST. HELENS NATIONAL VOLCANIC MONUMENT

37  Harmony Falls

38  Norway Pass

39  Smith Creek Trail

40  Windy Ridge

41  Hummocks Trail

42  Coldwater Lake Trail

43  Boundary Trail

44  Ape Caves

45  Lava Canyon

46  Ape Canyon Trail

# 37. Harmony Falls

| | |
|---:|:---|
| RATING | 🚶🚶🚶🚶 |
| DISTANCE | 2.0 miles round-trip |
| HIKING TIME | 1 hour, 30 minutes |
| ELEVATION GAIN | 700 feet |
| HIGH POINT | 4,000 feet |
| EFFORT | Prepare to Perspire |
| BEST SEASON | Summer, fall |
| PERMITS/CONTACT | Daily or annual fee required/ Mount St. Helens National Volcanic Monument, (360) 449-7800, www.fs.usda.gov/main/mountsthelens |
| MAPS | USGS Spirit Lake West, Spirit Lake East; Green Trails Spirit Lake 332 |
| NOTES | Dogs and bikes prohibited; good family walk; road closed in winter |

## THE HIKE
Walk down a moderately steep trail through a shady lane of young alder to the ashen shore of a lake where an entire forest floats.

## GETTING THERE
From I-5, take US Highway 12 to Randle and turn south on Forest Road 25, turning right on Forest Road 99 after passing Iron Creek Falls. Follow FR 99 for 12 miles to the parking area for Harmony Trail No. 224, on the right. GPS coordinates: N46°16′28″; W122°06′17″

## THE TRAIL
This short path was one of the very first trails built by US Forest Service crews after the 1980 eruption of Mount St. Helens and one I hiked with an escort before it was opened to the public. At that time, the ash had barely settled and evidence of that incredible blast was all around. Big shattered evergreens stripped of limbs and bark covered the ash, all pointing in unison away from the massive explosion that felled them.

So it was a big surprise when I returned in the late summer of 2014 to find that same trail surrounded by green alder and juvenile evergreens,

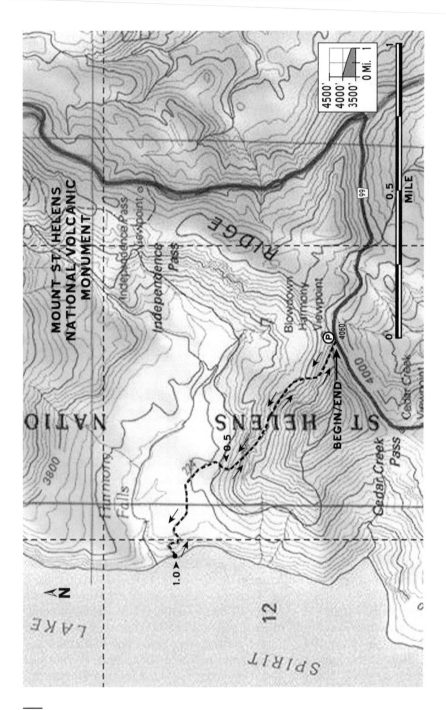

Harmony Falls trail leads across a volcanic plain to log-filled Spirit Lake.

sprouting along the hillside as if the blast nearly four decades ago never happened. Evidence that it had, however, was quickly obvious with a glance to the south and the gaping gray mound that was once a perfectly symmetrical snow giant.

The trail begins descending immediately on a moderate grade where views to Spirit Lake below are blocked by the young forest. You'll continue for a half mile before the trail takes a broad turn and then curves onto the ash and cinder plain above Spirit Lake, with a view to Harmony Falls, now half the height it was before the eruption. The final descent to the shoreline, 1.0 mile from the trailhead, is slightly steeper and loosely compacted.

Spirit Lake hosts a huge raft of logs that cover much of its surface, remnants of the ancient forest that surrounded the lake. When the mountain blew, a landslide rolled into the lake and created a wave that washed up and dragged the fallen timber into the water. It is a reminder to all that nobody can clear-cut a forest like Mother Nature.

If your knees don't remind you to take your time climbing back to the trailhead, I'll do so. Take your time climbing back to the trailhead.

# 38. Norway Pass

| | |
|---|---|
| RATING | 🧍🧍🧍🧍🧍 |
| DISTANCE | 4.2 miles round-trip |
| HIKING TIME | 3 hours |
| ELEVATION GAIN | 850 feet |
| HIGH POINT | 4,555 feet |
| EFFORT | Prepare to Perspire |
| BEST SEASON | Summer, fall |
| PERMITS/CONTACT | Daily or annual fee required/ |
| | Mount St. Helens National Volcanic Monument, |
| | (360) 449-7800, www.fs.usda.gov/main/mountsthelens |
| MAPS | USGS Spirit Lake West, Spirit Lake East; |
| | Green Trails Spirit Lake 332 |
| NOTES | Dogs and bikes prohibited; good family hike |

## THE HIKE

Start early for solitude on this climb to an unbeatable view of Mount St. Helens. If hiking in the late summer, you may never reach Norway Pass if you stop to pick huckleberries.

## GETTING THERE

From, take US Highway 12 to Randle and turn south on Forest Road 25, turning right on Forest Road 99 after passing Iron Creek Falls. Follow FR 99 to its junction with Forest Road 26 and turn right. Follow FR 26 for about a mile to the parking area and trailhead on the left, 3,710 feet above sea level. GPS coordinates: N46°18'17"; W122°04'58"

## THE TRAIL

A reader took me to task for describing this trail as an "easy walk" in an earlier guide, and she was correct. I blame an old analog altimeter; my wife, B. B. Hardbody, insists it was operator error.

Anyway, Norway Pass is no easy walk, but rather a steady climb that shouldn't be missed by anyone who is capable of climbing a moderately steep path for 2 miles. You'll drop a bit to cross a creek that may be dry in summer, then begin climbing over a hillock before turning south and starting up a brushy ridge, 0.2 mile from the trailhead.

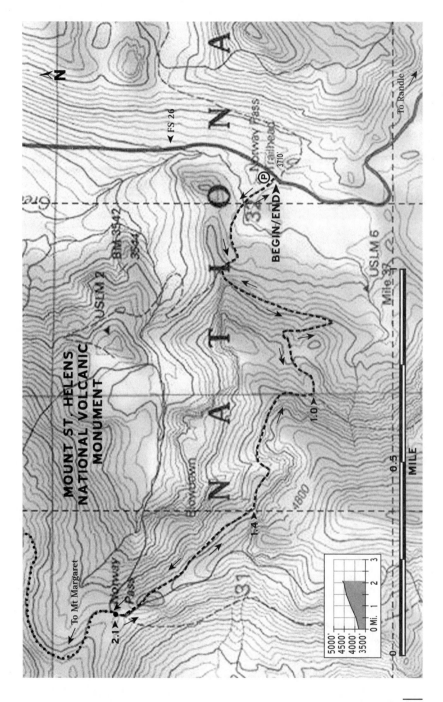

Spirit Lake and Mount St. Helens from Norway Pass.

Here the trail makes a broad switchback and begins a long ascending traverse to the south where you'll get views to the trailhead and Meta Lake below. After a half mile, switch back and round a small hill to a junction with the Independence Ridge Trail. Switch back to the right and continue climbing along the ridge, which in late summer is densely populated by huckleberries and the people who pick them. If you like huckleberries, expect to get purple hands and perhaps never reach Norway Pass.

The trail continues to climb, and you may notice that unlike many mountain trails, this one might be a bit smoother. The reason is that much of the former Mount St. Helens is under your feet and many rocks and roots are covered. You can look ahead to the broad and barren slopes of Mount Margaret, where the 1980 eruption leveled the forest.

At **2.1** miles, reach Norway Pass and a grand view of Mount St. Helens, hidden until now by the ridge you've been climbing. The best views are up the trail to your left, on the Independence Pass Trail.

## GOING FARTHER

You can make a loop trip of about 8.0 miles by hiking south on the Independence Pass Trail 227 to its junction with the Independence Ridge Trail 227A. Follow it back to the junction with the Norway Pass Trail and turn right to the trailhead. The Independence Ridge Trail was rough and not recently maintained in the fall of 2014.

Another more popular alternative is to climb another steep one-way mile to the right to Mount Margaret, where the view of St. Helens is even better than it is from Norway Pass.

# 39. Smith Creek Trail

| | |
|---|---|
| RATING | 🚶🚶 |
| DISTANCE | 4.6 miles round-trip |
| HIKING TIME | 3 hours |
| ELEVATION GAIN | 1,500 feet |
| HIGH POINT | 4,190 feet |
| EFFORT | Prepare to Perspire |
| BEST SEASON | Fall |
| PERMITS/CONTACT | None/Mount St. Helens National Volcanic Monument, (360) 449-7800, www.fs.usda.gov/main/mountsthelens |
| MAPS | USGS Spirit Lake West, Spirit Lake East; Green Trails Spirit Lake 332 |
| NOTES | Leashed dogs and mountain bikes welcome; carry water; road closed in winter |

## THE HIKE

Here's a great trail for views of the mountain that doesn't get as much pedestrian traffic as some of the other pathways in the blast zone but is popular with mountain bikers.

## GETTING THERE

From I-5, take US Highway 12 to Randle and turn south on Forest Road 25, turning right on Forest Road 99 after passing Iron Creek Falls. Follow FR 99 to its junction with Forest Road 26. Keep left and continue on FR 99 for 6 miles to the Donnybrook Viewpoint, 4,190 feet above sea level. GPS coordinates: N46°15′29″; W122°06′59″

Note: If parking is not available at the trailhead, drive 0.3 mile south on FR 99 to the Smith Creek Viewpoint parking area. A daily or annual fee is required for parking there.

## THE TRAIL

This trek isn't strenuous for most hikers with good knees until they reach the turnaround point, about 1,500 vertical feet below where you stand at the trailhead, all fresh and dewy. That's because the upper portion of the downhill trail isn't as steep as the lower sections, and if

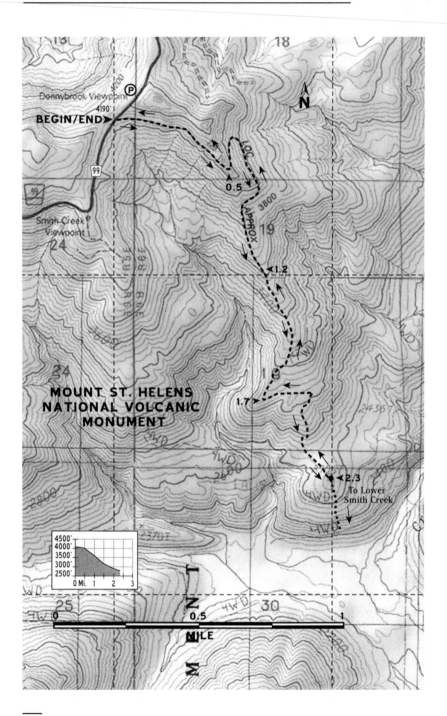

you've waited until autumn for this hike, it shouldn't be as hot or windy as it sometimes gets in the summer.

You'll get some great views of the crater of Mount St. Helens as you start down the trail, which begins with your back to the mountain on a gentle grade to the north. After hiking 0.5 mile, you'll round a prominent 4,300-foot-high rock sentinel on your left, and a quarter mile later, begin following a much steeper path that turns to the south and views of the mountain above. The path again traverses more gently for a bit, then turns and follows the crest of a ridge to a spot 400 vertical feet below and 1.2 miles from the trailhead.

Still in the blast zone of the 1980 eruption, the trail continues down along the ridge crest, curving slightly to the west before switching back to the east, 1.7 miles from the trailhead. The path again becomes a more gentle descent, but only long enough to give your knees a rest, then turns downhill, abandons the crest of the ridge, and drops in swooping curves to a saddle below a 2,700-foot-high knoll. This is your turnaround point, 2.3 miles from the trailhead. Drink water and have a bite to eat; you've a tough climb back to the trailhead.

## GOING FARTHER
This trail, No. 225, drops another 6.8 steep miles down the Smith Creek canyon to a trailhead at the end of Forest Road 8322. It's mainly a mountain bike route, although hikers who can con strong Norwegian tourists into a car- and key-exchange can make it a one-way walk.

# 40. Windy Ridge

| | |
|---|---|
| RATING | 🚶🚶🚶🚶🚶 |
| DISTANCE | 4.0 miles round-trip |
| HIKING TIME | 2 hours, 30 minutes |
| ELEVATION GAIN | 200 feet |
| HIGH POINT | 4,200 feet |
| EFFORT | Moderate Workout |
| BEST SEASON | Fall |
| PERMITS/CONTACT | Daily or annual fee required/ Mount St. Helens National Volcanic Monument, (360) 449-7800, www.fs.usda.gov/main/mountsthelens |
| MAPS | USGS Spirit Lake West, Spirit Lake East; Green Trails Spirit Lake 332 |
| NOTES | Leashed dogs and mountain bikes welcome; carry water and windbreaker; road closed in winter |

## THE HIKE

This is your best opportunity to get up close and personal with a volcano that literally blew its top not so long ago, across a landscape today littered with evidence of the power of that 1980 explosion.

## GETTING THERE

From I-5, take US Highway 12 to Randle and turn south on Forest Road 25, turning right on Forest Road 99 after passing Iron Creek Falls. Follow FR 99 to its end at the Windy Ridge Viewpoint and trailhead, 4,090 feet above sea level. GPS coordinates: N46°15'00"; W122°08'09"

## THE TRAIL

Two things make this hike more difficult than the grade and distance would suggest: the surface of the trail is pumice, which rolls underfoot; and the summer heat, which can be avoided by hiking in the fall or as early as possible in the morning. These difficulties are but minor annoyances given that this hike is one of the best in the monument for seeing what is left of a mountain that was 1,300 feet higher on May 17, 1980 than it was a day later.

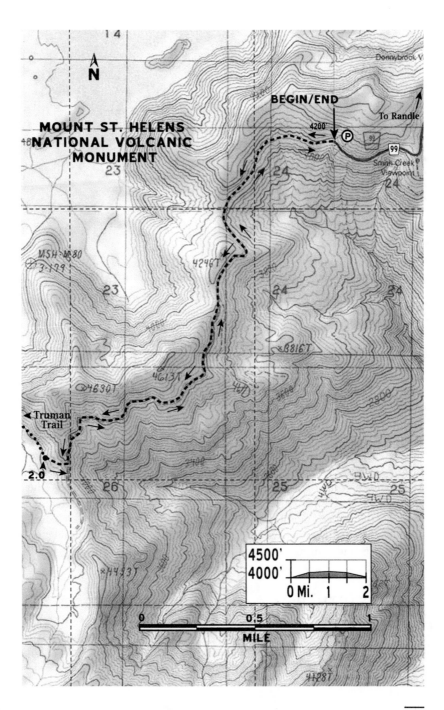

The trail along Windy Ridge serves hikers and bicyclists.

You'll climb past a gate on a logging road that was abandoned after the eruption and is a popular and rugged mountain bike adventure. As we climbed along the road, a mountain biker whizzed by toward the trailhead. "How was the ride?" I asked.

"Great!" he shouted back. Then he added, "For the survivors."

Take my word for it: the 26-mile ride is much tougher than the 4-mile walk. You'll climb, then drop around a hillside that temporarily blocks your view of the crater. At a saddle **0.5** mile from the trailhead, you'll see evidence of the blast—trunks of massive evergreens laid low and stripped of limbs and bark, all pointing neatly to the north like a compass, away from the crater.

You'll alternately climb and descend along the trail for another mile along a southeast-facing slope that can get hot and windy in the summer months, making cool mornings or evenings the best time to walk here. At **1.5** miles from the trailhead, you'll begin to drop to the very edge of the blast zone and the junction with the mountain bike trail leading down to the Ape Canyon, **1.7** miles from the trailhead. Stay right and enter a restricted area where dogs are prohibited, and walk another 0.3 mile to a second trail junction with the Truman Trail No. 207, your turn-around point.

## GOING FARTHER

Your best option for a longer hike is to follow the Truman Trail northwest across the blast plain, now filled with birdsong and occasional elk herds. You can hike about 1.5 miles one-way to a high plain above the southern end of Spirit Lake.

# 41. Hummocks Trail

| | |
|---|---|
| RATING | 🚶🚶 |
| DISTANCE | 2.3-mile loop |
| HIKING TIME | 1 hour, 30 minutes |
| ELEVATION GAIN | 220 feet |
| HIGH POINT | 2,500 feet |
| EFFORT | Moderate Workout |
| BEST SEASON | Summer, fall |
| PERMITS/CONTACT | None/Mount St. Helens National Volcanic Monument, (360) 449-7800, www.fs.usda.gov/main/mountsthelens |
| MAPS | USGS Elk Rock; Green Trails Spirit Lake 332 |
| NOTES | Dogs and bikes prohibited; good family hike; road closed in winter |

## THE HIKE

Walk around giant hills of volcanic rubble that covered an entire forest during the eruption of Mount St. Helens, home today to wildlife and a substantial number of bird species—enough to make this part of the Great Washington State Birding Trail.

## GETTING THERE

From I-5, follow Highway 505 exit 59 through Toledo to Highway 504, then take Highway 504 past the Coldwater Visitor Center 2.4 miles to the Hummocks Trail parking area, 2,500 feet above sea level. GPS coordinates: N46°17'11"; W122°12'43"

## THE TRAIL

This trail climbs over and around massive mounds of rock and sediment that blew out of Mount St. Helens. Short sections of the trail are steep and may present unstable footing for hikers wearing lightweight shoes.

Hike to the left from the trailhead to walk the path clockwise past a number of small ponds, climbing gently up and down but generally dropping toward the North Fork of the Toutle River. At 0.7 mile, the trail makes a wide turn at a junction with the Boundary Trail. Stay right and walk between two marshy ponds before turning downstream along the

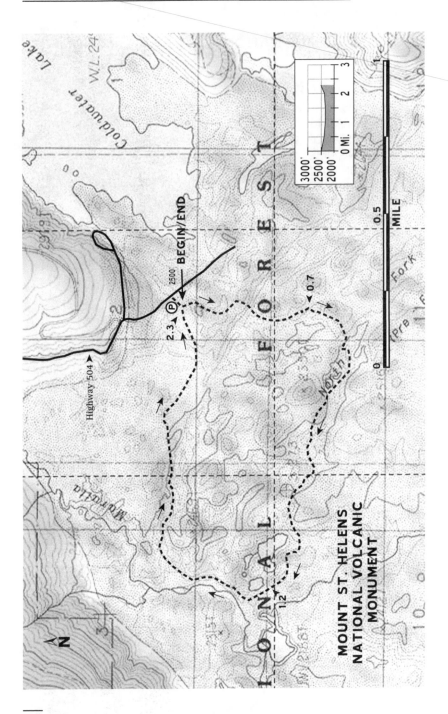

An interpretive sign explains how the hummocks were formed when Mount St. Helens blew her top.

river and winding between the mounds of debris. This area is home to a wide variety of wildlife, including elk, which are often seen in this area. Birds sing from pond borders and raptors float on thermals above.

After about a half mile, the pathway turns back to the north. You'll weave through hillocks and alder forest back to the trailhead.

## GOING FARTHER

The best alternative from the Hummocks trailhead is to begin a serious climb to the left at the junction with the Boundary Trail, following it 1.0 one-way mile up to the Loowit Viewpoint before turning back to the loop trail. This would make the total hike 4.3 miles.

# 42. Coldwater Lake Trail

| | |
|---|---|
| RATING | 🚶🚶🚶 |
| DISTANCE | 6.0 miles round-trip |
| HIKING TIME | 3 hours, 30 minutes |
| ELEVATION GAIN | 260 feet |
| HIGH POINT | 2,800 feet |
| EFFORT | Easy Walk |
| BEST SEASON | Summer, fall |
| PERMITS/CONTACT | Daily or annual fee required/ Mount St. Helens National Volcanic Monument, (360) 449-7800, www.fs.usda.gov/main/mountsthelens |
| MAPS | USGS Spirit Lake West, Elk Rock (trail not shown); Green Trails Spirit Lake 332 |
| NOTES | Dogs and bikes prohibited; good family hike; short wheelchair-accessible path at trailhead; road closed in winter |

## THE HIKE
Walk above the shores of a lake that is less than four decades old. Coldwater Lake was created by the eruption of Mount St. Helens, and much of the vegetation sprouting from the hillside is fodder for the elk herds you are likely to see along the trail.

## GETTING THERE
From I-5, follow Highway 505 from I-5 exit 59 through Toledo to Highway 504, then take Highway 504 to the Coldwater Lake boat launch and trailhead, 2,540 feet above sea level. GPS coordinates: N46°17′29″; W122°16′01″

## THE TRAIL
After an initial climb, this walk features a number of short ascents followed by an equal number of descents as you cross streams and gullies along the way. You'll cross a couple of streams that may be dry in the summer, and at **0.7** mile, arrive at a junction with the Elk Bench Trail. Stay right and continue another 0.3 mile to a spur trail leading down

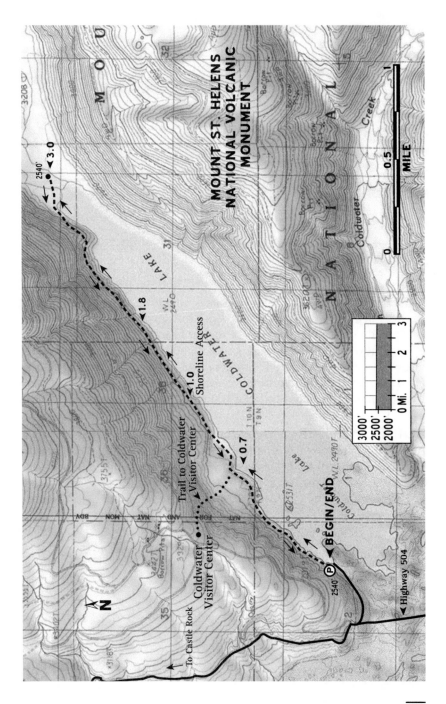

Coldwater Lake didn't exist before May 18, 1980.

to the lakeshore, one of only a few areas along the shore where public access is permitted. It's also a good spot to turn around for those with small children or who are seeking a shorter hike.

In the next 2.0 miles, the trail passes stands of cottonwood and alder where elk are often seen. You'll cross several more creeks and dry gullies and 1.8 miles from the trailhead, cross beneath a waterfall. Your turnaround point is the end of the lake, 3.0 miles from the trailhead.

## GOING FARTHER

You can hike another 0.8 mile to a second access point to the lake and a junction with a trail leading steeply a little over a mile one-way, up Coldwater Ridge to the South Coldwater Trail.

# 43. Boundary Trail

| | |
|---|---|
| RATING | 🚶🚶🚶🚶 |
| DISTANCE | 6.6 miles round-trip |
| HIKING TIME | 3 hours, 30 minutes |
| ELEVATION GAIN | 180 feet |
| HIGH POINT | 4,400 feet |
| EFFORT | Moderate Workout |
| BEST SEASON | Summer, fall |
| PERMITS/CONTACT | Daily or annual fee required/ Mount St. Helens National Volcanic Monument, (360) 449-7800, www.fs.usda.gov/main/mountsthelens |
| MAPS | USGS Spirit Lake West, Elk Rock (trail not shown); Green Trails Spirit Lake 332 |
| NOTES | Dogs and bikes prohibited; road closed in winter; carry a wind breaker |

## THE HIKE

Barren and traversing high ridges and steep sidehills, this windy hike gets about as close as you can get to the crater of Mount St. Helens.

## GETTING THERE

From I-5, follow Highway 505 exit 59 through Toledo to Highway 504, then take Highway 504 to the end of the road at the Johnston Ridge Observatory. This big parking area, 4,400 feet above sea level, can get crowded on summer weekends, so the earlier you get there, the better. GPS coordinates: N46°16′41″; W122°12′58″

## THE TRAIL

Even if you decide you don't want to hike the entire 6.6 miles, out and back, at least a portion of this trail is well worth the drive to the Johnston Ridge Observatory. The observatory is one of the finest close views you'll get of the Mount St. Helens crater, and it honors the geologist who lost his life on this very spot. An early starting time is advisable to avoid afternoon crowds, stay cooler on hot days, and decrease the likelihood of getting blown around by frequent winds.

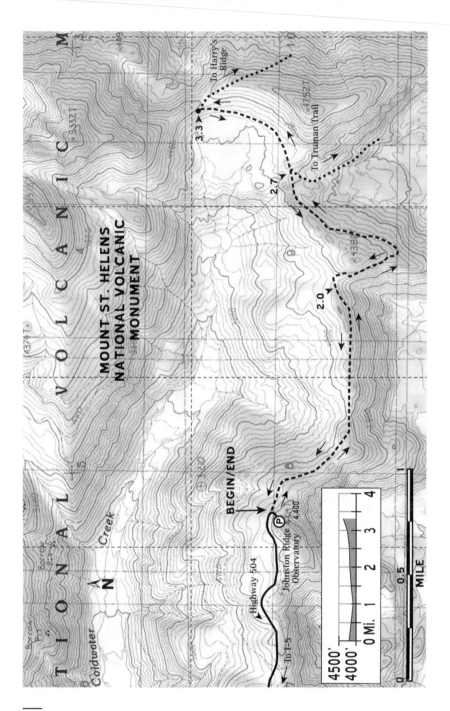

A memorial at the Johnston Ridge Observatory honors the fifty-seven people killed when Mount St. Helens erupted.

If you want the easiest hike, follow the Boundary Trail around and over the observatory hill where, at the end of the loop, the Boundary Trail swoops down a long ridge that drops steeply off to the devastated valley of the North Fork of the Toutle River. This ridge becomes very narrow 1.0 mile from the trailhead, but it widens quickly for another mile to a point where it turns south to traverse a very steep and loose volcanic slope around a sharp ridge.

This spot, 2.0 miles from the trailhead, gives you as good a view as you're going to get anywhere beyond, so if you or the kids don't feel comfortable hiking farther, make this the turnaround. Once you're around the steep ridge, the trail continues for another 0.7 mile to a junction with the Truman Trail. Stay left and continue along the ridge for 0.6 mile to Harry's Ridge, where a trail turns right and eventually affords a view of Spirit Lake. This junction is 3.3 miles from the trailhead, your turnaround.

## GOING FARTHER

You can hike Harry's Ridge Trail for another mile to make an 8.0-mile hike, out and back. Except for the view of Spirit Lake below, the scenery is pretty much the same.

# 44. Ape Caves

| | |
|---|---|
| **RATING** | 🚶🚶🚶🚶 |
| **DISTANCE** | 2.8 miles round-trip |
| **HIKING TIME** | 2 hours/3 hours (if exploring caves) |
| **ELEVATION GAIN** | 480 feet |
| **HIGH POINT** | 2,480 feet |
| **EFFORT** | Moderate Workout/Prepare to Perspire (in caves) |
| **BEST SEASON** | Summer |
| **PERMITS/CONTACT** | Daily or annual fee required/ Mount St. Helens National Volcanic Monument, (360) 449-7800, www.fs.usda.gov/main/mountsthelens |
| **MAPS** | USGS Mount Mitchell; Green Trails Mount St. Helens 364 |
| **NOTES** | Dogs and bikes prohibited |

## THE HIKE

It's not all about that hulking volcano to the north, as this mostly easy climb demonstrates. You'll walk through sparse forest to the exit of the highest of two lava tubes—the longest in North America—where you can return by trail or take the subterranean route back to the trailhead.

## GETTING THERE

Take Highway 503 from I-5 exit 21 at Woodland and drive east of Cougar on Forest Road 90 to Forest Road 83 and turn left. Follow FR 83 for 2 miles to Forest Road 8303 and turn left, arriving at the big parking area and trailhead in 1 mile, 2,120 feet above sea level. GPS coordinates: N46°06′25″; W122°12′43″

## THE TRAIL

Begin by joining the great majority of pedestrians touring the crowded visitor center, reading all about hiking in caves, and perhaps renting a lantern for cave exploration. Then leave most hikers as they plunge underground a few hundred feet away and continue past the entrance to the first Ape Cave on a nice trail that climbs gently up a lightly wooded hill tufted by bear grass. The trail generally follows above the underground

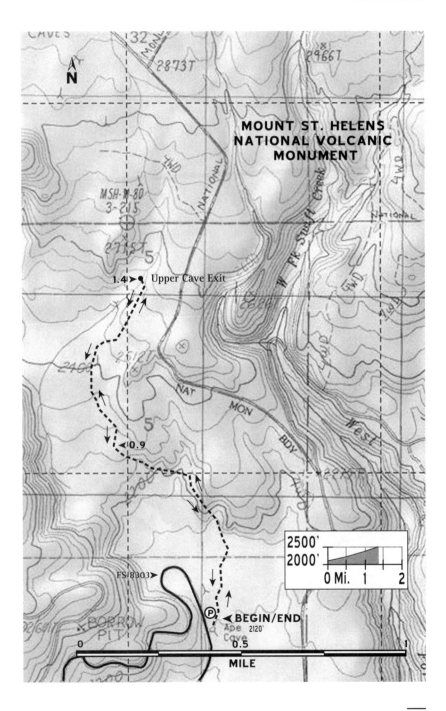

The exit to the upper Ape Cave begins with a ladder climb.

route through the caves, named after a local Boy Scout troop who called themselves "The Apes."

Where the pumice sand has filled the lava lumps from a long-ago eruption of Mount St. Helens, the trail is smooth and flat as a California beach. But when it scales the plateau-like benches, the lava underneath is sharp and exposed. You'll see their ropy masses frozen in exactly the spot they turned from liquid to rock 2,000 years ago.

At **0.9** mile, you'll climb along a lumpy lava mound marked by wide pits dotting the smoother rock surface. Another larger hole reaches to the tube below, where subterranean hikers in the upper cave get a window to the sky.

A side trail heads to the right to the entrance of the upper cave; you'll stay left and continue climbing over a hump of rock. The trail then climbs into a forest above the ancient lava flow and traverses to the exit of the second cave, **1.4** miles from the trailhead.

This is your turnaround point, a good spot for a picnic lunch in the sunshine and for donning the extra clothing and equipment you'll need if you plan to descend into the cave for the return trip. If that is your choice, you'll find a steep metal ladder that deposits you into the upper cave. Follow the rough rock tube down to the right, and be prepared to squeeze past hikers, scramble over lumpy lava, and climb in some tight places.

Perhaps the best advice is to return by the surface trail and take an easier walk through the lower tube. For either cave, bring a strong headlamp or flashlight and extra batteries. And put on a sweater or jacket before descending into the caves—the temperature is a constant 44 degrees. (Unless St. Helens sends another bunch of lava down the tube.)

## GOING FARTHER

The best way to extend your hike would be to take the 0.5-mile Trail of Two Forests, a half mile down Forest Road 8303 from the Lava Cave trailhead. This loop hike traverses both old growth and relatively younger forest that grew following the 2,000-year-old eruption of Mount St. Helens.

# 45. Lava Canyon

| | |
|---|---|
| RATING | 🚶🚶🚶 |
| DISTANCE | 1.4-mile loop |
| HIKING TIME | 1 hour, 30 minutes |
| ELEVATION GAIN | 300 feet |
| HIGH POINT | 2,800 feet |
| EFFORT | Moderate Workout |
| BEST SEASON | Summer, fall |
| PERMITS/CONTACT | Daily or annual fee required/ Mount St. Helens National Volcanic Monument, (360) 449-7800, www.fs.usda.gov/main/mountsthelens |
| MAPS | USGS Smith Creek; Green Trails Mount St. Helens 364 |
| NOTES | Dogs and bikes prohibited; wheelchair-accessible portion |

## THE HIKE

Get a look at two sides of a steep, rocky canyon carved in the lava of an ancient eruption of Mount St. Helens. Scramble across a swinging suspension bridge and climb steep metal stairs on the way back.

## GETTING THERE

Take Highway 503 from I-5 exit 21 at Woodland and drive east of Cougar on Forest Road 90 to Forest Road 83 and turn left. Follow FR 83 for a little more than 12 miles to the end of the road and trailhead, 2,800 feet above sea level. GPS coordinates: N46°09′56″; W122°05′32″

## THE TRAIL

Although the first 0.4 mile of this trail is paved and barrier-free, I'd not want to navigate the first five switchbacks aboard a wheelchair without some assistance or a "crash course" in navigation from a wheelchair athlete. It's not the steepness of the downhill grade that would do me in, but the sharp curves bounded by rock walls.

The paved path is much easier navigating on two feet, and I'd call it an easy walk except for the stair climb and suspension bridge ahead. Follow the pavement down the gentle grade to a fenced platform overlooking

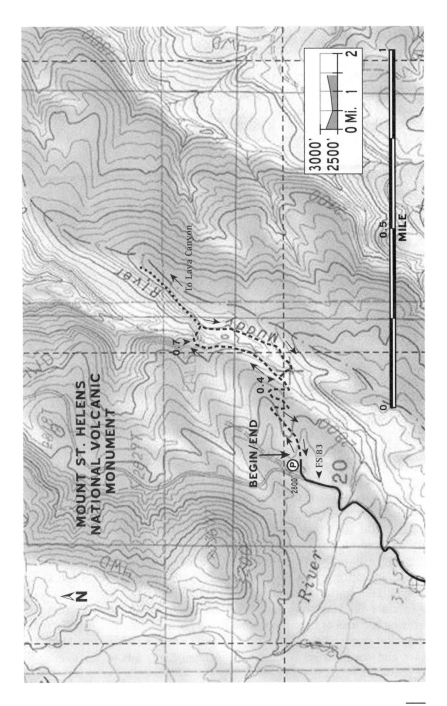

A suspension bridge crosses Lava Canyon.

the Muddy River as it crashes through a narrow lava canyon. The rock here, **0.4** mile from the trailhead, is polished and smooth from the water and the coarse pumice it carried down from the mountain, but it feels like you're walking on hard sandpaper. On rocks below, you'll see the steel bridge crossing the river, which is your return trail.

Look for the trail near the bottom of the rock as it leads downstream into forest above the canyon. The transition from rock to forest trail is the steepest you'll encounter on this side of the river, and it could be slippery going if it's wet. You'll walk another 0.3 mile in the forest above the river before arriving at a suspension bridge that dangles high above the river canyon.

Turn right and cross the bridge, which swings and bounces a bit and makes timid hikers like me thankful for sturdy handlines on each side. The bridge is fairly short, thanks to the steepness of the river canyon below, and once across the river you'll reach the junction of the Lava Canyon Trail to the left, and the Loop Trail to the right.

To close the loop, turn upstream and climb beside the river canyon, crossing sections of barren lava and forest for a quarter mile to a big rock lump and steel staircase. You'll climb the stairs to a rock overlooking the river and see the steel bridge just upstream that leads to the overlook.

Once you've snapped a selfie or two, cross the bridge and return to the trailhead.

## GOING FARTHER

For a longer walk, turn left at the suspension bridge junction and follow the trail as it descends steeply 0.5 mile to a steep 30-foot metal ladder that drops to the edge of the Lava Canyon. The trail beyond leads in another mile to a side trail and viewpoint on top of a lava formation called "The Ship." Turning around at this point would make a total hike of 4.4 miles; the Lava Canyon Trail continues another steep, exposed mile to a junction with the Smith Creek Trail.

# 46. Ape Canyon Trail

| | |
|---|---|
| RATING | 𝟘𝟘𝟘𝟘 |
| DISTANCE | 6.0 miles round-trip |
| HIKING TIME | 4 hours |
| ELEVATION GAIN | 850 feet |
| HIGH POINT | 3,720 feet |
| EFFORT | Moderate Workout |
| BEST SEASON | Fall |
| PERMITS/CONTACT | Daily or annual fee required/ Mount St. Helens National Volcanic Monument, (360) 449-7800, www.fs.usda.gov/main/mountsthelens |
| MAPS | USGS Smith Creek; Green Trails Mount St. Helens 364 |
| NOTES | Leashed dogs and mountain bikes welcome; carry water |

## THE HIKE
Share this scenic trail with mountain bike riders and climb along one of the mighty mudflows that vomited from Mount St. Helens when it erupted in a mile-wide lahar.

## GETTING THERE
Take Highway 503 from I-5 exit 21 at Woodland and drive east of Cougar on Forest Road 90 to Forest Road 83 and turn left. Follow FR 83 for 11.8 miles to the trailhead on the left, 2,800 feet above sea level. GPS coordinates: N46°09′55″; W122°05′31″

## THE TRAIL
One of the best trails in the lower portion of the Mount St. Helens National Volcanic Monument, this path takes you beside a massive landslide that swept from the erupting volcano in a matter of minutes. You'll begin in a young fir and cedar forest on a dry path that climbs at a moderate and steady grade that makes mountain bikers sweat on hot summer days and hikers happy for the limited shade along the route.

Once past an alder grove, you'll find a spur trail leading left at **0.6 mile** to a view of the lahar that avalanched down the **Muddy River** like a mile-wide bulldozer. Stay right and continue on the main trail, which

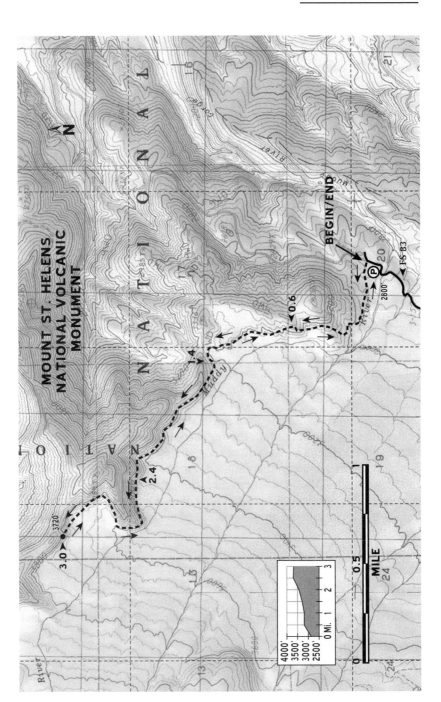

A massive lahar spit from Mount St. Helens beside the Ape Canyon Trail.

offers a number of side trips to look down on the rocky, treeless plain. At 1.4 miles from the trailhead, you'll transition from young forest to deep woods of old fir and hemlock. You can feel the temperature drop in these shady glades.

That is good, because the grade gets steeper here and switches back while climbing the ridge, alternating between views of the mudflow below and St. Helens above and old forest shade and alder brush. After climbing another mile, you'll find a view that provides a look to the north and east to Mount Rainier and Mount Adams. Continue climbing in switchbacks another half mile to your turnaround point at 3.0 miles, where you can look down on the expanse of the mudflow and East Dome.

## GOING FARTHER

If your knees aren't wobbling like pudding yet, this hike is one of the best for getting more exercise. You can climb another 2.5 miles and 400 vertical feet to the junction with the Loowit Trail or beyond to the base of Pumice Butte, where the views are barely worse than from the crater rim.

## MORE MOUNT ST. HELENS
## NATIONAL VOLCANIC MONUMENT HIKES

🏃 **West Boundary Trail**, 4.0 miles round-trip, Knee-Punishing. Trailhead at Johnston Ridge Observatory.

🏃 **South Coldwater Trail**, 10.0 miles round-trip, Knee-Punishing. Trailhead 1 mile south of Coldwater Lake boat launch off Highway 504.

🏃 **Jackpine Shelter**, 1.0 mile round-trip, Easy Walk. Trailhead 10.5 miles from Forest Road 90–Forest Road 83 intersection off FR 83.

🏃 **Trail of Two Forests**, 0.5 mile round-trip, Stroll in the Park. Trailhead 0.5 mile from the Forest Road 83–Forest Road 8303 junction off FR 8303.

🏃 **June Lake**, 2.8 miles round-trip, Easy Walk. Trailhead 10.0 miles from the Forest Road 90–Forest Road 83 junction off FR 83.

Paulina Lake from Big Obsidian Flow Trail (#53).

# NEWBERRY NATIONAL VOLCANIC MONUMENT

Basking in alpine desert sunshine, the Newberry National Volcanic Monument in Central Oregon is among my favorite hiking destinations. Because most of the 17-square-mile Newberry caldera rests above 6,000 feet, summer days don't make for unbearably hot trekking and nights are ideal for campfires and s'mores. It's not surprising that more than 200,000 visitors head for the monument every year, although you can still find plenty of lonesome trails on early summer mornings and late evenings. In the autumn, you'll likely walk miles on easy trails without encountering another hiking party.

Newberry Crater is the perfect place for those who take their hikes day by day. It's a short trip from Bend and even closer to Sunriver, now with a paved, 5-mile accessible trail that passes through the lower-elevation parts of the monument. You'll find hikes of every description, from knee-crunching climbs to shoreline strolls, from rock scrambles to cave crawling.

The Deschutes National Forest manages the 56,400-plus-acre monument, which means that leashed pets are welcome on many of the trails. You'll share some pathways with mountain bike enthusiasts and the two beautiful lakes—Paulina and East—serve up excellent fishing, paddling, and watersports. Winter closes portions of the monument to hikers, but snowshoe trekking, snowmobiling, and cross-country skiing are popular.

The network of trails offers a rare opportunity for the day hiker: a single trailhead can access as many as five or six different treks. By walking to a long, easy forest path that connects more trails, you can park at one location and hike virtually every trail in the Newberry Crater.

All of the hikes suggested here can be found along Highway 97, south of Bend. So, let's lace 'em up and get going on any of the eight hikes that follow.

# NEWBERRY NATIONAL VOLCANIC MONUMENT

47  Benham Falls Trail

48  Lava Cast Forest

49  Paulina Falls

50  Paulina Creek Trail

51  Little Crater Trail

52  Paulina Lakeshore Loop

53  Silica and Big
    Obsidian Flow Trails

54  Newberry Crater Trail

# 47. Benham Falls Trail

| | |
|---|---|
| RATING | 🚶🚶🚶🚶 |
| DISTANCE | 5.2 miles round-trip |
| HIKING TIME | 3 hours, 30 minutes |
| ELEVATION GAIN | 60 feet |
| HIGH POINT | 4,180 feet |
| EFFORT | Easy Walk |
| BEST SEASON | Summer, fall |
| PERMITS/CONTACT | Daily or annual fee required/ Newberry National Volcanic Monument, (541) 383-5700, www.fs.usda.gov/main/deschutes |
| MAPS | USGS Benham Falls; Newberry National Volcanic Monument handout, Volcanic Vistas |
| NOTES | Leashed dogs and mountain bikes welcome (bikes on separate trail); good family hike |

## THE HIKE

This is a pleasing stroll along a portion of the Deschutes River Trail through a forest of giant old pines to a tumbling rapid and beyond, to a riverfront picnic area.

## GETTING THERE

Follow Highway 97 south from Bend about 11 miles to the Lava Lands Visitor Center and turn right. Continue straight at the stop sign on Forest Road 9702 where you'll see a sign indicating Deschutes River. Follow FR 9702 for 4 miles to the parking area along the river, 4,180 feet above sea level. GPS coordinates: N43°55′53″; W121°24′40″

## THE TRAIL

Although the views of 10,358-foot-high South Sister and its jagged neighbor, 9,175-foot Broken Top, are excellent on spots along this route, this might be an excellent hike to save for a less-than-perfect Central Oregon day—if there is such an animal. The pine forest is beautiful, the Deschutes River both raucous and silent, with opportunities for wildlife-watching.

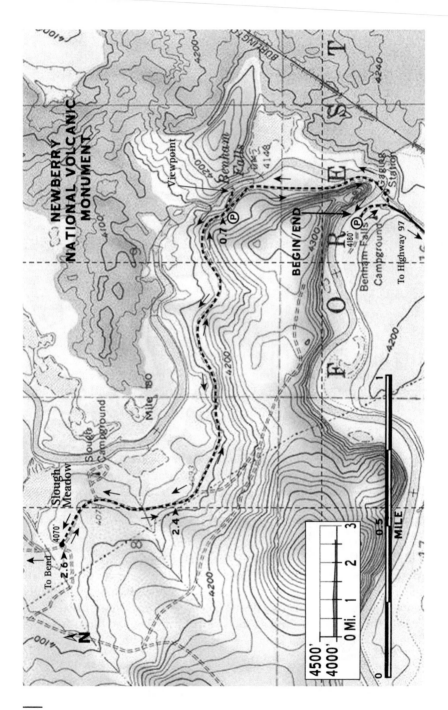

The Deschutes River rolls past the Benham Falls trailhead.

The hike begins by following the riverside downstream to a wide plank bridge that crosses the river above a wide curve, where you can look across the water to the dark sweep of a lava flow. Beyond, you'll share the wide old roadbed with bicyclists for a half mile before a separate pedestrian path splits to the right, closer to the river, **0.7** mile from the trailhead.

In another 150 yards, you'll arrive at a trail leading down to the right to a viewpoint of raging Benham Falls, which is a spectacular series of steep rapids. Families with younger children may wish to make this a turnaround point and a 1.4-mile hike, out and back. After viewing the falls, rejoin the main trail and turn right to Slough Meadow. A trailhead and parking area is located at Benham Falls.

On the trail to Slough Meadow, you pass by some huge pine trees, which make favorite roosting spots for ospreys that keep watch over the river. The giant birds nest in silver snags along the Deschutes, and if you watch them long enough, you'll discover ospreys are much better at catching fish than building nests. The trail climbs gently around a river slough at **2.4** miles from the trailhead, the one that likely gave the name to Slough Meadow, 0.2 mile beyond and your turnaround point, 2.6 miles from the trailhead.

## GOING FARTHER

The Deschutes River Trail is a wide, level path that leads all the way north through the city of Bend, and it makes an excellent bicycle ride or long hike. From Slough Meadow, the next section leads 1.8 miles one-way to the Dillon Falls day-use area.

Another option is to follow the recently paved accessible trail from the parking area south along the river for 1.5 miles to the resort community of Sunriver. Future plans call for the pavement to be extended all the way to Bend.

# 48. Lava Cast Forest

| | |
|---|---|
| RATING | 🥾🥾🥾 |
| DISTANCE | 1.1-mile loop |
| HIKING TIME | 1 hour, 30 minutes |
| ELEVATION GAIN | 100 feet |
| HIGH POINT | 5,765 feet |
| EFFORT | Stroll in the Park |
| BEST SEASON | Summer, fall |
| PERMITS/CONTACT | Daily or annual fee required/ Newberry National Volcanic Monument, (541) 383-5700, www.fs.usda.gov/main/deschutes |
| MAPS | USGS Lava Cast Forest; Newberry National Volcanic Monument handout, Volcanic Vistas |
| NOTES | Leashed dogs welcome; good family hike; paved trail too narrow or steep in places for wheelchairs |

## THE HIKE

This self-guiding walk on a paved trail offers a fascinating look at what happens when a river of molten liquid rock bubbles over a mighty forest.

## GETTING THERE

Follow Highway 97 from Bend for about 15 miles to the Sunriver exit, and after exiting, turn left and pass under the highway on Forest Road 9720, which turns to gravel in 0.2 mile. This road leads 10 miles on very rough washboard to a wide parking area and trailhead, 5,765 feet above sea level. GPS coordinates: N43°49′03″; W121°17′20″

## THE TRAIL

This hike leads across a massive flow of lava estimated to be around 7,000 years old where huge trees were consumed by the molten rock. As the lava cooled around the burned trees, it left casts of the trunks.

Given the fact that you're walking on top of a lava glacier, the paved trail is lumpy in spots. It climbs gently for about a half mile to a low lava ridge overlooking the flow before turning sharply and switching back down a steep but short grade. You'll weave through mounds of lava before climbing back to the trailhead.

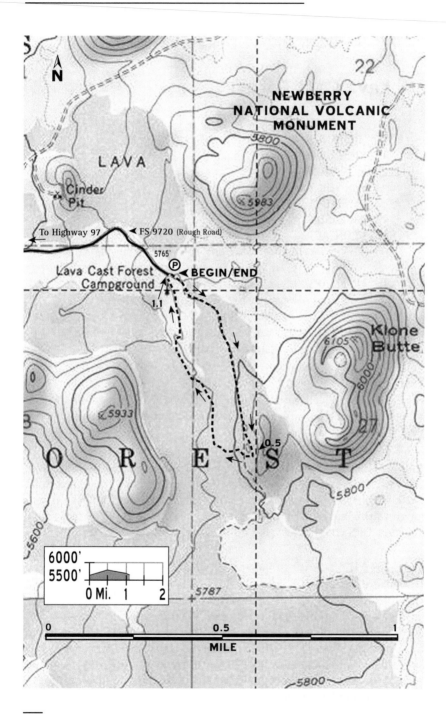

Molten lava vaporized this tree along the Lava Cast trail.

# 49. Paulina Falls

| | |
|---|---|
| RATING | 🧍🧍🧍 |
| DISTANCE | 1.8 miles round-trip |
| HIKING TIME | 1 hour, 30 minutes |
| ELEVATION GAIN | 160 feet |
| HIGH POINT | 6,340 feet |
| EFFORT | Easy Walk |
| BEST SEASON | Summer, fall |
| PERMITS/CONTACT | Daily or annual fee required/ Newberry National Volcanic Monument, (541) 383-5700, www.fs.usda.gov/main/deschutes |
| MAPS | USGS La Pine; Newberry National Volcanic Monument handout, Volcanic Vistas |
| NOTES | Leashed dogs welcome; good family hike; wheelchair access to falls viewpoint |

## THE HIKE

This short hike provides two views of 80-foot-high Paulina Falls; one from above and one from below. You can also take a walk upstream to the mouth of Paulina Creek at Paulina Lake.

## GETTING THERE

From Bend, follow Highway 97 for about 23 miles to the Paulina Lake Road and turn left. Continue on the Paulina Lake Road as it turns to Forest Road 21 on entering Deschutes National Forest and drive 12.5 miles to the Newberry Welcome Station, where you'll be asked to pay a fee.

Drive past the center about a half mile to the Paulina Falls Viewpoint parking area on the left, 6,300 feet above sea level. GPS coordinates: N43°42′35″; W121°16′58″

## THE TRAIL

Paulina Falls is the highest waterfall along Paulina Creek, which is born a short distance upstream in the lake of the same name. It makes an excellent though short journey for those who do their hiking aboard a wheelchair.

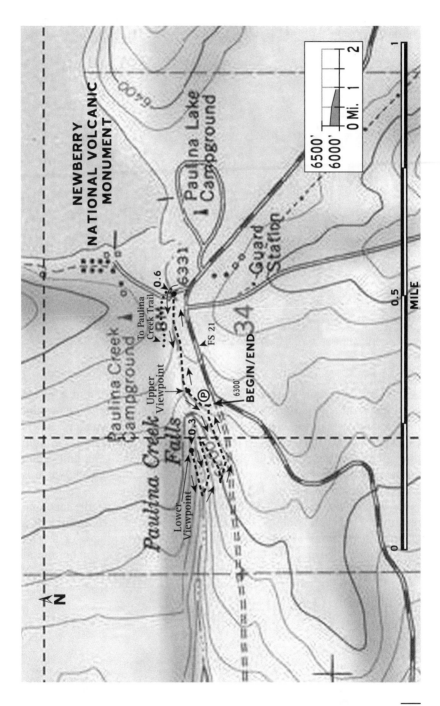

Paulina Falls from the lower trail.

The short trail from the parking area to the upper viewpoint is paved and only about 120 yards long, ending in a wide, stone-walled viewpoint for the falls, which tumbles down lava cliffs in several streams. Hikers choosing to walk farther can find the path leading upstream to an auto bridge crossing the creek at Paulina Lake. Turn around here, unless you are headed for the Paulina Creek Trail (hike #50 in this guide), which is across the bridge and to the left.

To walk to the bottom of Paulina Falls, turn around at the lake and return the way you came. Keep right at the parking area and begin a gentle descent along a wide trail above the falls, switching back as you drop through the woods. In 0.3 mile, reach a viewpoint at the bottom of the falls and return the way you came.

# 50. Paulina Creek Trail

| | |
|---|---|
| RATING | 🚶🚶🚶 |
| DISTANCE | 6.0 miles round-trip |
| HIKING TIME | 4 hours |
| ELEVATION GAIN | 950 feet |
| HIGH POINT | 6,340 feet |
| EFFORT | Prepare to Perspire |
| BEST SEASON | Summer, fall |
| PERMITS/CONTACT | Daily or annual fee required/ Newberry National Volcanic Monument, (541) 383-5700, www.fs.usda.gov/main/deschutes |
| MAPS | USGS La Pine; Newberry National Volcanic Monument handout, Volcanic Vistas |
| NOTES | Leashed dogs, horses, and mountain bikes (uphill only) welcome |

## THE HIKE

The best part of this walk is that it's downhill along a pretty creek for the first 3 miles; the worst part of the trail is that it's uphill the next 3 miles on the return.

## GETTING THERE

From Bend, follow Highway 97 for about 23 miles to the Paulina Lake Road and turn left. Continue on the Paulina Lake Road as it turns to Forest Road 21 on entering Deschutes National Forest and drive 12.5 miles to the Newberry Welcome Station, where you'll be asked to pay a fee.

Drive past the center about a half mile to the Paulina Falls Viewpoint parking area on the left, 6,300 feet above sea level. GPS coordinates: N43°42′35″; W121°16′58″

## THE TRAIL

Begin this hike by walking past the upper Paulina Falls Viewpoint (hike #49 in this guide) and following the trail upstream to the auto bridge crossing the creek at its mouth. Cross the bridge and turn left on the trail leading uphill for a hundred feet to a junction with the Lakeshore Loop and Crater Rim Trails. Stay left here, on the Paulina Creek Trail, also

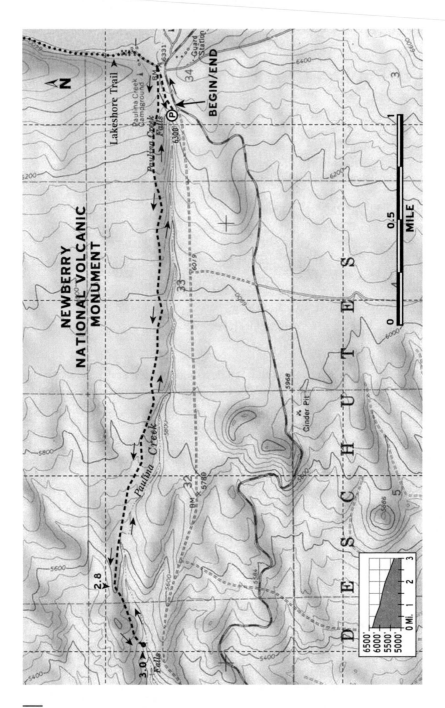

Paulina Creek Trail is closed to mountain bikers riding downhill.

called the Peter Skene Ogden National Scenic Trail No. 56. It's named after the Hudson's Bay Company trapper and explorer who discovered Paulina Lake.

This trail was once a very popular single-track adventure with mountain bike riders, but their activity on this path is limited to uphill travel and they get their downhill thrills on a forest road across the creek. You'll start downhill to a spot overlooking Paulina Falls, on the left, before beginning a moderate downhill grade along a ridge above Paulina Creek.

The trail never strays far from the watercourse, descending through pine forest above the creek canyon for 2.8 miles. The path is smooth and packed with pumice in spots. Paulina Creek drops over several small waterfalls before arriving at a trail junction 3.0 miles from the trailhead. Turn left and walk to a creek crossing just above a higher waterfall, your turnaround point. Take a nice break here—it's a long climb back.

## GOING FARTHER

The trail continues downhill for another 5.0 miles and makes a nice key-and-car exchange walk if you can persuade a strong Norwegian tourist to hike up the trail. For a loop option, you can cross Paulina Creek and turn left on the old Forest Road 500—but remember, this is the downhill route for mountain bike riders, and they don't usually dally.

# 51. Little Crater Trail

| | |
|---|---|
| RATING | 🚶🚶🚶🚶🚶 |
| DISTANCE | 1.8-mile loop |
| HIKING TIME | 2 hours, 30 minutes |
| ELEVATION GAIN | 520 feet |
| HIGH POINT | 6,850 feet |
| EFFORT | Moderate Workout |
| BEST SEASON | Summer, fall |
| PERMITS/CONTACT | Daily or annual fee required/ Newberry National Volcanic Monument, (541) 383-5700, www.fs.usda.gov/main/deschutes |
| MAPS | USGS East Lake; Newberry National Volcanic Monument handout, Volcanic Vistas |
| NOTES | Leashed dogs welcome; carry water |

## THE HIKE

Climb through a pine forest above splendid Paulina Lake for a view that stretches across the massive Newberry caldera and to a river of volcanic glass.

## GETTING THERE

From Bend, follow Highway 97 for about 23 miles to the Paulina Lake Road and turn left. Continue on the Paulina Lake Road as it turns to Forest Road 21 on entering Deschutes National Forest, driving 12.5 miles to the Newberry Welcome Station, where you'll be asked to pay a fee.

Drive about 2.8 miles beyond the station on Paulina Lake Road to the Little Crater Campground entrance on the left. Turn left and drive to the day-use parking area and boat launch. The trailhead is on the right, 6,359 feet above sea level. GPS coordinates: N43°41′16″; W121°14′48″

## THE TRAIL

This hike is a perfect way to begin a visit to the Newberry National Volcanic Monument, because it introduces you to all the trekking possibilities in the area. To the north, you'll see shoreline hikes and mountain trails; to the south, frozen rivers of black glass and rocky ridge trails—all available from this single trailhead.

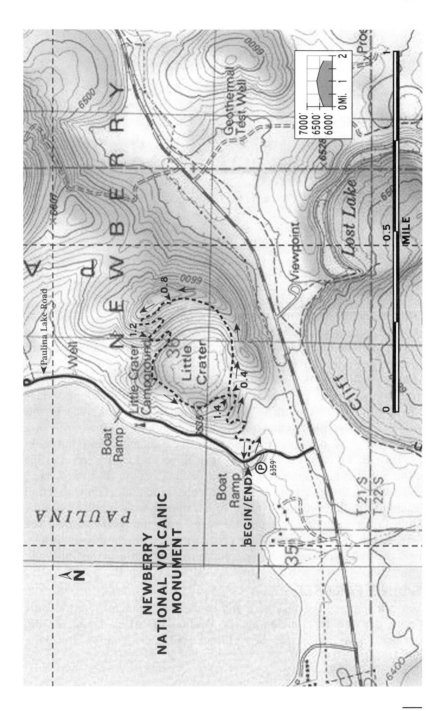

The Little Crater Trail climbs to a viewpoint of Paulina Lake.

Begin by climbing into the sparse pine forest and switching back before climbing underneath a big rock face where you can look down to Paulina Lake below. It's not worth scrambling around on the boulder, because you'll be on top of it on the way back.

At **0.4** mile from the trailhead, find the junction with the Little Crater Trail and stay right, continuing to climb more moderately along a ridge where you can look south to the Big Obsidian Flow (hike #53 in this guide). You'll continue climbing along the ridge as it turns north to a 6,850-foot peak, **0.8** mile from the trailhead. This high viewpoint looks out on Paulina and East Lakes, the lava flows and cinder cones to the north and the rocky spire of 7,984-foot Paulina Peak to the southwest.

From here, the trail drops in long switchbacks to a junction with a trail leading right that eventually drops to a trailhead at the north end of the Little Crater Campground loop, 1.2 miles from the trailhead. Stay left here, and at **1.4** miles, cross the big rock above the trailhead switchbacks. Find the trail junction just beyond and turn right down to the trailhead.

## GOING FARTHER

You can combine this hike with any of the trails leading from the Little Crater day-use area, including the Paulina Lakeshore Loop, the Big Obsidian Flow Trail, or Newberry Crater Trail (hikes #52, 53, and 54 in this guide).

# 52. Paulina Lakeshore Loop

|  |  |
|---|---|
| RATING | 👣👣👣 |
| DISTANCE | 7.2-mile loop |
| HIKING TIME | 4 hours, 30 minutes |
| ELEVATION GAIN | 230 feet |
| HIGH POINT | 6,560 feet |
| EFFORT | Moderate Workout |
| BEST SEASON | Summer, fall |
| PERMITS/CONTACT | Daily or annual fee required/ Newberry National Volcanic Monument, (541) 383-5700, www.fs.usda.gov/main/deschutes |
| MAPS | USGS East Lake; Newberry National Volcanic Monument handout, Volcanic Vistas |
| NOTES | Leashed dogs welcome; great family hike; portions are wheelchair accessible |

## THE HIKE

This is a long but mostly gentle walk around Paulina Lake, the largest of the Newberry lakes, where parts of the trail can be broken into sections for younger walkers.

## GETTING THERE

From Bend, follow Highway 97 for about 23 miles to the Paulina Lake Road and turn left. Continue on the Paulina Lake Road as it turns to Forest Road 21 on entering Deschutes National Forest and drive 12.5 miles to the Newberry Welcome Station, where you'll be asked to pay a fee.

Drive about 2.8 miles beyond the station on Paulina Lake Road to the Little Crater Campground entrance on the left. Turn left and drive to the day-use parking area and boat launch. The trailhead is on the right, 6,359 feet above sea level. GPS coordinates: N43°41′16″; W121°14′48″

## THE TRAIL

Although several trailheads provide access to the Paulina Lakeshore Loop, the Little Crater day-use parking area makes a good beginning, especially if you are camped at the Little Crater Campground, which offers fine lakefront spots. From the parking area, walk down to the

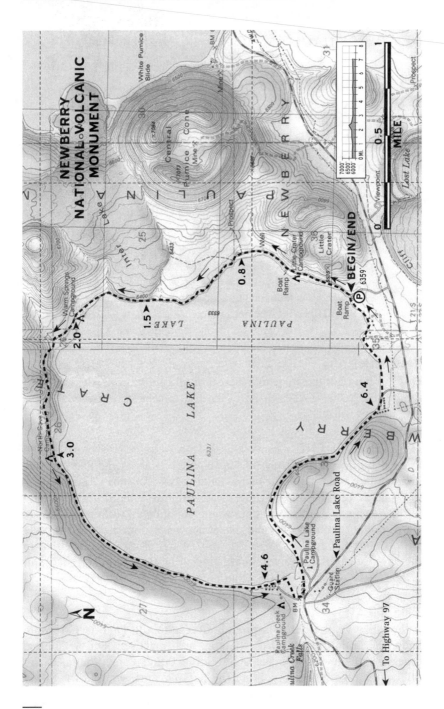

Parts of the Paulina Lakeshore Loop trail follow the beach.

lakeshore and turn right, or east, along the shore. You'll hike counter-clockwise around the lake.

The trail alternately follows the beach and the campground road to a trailhead at the end of the campground loop, **0.8** mile from your starting point. The trail then leaves the roadway and becomes a pine-forested shoreline path along the edge of the lake. At **1.5** miles from the trailhead, you'll cross the Interlake Lava Flow, which as you might guess from the name, flows between Paulina and East Lakes.

In another half mile, you'll arrive at one of the places that demonstrates that the Newberry caldera is still percolating: hot springs bubble forth from gravel along the shore, serving up a nice place to soak in a lake where water temperatures aren't always so hospitable. The hike to this spot and returning the way you came would make a 4.0-mile trek for the youngsters.

A mile beyond the hot springs is the North Cove picnic area, which would make returning the way you came a 6.0-mile hike, the point of no return for the entire loop hike. The trail continues along the lakeshore from this point, never climbing or descending more than 40 feet above the lake.

Beyond the picnic area, walk another 1.6 miles to the road and trailhead at the Paulina Lake Resort, following the road or shoreline across Paulina Creek to the Paulina Lake Campground. The trail leaves the campground just past the boat launch and circles around two forested hills along the lake before passing private residences along the shore, **6.4** miles from the trailhead. Walk another 0.8 mile along the shore to close the loop.

# 53. Silica and Big Obsidian Flow Trails

| | |
|---|---|
| RATING | 🏃🏃🏃🏃🏃 |
| DISTANCE | 3.2 miles round-trip |
| HIKING TIME | 3 hours, 30 minutes |
| ELEVATION GAIN | 520 feet |
| HIGH POINT | 6,850 feet |
| EFFORT | Moderate Workout |
| BEST SEASON | Summer, fall |
| PERMITS/CONTACT | Daily or annual fee required/ Newberry National Volcanic Monument, (541) 383-5700, www.fs.usda.gov/main/deschutes |
| MAPS | USGS East Lake; Newberry National Volcanic Monument handout, Volcanic Vistas |
| NOTES | Dogs not advised; great family hike; wear hiking shoes or boots |

## THE HIKE

Walk through a pumice-floored forest to a volcanic glacier of black glass that oozed out of the Newberry caldera only yesterday—by the geologic clock.

## GETTING THERE

From Bend, follow Highway 97 for about 23 miles to the Paulina Lake Road and turn left. Continue on the Paulina Lake Road as it turns to Forest Road 21 on entering Deschutes National Forest and drive 12.5 miles to the Newberry Welcome Station, where you'll be asked to pay a fee.

Drive about 2.8 miles beyond the station on Paulina Lake Road to the Little Crater Campground entrance on the left. Turn left and drive to the day-use parking area and boat launch. The trailhead is on the right, 6,359 feet above sea level. GPS coordinates: N43°41′16″; W121°14′48″

## THE TRAIL

It's not a good idea to take dogs on this hike, and those with sturdy hiking boots or shoes will be more comfortable walking on the sharp shards of obsidian—volcanic glass—that make up the trail climbing up the Big Obsidian Flow. The trail is aptly named—more than 170 million cubic

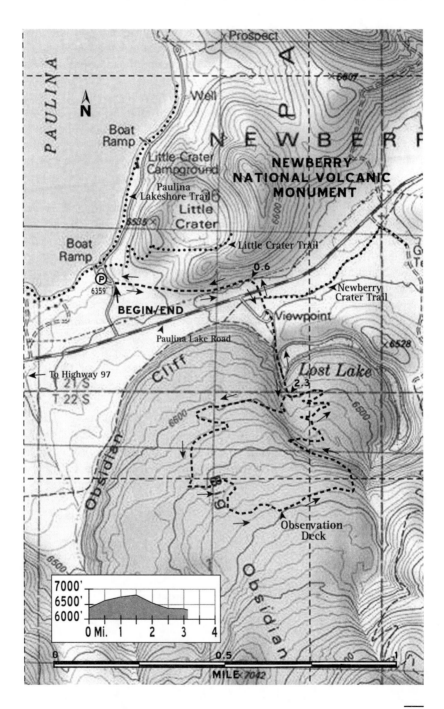

yards of the stuff was molten liquid only 1,300 years ago, during Oregon's youngest lava eruption. Boulders of obsidian as big as Volkswagen Beetles line the trail and glass sand crunches underfoot; the sun reflects from their concave, mirrorlike fractures.

All of that welcomes you after about a half mile of walking the Silica Trail 58.5, which takes you from the trailhead through a sparse pine forest over a low ridge before descending to cross the Paulina Lake Road, just east of a road leading to the Big Obsidian Flow trailhead. Across the road, you'll find a junction with the Newberry Crater Trail (hike #54 in this guide) at 0.6 mile before reaching the Big Obsidian Flow trailhead.

Find the Flow Trail at the southern end of the parking area. The first portion of this trail is paved and accessible to a viewpoint just below the toe of the flow. From there, you'll climb a wide metal staircase up the north face of the flow to a bench formation and trails leading right and left—the beginning and end of the trail loop. Turn right and continue climbing at a moderate grade up the face of the formation as views of the surrounding territory get wider. Look to the southwest for the signature Paulina Peak and its overlook, or north to Paulina Lake basin. Directly below is Lost Lake, a narrow pond that is home to ducks and frogs.

After reaching a high observation platform, descend the trail to the right in steep switchbacks before arriving at the junction of the loop, 2.3 miles from the trailhead. Climb back down the stairs and return the way you came.

## GOING FARTHER
You can combine this hike with any of the trails leading from the Little Crater day-use area, including the Little Crater Loop, Paulina Lakeshore Loop, or Newberry Crater Trail (hike #51, 52, and 54 in this guide.).

# 54. Newberry Crater Trail

| | |
|---|---|
| RATING | 🚶🚶 |
| DISTANCE | 3.6 miles round-trip |
| HIKING TIME | 3 hours |
| ELEVATION GAIN | 150 feet |
| HIGH POINT | 6,500 feet |
| EFFORT | Easy Walk |
| BEST SEASON | Summer, fall |
| PERMITS/CONTACT | Daily or annual fee required/ Newberry National Volcanic Monument, (541) 383-5700, www.fs.usda.gov/main/deschutes |
| MAPS | USGS East Lake; Newberry National Volcanic Monument handout, Volcanic Vistas |
| NOTES | Leashed dogs, horses, and mountain bikes welcome |

## THE HIKE

Save this hike for that rare cloudy or rainy day when exercise and potential wildlife viewing is the main objective, or plan a longer and much more strenuous and spectacular climb to the Newberry Crater rim.

## GETTING THERE

From Bend, follow Highway 97 for about 23 miles to the Paulina Lake Road and turn left. Continue on the Paulina Lake Road as it turns to Forest Road 21 on entering Deschutes National Forest and drive 12.5 miles to the Newberry Welcome Station, where you'll be asked to pay a fee.

Drive about 2.8 miles beyond the station on Paulina Lake Road to the Little Crater Campground entrance on the left. Turn left and drive to the day-use parking area and boat launch. The trailhead is on the right, 6,359 feet above sea level. GPS coordinates: N43°41′16″; W121°14′48″

## THE TRAIL

Begin by walking the half-mile Silica Trail 58.5, which takes you from the trailhead through a sparse pine forest over a low ridge before descending to cross the Paulina Lake Road, just east of a road leading to the Big Obsidian Flow trailhead. Across the road, you'll find a junction with the

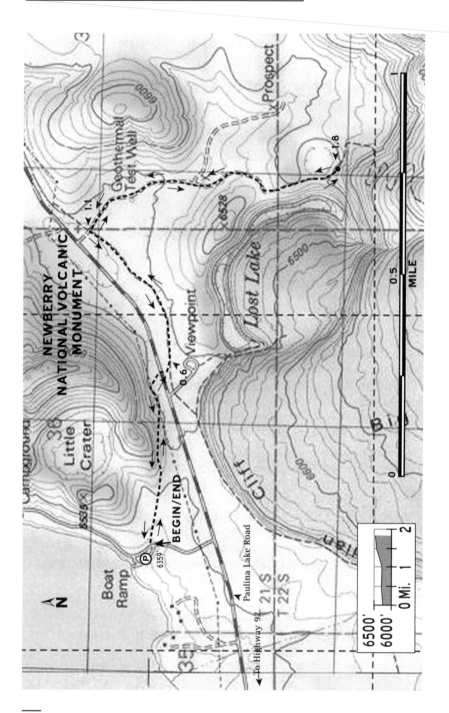

The Newberry Crater Trail links a series of pathways ranging from gentle for very steep.

Newberry Crater Trail 3958. Turn left onto the Newberry Crater Trail as it parallels the Paulina Lake Road in a pine forest for 0.6 mile.

After hiking 1.1 miles from the trailhead, you'll strike a junction with the Lost Lake Trail. Turn right and begin a gentle climb on an old road through open pine forest. The trail steepens slightly and the forest begins to yield more shade as you climb along the edge of a steep ridge that tumbles down to the wetland of narrow Lost Lake. You can look across through the trees to the Big Obsidian Flow that stretches east for almost a mile.

The trail begins a steep take-no-prisoners switchback climb in forest above the lava flow, 1.8 miles from the trailhead. This is your turn-around point, unless you are looking for a much more strenuous hike.

## GOING FARTHER

It's a 1.7-mile, 640-vertical-foot climb on a steep switchback trail to a 7,100-foot pumice plain overlooking the Newberry Crater. A trail junction here follows the Lost Lake Trail to the left or the South Lost Lake Trail to the right.

If you'd like to make certain your knees turn to the consistency of polenta, take the trail to the right, which climbs 315 vertical feet in 0.7 mile to the summit of the crater rim, 7,450 feet above sea level. Your total elevation gain from the trailhead would be 1,100 feet and round-trip distance 8.5 miles.

## MORE NEWBERRY NATIONAL VOLCANIC MONUMENT HIKES

🚶 **Lava River Cave**, 2.0 miles underground round-trip, Moderate Workout. Open summer to early fall. Cave located off Forest Road 9703 from Lava Lands Visitor Center entrance off Highway 97.

🚶 **Trail of the Molten Land**, 1.25-mile loop, paved and partially accessible, Moderate Workout. Trailhead at Lava Lands Visitor Center off Highway 97.

🚶 **Black Rock Trail**, 4.0 miles round-trip, Moderate Workout. Trailhead at Lava Lands Visitor Center off Highway 97.

🚶 **Lava Butte Trail**, 0.3-mile loop, Stroll in the Park. Trailhead at end of Red Cinder Road (no RVs) from Lava Lands Visitor Center off Highway 97.

🚶 **Parallel Trail**, 4.0 miles round-trip, Moderate Workout. Trailhead at end of Paulina Lake Road.

🚶 **Crater Rim Trail**, 21-mile loop can be done in sections, Prepare to Perspire. Closest large trailhead at Paulina Falls parking area.

🚶 **Paulina Peak Trail**, 0.5 mile round-trip, Stroll in the Park. Trailhead at end of Paulina Peak Road.

Using its peculiar beak, the red crossbill feeds on seeds from cones of Newberry trees.

Arch Trail (#56).

# JOHN DAY FOSSIL BEDS NATIONAL MONUMENT

The distance from the three units of the John Day Fossil Beds National Monument to Bend, Oregon, might seem a long 75 to 125 miles. Trust me: the distance in geologic time and scenery is light-years farther. Looking across the camel- and russet-striped Painted Hills, you'll swear you're on another planet. In contrast to the noble pine forests and 7,000-year-old volcanic rubble of the Newberry Crater, the 5- to 45-million-year-old fossils and landforms of the monument tell a tale you've not likely heard before.

With a few exceptions, the 13,944-acre monument offers little to day hikers in the way of challenge or long treks. Yet the shorter walks in the monument provide spectacular, unique scenery as well as the chance to stretch your legs from what for some may be a long drive. It's definitely worth the visit.

More than 150,000 people visit the monument every year, but even on the busiest weekends the wide expanse of John Day country might make you feel downright lonesome. The three units of the monument—Painted Hills, Sheep Rock, and Clarno—are managed by the National Park Service. They are distant from one another but can all be visited in a long day from Oregon cities such as Bend, Redmond, Prineville, or Madras. Plan to spend 2 days or longer for more thorough exploring.

You'll find the two hikes outlined here in the Clarno and Sheep Rock Units, but don't miss the short side trip to the Painted Hills Unit and its short walks to views of hills the likes of which you won't see anywhere in the Northwest. To reach the Painted Hills Unit, follow Highway 26 for 47 miles east from Prineville to the National Park Service John Day Monument sign and turn left. Drive about 5.5 miles to the end of the pavement and turn left to short loop trails and a picnic area.

For the Sheep Rock Unit, return to Highway 26 and drive east 32 miles to Highway 19. Turn left along the John Day River to the Sheep Rock Unit, and don't miss stopping at the Thomas Condon Paleontology Center before continuing to Blue Basin. To complete the loop drive, follow Highway 19 north through Kimberly and Spray to Fossil, then take Highway 218 west to the Clarno Unit. Highway 218 leads west to Shaniko and Highway 97.

# JOHN DAY FOSSIL BEDS
# NATIONAL MONUMENT

**55** Blue Basin Overlook Trail

**56** Geologic Time–Clarno
Arch Trail

# 55. Blue Basin Overlook Trail

| | |
|---|---|
| RATING | 🚶🚶🚶🚶🚶 |
| DISTANCE | 3.3-mile loop |
| HIKING TIME | 2 hours, 30 minutes |
| ELEVATION GAIN | 760 feet |
| HIGH POINT | 2,920 feet |
| EFFORT | Prepare to Perspire |
| BEST SEASON | Summer, fall |
| PERMITS/CONTACT | None/John Day Fossil Beds National Monument, (541) 987-2333, www.nps.gov/joda |
| MAPS | USGS Mount Misery; national monument trail map |
| NOTES | Leashed pets welcome; very hot in summer—carry water (available May–September at trailhead); trail slippery when wet |

## THE HIKE

See more blue earth here than anywhere, including Blue Earth, Minnesota, and climb a steep trail to a viewpoint over the John Day River valley.

## GETTING THERE

From Prineville, Oregon, drive 80 miles east on Highway 26 to its intersection with Highway 19 and turn left. Follow Highway 19 north for about 6 miles to the Blue Basin trailhead and picnic area on the right, 2,160 feet above sea level. GPS coordinates: N44º35′44″; W119º37′51″

## THE TRAIL

This is the longest and most strenuous hike in the John Day Monument, but it's well worth the sweat and NSAIDs you might need upon your return. You'll climb beneath a wall of grayish-blue rock streaked with rust and green to a viewpoint overlooking the basin and colored canyon walls.

Begin by following the trail to the left for a clockwise hike of the loop around a 2,680-foot-high promontory on your right. The grade begins to steepen at **1.0** mile, climbing up a narrow canyon for about a half mile before easing slightly and turning up the other side and climbing again before reaching the high point of the hike, **1.7** miles from the trailhead. Beyond is a short trail leading to a spectacular basin viewpoint.

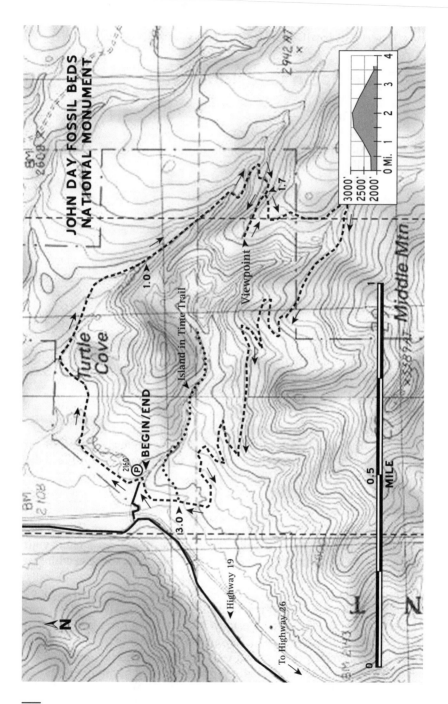

The Blue Basin in John Day Fossil Beds National Monument.

Back on the main trail to the right, you'll begin a long and steep descent down the north slope of 5,587-foot-high Middle Mountain. The trail drops in switchbacks before rounding a ridge and turning north to a junction with the Island in Time Trail, 3.0 miles from the trailhead. Stay left and return to the parking area in 0.3 mile.

## GOING FARTHER
The Island in Time Trail is a 0.8-mile hike, out and back, and a more gentle climb into the Blue Basin, but be forewarned: the bottom of the canyon is an oven compared to the surrounding hillsides. The Island in Time Trail is the most popular in the monument, with replica fossil skeletons on display along the route. The National Park Service also advises pet owners that some dogs might not enjoy crossing the thirteen metal grate bridges along the trail.

# 56. Geologic Time–Clarno Arch Trail

| | |
|---|---|
| RATING | 🚶🚶🚶🚶 |
| DISTANCE | 1.25 miles round-trip |
| HIKING TIME | 1 hour, 30 minutes |
| ELEVATION GAIN | 80 feet |
| HIGH POINT | 1,560 feet |
| EFFORT | Moderate Workout |
| BEST SEASON | Spring, fall |
| PERMITS/CONTACT | None/John Day Fossil Beds National Monument, (541) 987-2333, www.nps.gov/joda |
| MAPS | USGS Clarno; national monument trail map |
| NOTES | Leashed dogs welcome; very hot in summer—carry water (available May–September at trailhead picnic area); trail slippery when wet |

## THE HIKE

A beautiful desert walk under the Palisades, colorful cliffs where you can practically count down the centuries from rock layers formed by multiple volcanic mudslides, like tree rings.

## GETTING THERE

From Madras, Oregon, follow Highway 97 north 39 miles to Shaniko and turn right on Highway 218. Drive 44 miles to the Palisades picnic area and trailhead, 1,545 feet above sea level. GPS coordinates: N44°54'48"; W120°24'55"

## THE TRAIL

This walk combines three short trails under the Palisades, which tower like castles 400 feet above the pathway. Look for the Geologic Time Trail at the west end of the picnic area and climb over a gentle hump along the base of the cliff for **0.3** mile to a junction with the Trail of the Fossils.

This is a rough loop trail, which climbs steeply to the right in switchbacks. Turn right and look for leaf and wood fossils on boulders beside the winding path. The trail climbs for a hundred yards before turning and traversing underneath the Palisades, then begins a series of short, steep switchbacks down to rejoin the loop trail, **0.8** mile from the trailhead.

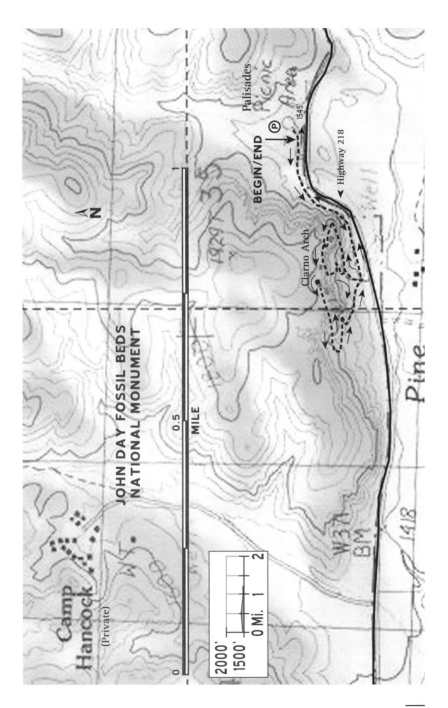

Turn right at the Clarno Arch trailhead parking area on the Arch Trail, which climbs steeply for 0.2 mile before switching back a couple of times and then passing a fossilized log and ending underneath a steep gully. Look up to see the arch, a bridge carved by wind and water in the cliffs of the Palisades.

Return the way you came, bypassing the Trail of the Fossils loop—unless you haven't had enough exercise. If that's the case, you've better knees than your faithful correspondent.

## MORE JOHN DAY FOSSIL BEDS
## NATIONAL MONUMENT HIKES

- ⚐ **Carroll Rim Trail**, 1.6 miles round-trip, Prepare to Perspire. Painted Hills Unit.

- ⚐ **Painted Hills Overlook Trail**, 0.5 mile round-trip, Moderate Workout. Painted Hills Unit.

- ⚐ **Red Scar Knoll Trail**, 0.25 mile round-trip, Stroll in the Park. Painted Hills Unit.

- ⚐ **River Trail**, 0.6 mile round-trip, Easy Walk. Sheep Rock Unit.

- ⚐ **Sheep Rock Overlook**, 0.5 mile round-trip, Stroll in the Park. Sheep Rock Unit.

- ⚐ **Story in Stone Trail**, 0.3 mile round-trip, partially paved, Stroll in the Park. Sheep Rock Unit (Foree).

- ⚐ **Flood of Fire Trail**, 0.4 mile round-trip, Easy Walk. Sheep Rock Unit (Foree).

Crater Lake from Mount Scott. Wizard Island is at left center.

# CRATER LAKE NATIONAL PARK

Crater Lake, Oregon's only national park, provides an excellent destination for those who take their hiking one day at a time. You'll find everything from short wooded walks that reveal a forest nymph of granite to high-altitude climbs to fire lookouts. If that's not enough variety, stroll down a path to the edge of that liquid sapphire bowl that is the center of the park, and huff and puff back up to the trailhead.

Nearly a half million people visit Crater Lake National Park every year. Although the park is open year-round, the crowds arrive after the annual 44-foot-high snow blanket melts in late spring. Visitors enjoy the sunshine and dry weather of summer and may linger into early fall, but except for a few popular pathways, they don't wander far from the wide variety of viewpoints along the East and West Rim Drives around the 8,000-foot-high cliffs of Mount Mazama. That's the volcano that around 7,700 years ago blew her top to create the nearly 2,000-foot-deep lake, lying like a lapis ring in a pewter and emerald setting.

The walks suggested here begin along the Highway 62 entrance from Medford and I-5, then proceed clockwise around the West Rim Drive to the North Entrance Road and East Rim Drive. One of these fifteen hikes is certain to be one of your favorites for a long, long time. If you find a trek here that you liken to a visit to the gates of hell, please forget who told you about it.

# CRATER LAKE NATIONAL PARK

57 Pacific Crest Trail North

58 Annie Spring–Pacific Crest Trail

59 Godfrey Glen

60 Lady of the Woods and Castle Crest Wildflower Loops

61 Garfield Peak Trail

62 Discovery Point Trail

63 Watchman Peak

64 Crater Rim Trail

65 Pacific Crest Trail–Red Cone Spring

66 Pacific Crest Trail– Pumice Desert

67 Cleetwood Cove

68 Mount Scott

69 Crater Peak

70 Sun Notch

71 Plaikni Falls

# 57. Pacific Crest Trail North

|  |  |
|---|---|
| RATING | 🚶🚶 |
| DISTANCE | 5.8 miles round-trip |
| HIKING TIME | 3 hours, 30 minutes |
| ELEVATION GAIN | 380 feet |
| HIGH POINT | 6,560 feet |
| EFFORT | Easy Walk |
| BEST SEASON | Summer, fall |
| PERMITS/CONTACT | Daily or annual entrance fee required/ Crater Lake National Park, (541) 594-3000, www.nps.gov/crla |
| MAPS | USGS Union Peak; National Park Service Crater Lake |
| NOTES | Leashed dogs (one per hiker) and horses welcome; carry water |

## THE HIKE

Here's a fine hike for those looking to find what will probably be a solitary walk in the woods, where scenery isn't as important as filling your lungs with clean mountain air.

## GETTING THERE

Follow Highway 62 from I-5 in Medford to the Crater Lake National Park entrance, then continue 7.2 miles to the Pacific Crest Trail crossing and trailhead, 6,170 feet above sea level. GPS coordinates: N45°52'17"; W122°10'48"

## THE TRAIL

This is essentially a very gentle climb in a forest of lodgepole pine until you arrive at a trail leading to 7,709-foot Union Peak, where it becomes the evil fiend ready to smash your knees with a ball-peen hammer. Don't worry; you get to turn around at this junction unless you're in charge of the kids or grandkids and want to exhaust their sugar high.

There are several good reasons to include this hike on your visit to Crater Lake National Park. First and foremost, you can tell friends you've hiked the Pacific Crest Trail and like Cheryl Strayed, the author of *Wild*, you don't need to mention that you only hiked part of the path.

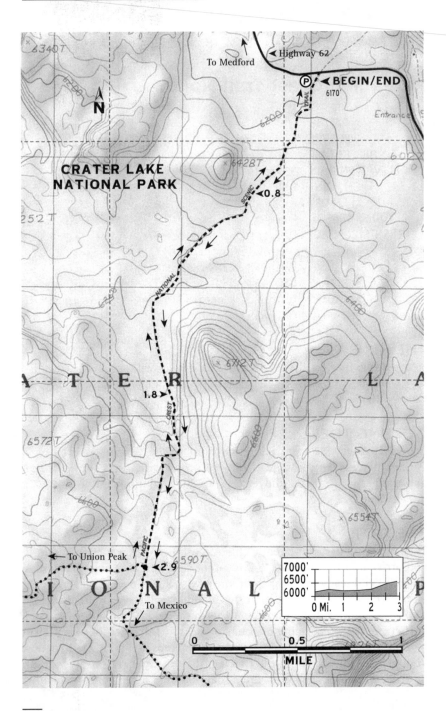

A tree grows around a Pacific Crest Trail marker on the Union Peak Trail.

Second, if you have unsettled guilt over your mother's death, this is the hike for you, and you can mumble and pant about it like Reese Witherspoon did in the movie version. Third and best—unless you are hiking sometime in August when all those PCT thru-hikers are racing by—you may be the only person or party on this trail.

The scenery doesn't change much as you climb past a 6,428-foot cone on your right, 0.8 mile from the trailhead. Beyond, the route descends a bit into a glade, then climbs once more along a forested ridge for 1.0 mile before heading up a wide draw where the trail steepens and climbs 300 feet in the last mile, reaching your turnaround point and junction with the Union Peak Trail on your right, 2.9 miles from the trailhead.

## GOING FARTHER

It's 2.2 miles one-way and 1,150 vertical feet to the summit of 7,709-foot Union Peak, a strenuous but rewarding climb for strong hikers in very good shape. Dogs are prohibited on this section of the trail. Besides the expansive view from the summit of this prominent peak, you've got bragging rights when you point the summit out to tourists at the park's Rim Village.

# 58. Annie Spring–Pacific Crest Trail

| | |
|---:|:---|
| RATING | 𝋌𝋌𝋌 |
| DISTANCE | 2.0 miles round-trip |
| HIKING TIME | 1 hour, 30 minutes |
| ELEVATION GAIN | 200 feet |
| HIGH POINT | 6,340 feet |
| EFFORT | Easy Walk |
| BEST SEASON | Summer, fall |
| PERMITS/CONTACT | Daily or annual entrance fee required/ Crater Lake National Park, (541) 594-3000, www.nps.gov/crla |
| MAPS | USGS Union Peak; National Park Service Crater Lake |
| NOTES | Dogs prohibited on trails |

## THE HIKE

This is a quiet, solitary stroll along a forested hillside to a junction with the Pacific Crest Trail, an alternate walk to the steeper and more crowded Annie Creek Canyon Trail.

## GETTING THERE

Follow Highway 62 from I-5 in Medford to Crater Lake National Park and turn left to Mazama Village. After stopping to pay a fee at the Annie Spring Entrance Station, continue to the wide parking area at Mazama Village, or continue to a new parking area just across the Annie Creek bridge, signed Annie Creek Canyon, 6,030 feet above sea level. GPS coordinates: N42°52'17"; W122°10'04"

## THE TRAIL

This hike begins on the opposite side of the road from the new trailhead with a short side path that leads down to Annie Spring, a bubbling pool of clear water that was named Oregon's Best Tasting Water in 2004. Once you've visited the spring, climb back to the main trail and turn right.

You'll climb past two long switchbacks on a moderately steep grade before turning along a hillside above a shaded glade, where the trail begins a climbing traverse to the northwest, 0.5 mile from the trailhead.

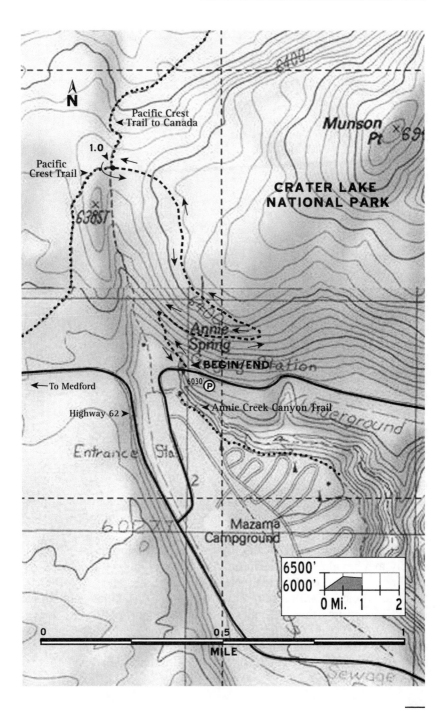

N

Pacific Crest
Trail to Canada

Munson
Pt. ×69

1.0

Pacific
Crest Trail ►

×
6385T

CRATER LAKE
NATIONAL PARK

Annie ◄
Spring ►

BEGIN/END ation

◄ To Medford

6030 Ⓟ

◄ Annie Creek Canyon Trail

Highway 62 ►

Entrance Sta

erground

Mazama
Campground

6500'
6000'

0 Mi.    1    2

0                    0.5                    1
MILE

Sewage

Annie Springs.

The trail levels and begins dropping gently in a mixed forest to join the Pacific Crest Trail in another half mile. Return the way you came.

## GOING FARTHER

Two options for stretching your hike and legs are available: you can turn right on the Pacific Crest Trail or return to the trailhead and walk the Annie Creek Canyon Trail.

For the first, turn right on the Pacific Crest Trail and begin climbing steeply to a broad ridge to the north, then descend into a gully and cross a tributary of Dutton Creek. Climb out of the gully and cross Dutton Creek to a junction with a trail that climbs up to Rim Village and drops to a PCT campsite below, 1.3 miles from the junction.

The Annie Creek Canyon Trail is a 1.7-mile loop that contours along the canyon from the Mazama Campground and drops in steep switchbacks down to the creek, following it back upstream to the Mazama Village.

# 59. Godfrey Glen

| | |
|---|---|
| **RATING** | 👫 |
| **DISTANCE** | 1.2-mile loop |
| **HIKING TIME** | 1 hours, 30 minutes |
| **ELEVATION GAIN** | 50 feet |
| **HIGH POINT** | 6,050 feet |
| **EFFORT** | Stroll in the Park |
| **BEST SEASON** | Summer, fall |
| **PERMITS/CONTACT** | Daily or annual entrance fee required/Crater Lake National Park, (541) 594-3000, www.nps.gov/crla |
| **MAPS** | USGS Union Peak; National Park Service Crater Lake |
| **NOTES** | Leashed dogs welcome; good family hike; dirt path accessible to wheelchair hikers with assistance |

## THE HIKE

This pleasant self-guided walk descends gently above Munson Creek to overlook the sculpted canyon walls and hear the rush of Duwee Falls, below. It's one of three trails in the park where leashed pets are welcome.

## GETTING THERE

Follow Highway 62 from I-5 in Medford to Crater Lake National Park and turn left to Mazama Village. After stopping to pay a fee at the Annie Spring Entrance Station, continue 2.0 miles to the trailhead parking area on your right, 6,050 feet above sea level. GPS coordinates: N42°52′01″; W122°08′43″

## THE TRAIL

Before setting out, pick up a self-guiding brochure at the trailhead to learn all about the splendid forest that surrounds you and the carved hoodoos and pinnacles that jut from the floor of Munson and Annie Creeks. The trail is reportedly wheelchair accessible with assistance; I'd emphasize the assistance part.

From the parking area, drop to the junction of the loop trail and continue to the right, which descends gently through the forest to the edge of the cliffs above Duwee Falls, which you can hear but not see. The trail continues to descend along the canyon wall for 0.4 mile, then turns and

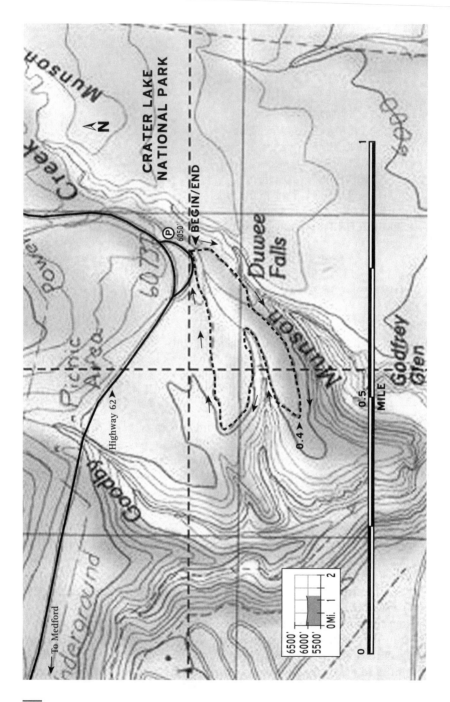

The trail at Godfrey Glen passes hoodoo formations above Duwee Falls.

crosses a bench to a second canyon, where wind and water have carved pinnacles in the cliffside. The trail crosses the canyon near its mouth, then circles into the forest to climb back to the trailhead.

# 60. Lady of the Woods and Castle Crest Wildflower Loops

| | |
|---|---|
| RATING | 🚶🚶🚶🚶 |
| DISTANCE | 2.0 miles round-trip |
| HIKING TIME | 1 hour, 30 minutes |
| ELEVATION GAIN | 220 feet |
| HIGH POINT | 6,400 feet |
| EFFORT | Easy Walk |
| BEST SEASON | Summer, fall |
| PERMITS/CONTACT | Daily or annual entrance fee required/Crater Lake National Park, (541) 594-3000, www.nps.gov/crla |
| MAPS | USGS Union Peak; National Park Service Crater Lake |
| NOTES | Leased dogs welcome on Lady of the Woods trail; portion wheelchair accessible; splendid wildflowers in season |

## THE HIKE

This easy trek combines two short trails around Crater Lake National Park Headquarters and Steel Visitor Center. One leads to a 1917 rock sculpture; the second to a meadow of spring-fed wildflowers.

## GETTING THERE

Follow Highway 62 from I-5 in Medford to Crater Lake National Park and turn left to Mazama Village. After stopping to pay a fee at the Annie Spring Entrance Station, continue 4.2 miles to the Crater Lake National Park Headquarters and Steel Visitor Center on your left, 6,450 feet above sea level. GPS coordinates: N42°53'47"; W122°08'02"

## THE TRAIL

Before setting out on the 0.7-mile Lady of the Woods loop, pick up a self-guiding brochure at the trailhead next to the park library—itself a fascinating collection of park history. Stay left at the trail junction and walk through a forest of hemlocks to the spot where the trail turns right to climb uphill around a huge boulder that blocks the way.

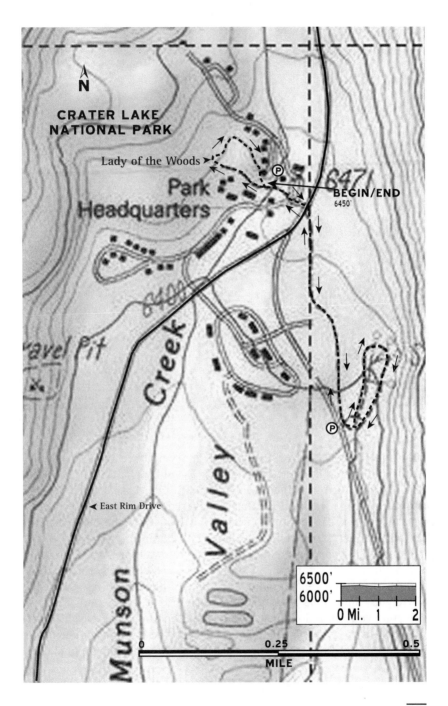

The Lady of the Woods.

Now look at the top of the boulder and you'll see the *Lady of the Woods*, a reclining nude sculpture almost a century old. Dr. Earl R. Bush, who was stationed with the US Engineers at Crater Lake, carved her out of the volcanic rock in 1917. Once you've admired the surgeon's only rock work, you can continue around the loop trail another 0.4 mile, climbing above the park buildings in a hemlock forest.

Return to the parking area and find the crosswalk on West Rim Drive leading to a connector trail to the Castle Crest Wildflower Trail. This trail descends on a gentle grade for 0.3 mile to the Castle Crest trailhead, where you can pick up a self-guiding brochure.

Beyond you can follow the half-mile loop that drops to a meadow that is usually carpeted with wildflowers of every description around mid-July. Springs feed the meadow and also make the trail slippery in places.

# 61. Garfield Peak Trail

| | |
|---|---|
| RATING | 🚶🚶🚶🚶 |
| DISTANCE | 3.0 miles round-trip |
| HIKING TIME | 3 hours |
| ELEVATION GAIN | 1,010 feet |
| HIGH POINT | 8,054 feet |
| EFFORT | Knee-Punishing |
| BEST SEASON | Summer, fall |
| PERMITS/CONTACT | Daily or annual entrance fee required/Crater Lake National Park, (541) 594-3000, www.nps.gov/crla |
| MAPS | USGS Crater Lake East, Crater Lake West; National Park Service Crater Lake |
| NOTES | Dogs and bikes prohibited; carry water; road closed in winter |

## THE HIKE

This climb is one of the toughest in the park, but well worth the effort in scenic reward for those in good physical condition.

## GETTING THERE

Follow Highway 62 from I-5 in Medford to Crater Lake National Park and turn left on East Rim Drive to Mazama Village. After stopping to pay a fee at the Annie Spring Entrance Station, continue 7.2 miles to the Rim Village and turn right to trailhead parking. It gets crowded here in the summer, but any spot in Rim Village can give you access to the trail to Garfield Peak. The trailhead giving you the shortest walk begins along the wide parking area west of Crater Lake Lodge, 7,100 feet above sea level. GPS coordinates: N42°55′13″; W122°09′44″

## THE TRAIL

This hike might feel longer than it actually is because if you are in the kind of condition your ancient correspondent is, you will return to the trailhead resembling a gelatinous, sweaty lutefisk. On the other hand, this hike could actually be longer than 3.0 miles, out and back, because park brochures and maps note the distance as 3.4 and 3.6 miles. My antique Fitbit recorded the distance as 2.8 miles, but I attribute that to

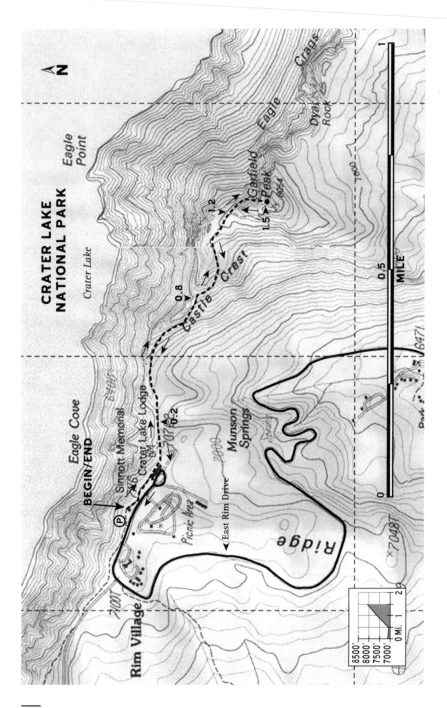

The Garfield Peak Trail passes under crags looking down on Crater Lake.

the fact that my typical 28-inch stride shrunk to a few millimeters as I gained altitude and lost oxygen.

The paved trail skirts the view deck of the historic Crater Lake Lodge and begins with a surprising descent to a wide meadow and saddle that is a wildflower showpiece in season, 0.2 mile from the lodge. The path climbs from this point, first up a gentle hillside to the first of several viewpoints down to Crater Lake.

You'll find opportunities to rest and catch your breath on the pretext of admiring the view at notches in the ridge at 0.8 mile. Regain the Castle Crest ridge at a wide rocky viewpoint, 1.2 miles from the trailhead.

The trail continues up the ridge to a series of short, steep switchbacks that lead to the summit of Garfield Peak. The upper portion of the trail sometimes holds snow until the middle of July, and the summit is often windy. The view includes Mount Shasta to the south, Union Peak to the west, and the tip of 10,358-foot South Sister to the north.

# 62. Discovery Point Trail

| | |
|---|---|
| RATING | 🚶🚶🚶 |
| DISTANCE | 5.2 miles round-trip |
| HIKING TIME | 3 hours |
| ELEVATION GAIN | 220 feet |
| HIGH POINT | 7,310 feet |
| EFFORT | Moderate Workout |
| BEST SEASON | Summer, fall |
| PERMITS/CONTACT | Daily or annual entrance fee required/Crater Lake National Park, (541) 594-3000, www.nps.gov/crla |
| MAPS | USGS Crater Lake West; National Park Service Crater Lake |
| NOTES | Dogs prohibited on trails; good Wizard Island view |

## THE HIKE

This is the best way to see the cliffs and rocky ridges of the Mazama crater—on foot, where you can get a feel for the size of the explosion that created it. You'll share the path with far fewer folks than move quickly past in cars below.

## GETTING THERE

Follow Highway 62 from I-5 in Medford to Crater Lake National Park and turn left on East Rim Drive to Mazama Village. After stopping to pay a fee at the Annie Spring Entrance Station, continue 7.2 miles to the Rim Village and turn right to trailhead parking. It gets crowded here in the summer, but any spot in Rim Village can give you access to the trail to Discovery Point. The trailhead giving you the longest walk begins west of Crater Lake Lodge near the Sinnott Memorial, 7,100 feet above sea level. GPS coordinates: N42°55′13″; W122°09′44″

## THE TRAIL

The Discovery Point Trail leads to the rock where, in 1853, a party of miners first looked down upon Crater Lake. It's still one of the best places in the park to do just that.

Begin by finding the trail along the rim of the crater just west of Crater Lake Lodge. There are no designated trailheads, but the trail is easily

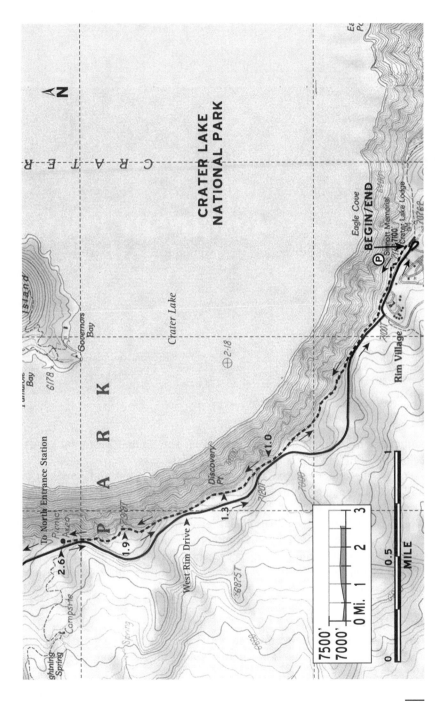

Discovery Point Trail travels along a portion of the Crater Lake rim.

found as a promenade along the crater rim. The Sinnott Memorial hangs below the trail and offers a cliffside view of the lake.

Follow the crater rim as it curves gently to the west and north on a trail that alternately skirts whitebark pine forest and viewpoints along the crater for 1.0 mile. You'll drop to a wide parking area along West Rim Drive, where a second trailhead leads to Discovery Point, 0.3 mile beyond. Continue past the point another 0.6 mile to a 7,318-foot promontory overlooking the lake, then descend to a picnic area overlooking Wizard Island and Fumarole Bay, your turnaround point 2.6 miles from the trailhead.

## GOING FARTHER

The trail continues along the crater rim for 0.9 mile to join the trail up Watchman Peak (hike #63 in this guide) and 2.4 miles beyond to Merriam Point.

# 63. Watchman Peak

| | |
|---|---|
| RATING | 🚶🚶🚶🚶🚶 |
| DISTANCE | 1.6 miles round-trip |
| HIKING TIME | 1 hour, 45 minutes |
| ELEVATION GAIN | 420 feet |
| HIGH POINT | 8,013 feet |
| EFFORT | Prepare to Perspire |
| BEST SEASON | Summer, fall |
| PERMITS/CONTACT | Daily or annual entrance fee required/Crater Lake National Park, (541) 594-3000, www.nps.gov/crla |
| MAPS | USGS Crater Lake West; National Park Service Crater Lake |
| NOTES | Dogs prohibited on trails; spectacular view; trail usually snow-free by early July |

## THE HIKE
Here's the shortest climb to one of the peaks that provides a territorial view of the entire Crater Lake National Park, one of the must-do hikes.

## GETTING THERE
Follow Highway 62 from I-5 in Medford to Crater Lake National Park and turn left on East Rim Drive to Mazama Village. After stopping to pay a fee at the Annie Spring Entrance Station, continue 7.2 miles to the Rim Village and turn left on West Rim Drive. Follow West Rim Drive for 4.0 miles to the Watchman Peak trailhead on the right, 7,590 feet above sea level. GPS coordinates: N42°56'46"; W122°10'9"

## THE TRAIL
Even those who qualify for the Creakiest Knees Medal of Honor should attempt this climb to a lookout almost 2,000 feet above Crater Lake. The trail is wide and smooth and follows a moderate grade nearly to the top before it officially qualifies as steep—at least to this old man's quads.

The trail contours around the sharp rocky boulders of the Watchman, climbing to the south at a steady grade above the West Rim Drive. At **0.4** mile, you'll arrive at a junction with the Discovery Point Trail

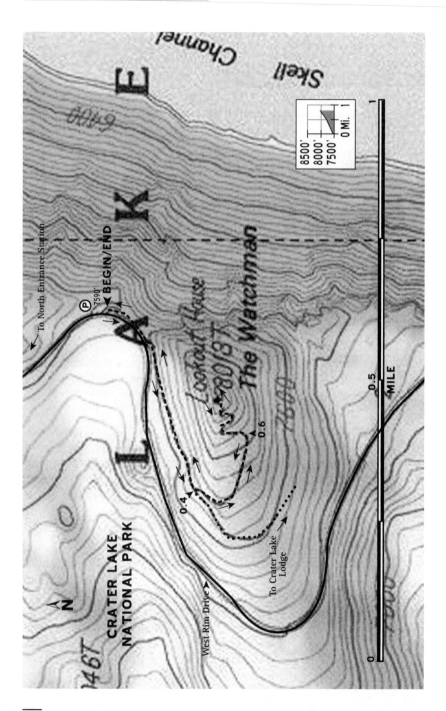

The view from Watchman Peak looks down on Crater Lake, the West Rim Drive, and Hillman Peak, center.

(hike #62 in this guide). Turn left here and climb another 0.2 mile to the first of seven switchbacks leading to the lookout atop the Watchman.

The pathway gets steeper here, so it's important to remember that you've got less than a quarter-mile climb to the summit. A good measure of your progress is to count the switchbacks as you round them; this old man may have been in an altitude-induced delirium at this point and miscounted.

## GOING FARTHER
The best way to extend this hike is to combine it with the Discovery Point Trail from Crater Lake Lodge. Round-trip would be 7.8 miles.

# 64. Crater Rim Trail

| | |
|---|---|
| RATING | 🚶🚶🚶 |
| DISTANCE | 4.8 miles round-trip |
| HIKING TIME | 3 hours |
| ELEVATION GAIN | 300 feet |
| HIGH POINT | 7,800 feet |
| EFFORT | Moderate Workout |
| BEST SEASON | Summer, fall |
| PERMITS/CONTACT | Daily or annual entrance fee required/Crater Lake National Park, (541) 594-3000, www.nps.gov/crla |
| MAPS | USGS Crater Lake West; National Park Service Crater Lake |
| NOTES | Dogs prohibited on trails; carry water |

## THE HIKE

Follow this pathway above the West Rim Drive to the jagged, sharp ridge of rock called the Devil's Backbone past Hillman Peak, the highest point on the Mazama crater rim at 8,151 feet above sea level.

## GETTING THERE

Follow Highway 62 from I-5 in Medford to Crater Lake National Park and turn left on East Rim Drive to Mazama Village. After stopping to pay a fee at the Annie Spring Entrance Station, continue 7.2 miles to the Rim Village and turn left on West Rim Drive. Follow West Rim Drive for 6.3 miles to the junction with the North Entrance Road. The trailhead is just beyond the Y intersection, 7,300 feet above sea level. GPS coordinates: N42°57′58″; W122°09′01″

## THE TRAIL

This wide pathway follows the crater rim south along the steep cliffs of the Mazama crater, first passing Merriam Point, the rock ridge that plunges into Crater Lake below. Continue another 0.7 mile to one of the most prominent rock features of the crater, the Devil's Backbone, a sharp ridge of rock that must have made US Geological Survey mapmakers cross-eyed trying to depict the ridge on a topographic map.

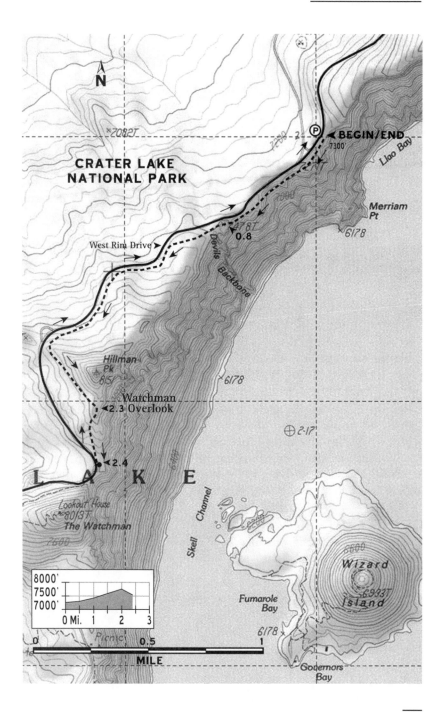

N

CRATER LAKE
NATIONAL PARK

BEGIN/END

Llao Bay

Merriam
Pt

West Rim Drive

0.8

Devils Backbone

Hillman
Pk
8151

Watchman
2.3 Overlook

2.4

L A K E

Lookout House

The Watchman

Skell Channel

Wizard
Island

Fumarole
Bay

Picnic

Governors
Bay

8000'
7500'
7000'

0 Mi.    1    2    3

0                    0.5                    1
MILE

The Crater Rim Trail follows the crater's edge for more than 6 miles.

Past the ridge, the trail begins a moderate climb around Hillman Peak, which rises nearly 400 feet above the trail. Besides the West Rim Drive below, you'll look across the broad hollow and hillock, Williams Crater. You'll round the sharp ridge west of Hillman Peak and begin a gentle descent to the south, arriving at the Watchman Peak trailhead after hiking 2.4 miles. Return the way you came.

## GOING FARTHER
The best way to extend this hike is to follow the Watchman Peak Trail (hike #63 in this guide). That would add 1.6 miles to the hike for a total of 6.4 miles.

# 65. Pacific Crest Trail—Red Cone Spring

| | |
|---|---|
| RATING | 🚶🚶 |
| DISTANCE | 7.6 miles round-trip |
| HIKING TIME | 5 hours, 30 minutes |
| ELEVATION GAIN | 380 feet |
| HIGH POINT | 6,480 feet |
| EFFORT | Moderate Workout |
| BEST SEASON | Summer, fall |
| PERMITS/CONTACT | Daily or annual entrance fee required/Crater Lake National Park, (541) 594-3000, www.nps.gov/crla |
| MAPS | USGS Pumice Desert West; National Park Service Crater Lake |
| NOTES | Leashed dogs and horses welcome |

## THE HIKE
Here's a gentle forested climb along the Pacific Crest Trail, best saved for a day when you'd like to give Fido some exercise—or get some yourself.

## GETTING THERE
Follow Highway 62 from I-5 in Medford to Crater Lake National Park and turn left on East Rim Drive to Mazama Village. After stopping to pay a fee at the Annie Spring Entrance Station, continue 7.2 miles to the Rim Village and turn left on West Rim Drive. Follow West Rim Drive for 6.3 miles to the junction with the North Entrance Road. Turn left on the North Entrance Road and drive 2.7 miles to the Pacific Crest Trail parking area on the left, 6,480 feet above sea level. GPS coordinates: N42°59′45″; W122°08′10″

## THE TRAIL
The Pacific Crest Trail is the granddaddy of all trails, stretching more than 2,650 miles from Mexico to Canada, now enjoying more popularity due to the book by Cheryl Strayed, who hiked a portion of the trail decades ago and then wrote a best-selling book about her misadventures, which was also adapted for film.

So while you are walking this gentle section of the PCT in a few hours—especially if you're hiking around mid-July to mid-August—

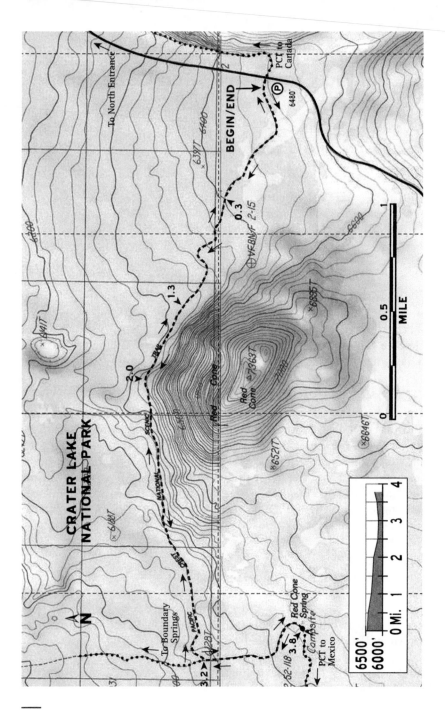

The Red Cone hides in clouds along the Pacific Crest Trail.

you might meet one of the sturdy hikers who plan to finish the entire trail in a single season. These thru-hikers begin at the Mexican border in early spring and hope to finish the hike at the Canadian border by the end of September. That's an incredible feat for anyone. Imagine, then, the kind of stamina and drive it would take to hike the entire distance in 53 days, as was done in 2014 by Joe McConaughy of Seattle.

This part of the PCT begins with a walk through pine forests on a wide trail that appears to get fairly heavy equestrian use. The trail wanders uphill on a gentle grade for **0.3** mile before turning downhill on an equally gentle slope for a mile. Here the forest closes in as you circle around the bald ochre summit of 7,363-foot Red Cone.

At **2.0** miles from the trailhead, climb over a round ridge on the north side of Red Cone and begin a gentle descent through the forest to a junction with a trail leading north to Boundary Springs, **3.2** miles from the trailhead. Dogs are prohibited on this trail. So turn left and continue on the PCT for another 0.6 mile to Red Cone Spring, a designated PCT campsite and your turnaround point.

# 66. Pacific Crest Trail—Pumice Desert

| | |
|---|---|
| RATING | 🚶🚶 |
| DISTANCE | 11.8 miles |
| HIKING TIME | 6 hours, 30 minutes |
| ELEVATION GAIN | 390 feet |
| HIGH POINT | 6,249 feet |
| EFFORT | Prepare to Perspire |
| BEST SEASON | Summer, fall |
| PERMITS/CONTACT | Daily or annual parking pass required/ Crater Lake National Park, (541) 594-3000, www.nps.gov/crla |
| MAPS | USGS Pumice Desert East |
| NOTES | Leashed dogs and horses welcome; carry water |

## THE HIKE

This is a long, very gentle climb to the edge of a pumice plain deposited onto the land when Mount Mazama blew her top more than 7,000 years ago.

## GETTING THERE

Follow Highway 62 from I-5 in Medford to Crater Lake National Park and turn left on East Rim Drive to Mazama Village. After stopping to pay a fee at the Annie Spring Entrance Station, continue 7.2 miles to the Rim Village and turn left on West Rim Drive. Follow West Rim Drive for 6.3 miles to the junction with the North Entrance Road. Turn left on the North Entrance Road and drive 9.4 miles to the junction with Highway 138, leaving the park at the North Entrance Station. (Show the pass you received at the Annie Spring entrance to reenter the park.)

Turn right at the junction on Highway 138 and drive 0.9 mile on the gravel road leading to the PCT trailhead, on the left. Turn left and drive 0.4 mile to the trailhead.

Alternate routes lead east from I-5 at Roseburg on Highway 230 and south on Highway 97 and west on Highway 138 from Bend. The trailhead is 5,858 feet above sea level. GPS coordinates: N43°05′37″; W122°05′38″

## THE TRAIL

Eleven-plus miles might seem too long for some, but those who are looking for a shorter hike should still consider this pretty hike in the pines.

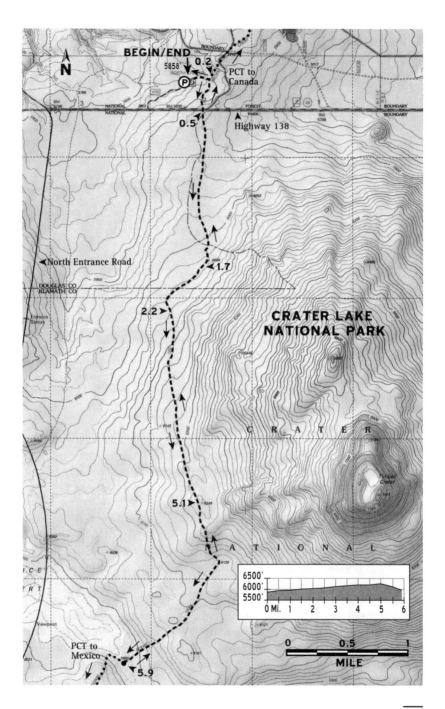

The Pacific Crest Trail to Pumice Desert begins outside the park.

Simply turn back at a point you choose short of the Pumice Desert, and you'll still get an excellent walk with your leashed dog on the Pacific Crest Trail.

An added plus to this walk is that it may be one of the least crowded hikes in Crater Lake National Park, since it is so distant from the main attraction and its heaviest use is during midsummer, when Pacific Crest Trail thru-hikers are chugging north. If you walk this trail in the fall, you may find yourself the only company you'll keep.

The trail leads east out of the parking lot for **0.2** mile before it intersects the Pacific Crest Trail. Turn right on the PCT and walk another 0.3 mile to a crossing of Highway 138. Pick up the trail on the opposite side of the highway at the park boundary and begin a gentle climb into the forest on a wide, sandy trail, which may be eroded in spots below occasional water bars.

You'll continue to climb on a very gentle grade for 1.7 miles, with occasional openings in the trees to view the broad cone of Mount Mazama in front of you. The trail at this point now levels briefly before climbing again after a half mile. You'll continue to climb at the same gentle grade for another 1.8 miles to the high point of the trek on a 6,249-foot-high knoll, 5.1 miles from the trailhead.

From here, the trail begins to descend on a slightly steeper grade to the edge of the Pumice Desert, a vast plain of that volcanic foam rock you drove through on the way to the trailhead. The North Entrance Road is less than a mile to the west. Park rules prohibit collecting any of the pumice rocks or objects.

# 67. Cleetwood Cove

| | |
|---|---|
| RATING | ♪♪♪♪ |
| DISTANCE | 2.2 miles round-trip |
| HIKING TIME | 2 hours |
| ELEVATION GAIN | 700 feet |
| HIGH POINT | 6,850 feet |
| EFFORT | Prepare to Perspire |
| BEST SEASON | Summer, fall |
| PERMITS/CONTACT | Daily or annual entrance fee required/Crater Lake National Park, (541) 594-3000, www.nps.gov/crla |
| MAPS | USGS Crater Lake East; National Park Service Crater Lake |
| NOTES | Dogs and bikes prohibited; carry water; road closed in winter |

## THE HIKE

This strenuous trek is the only access to Crater Lake and the boat ride to Wizard Island, not to be missed by all who feel up to the steep but short trail.

## GETTING THERE

Follow Highway 62 from I-5 in Medford to Crater Lake National Park and turn left on East Rim Drive to Mazama Village. After stopping to pay a fee at the Annie Spring Entrance Station, continue 7.2 miles to the Rim Village and turn left on West Rim Drive. Follow West Rim Drive for 6.3 miles to the junction with the North Entrance Road. Stay right at this junction and drive 4.6 miles on the East Rim Drive to the Cleetwood Cove trailhead and Wizard Island ticket booth on the left.

Alternate routes lead east from I-5 at Roseburg on Highway 230 and south on Highway 97 and west on Highway 138 from Bend, then up the North Entrance Road. The trailhead is 6,850 feet above sea level. GPS coordinates: N42°58′48″; W122°05′0″

## THE TRAIL

This is not a trail for folks who don't walk regularly or aren't accustomed to hiking steep trails, but hundreds of visitors who aren't regular hikers

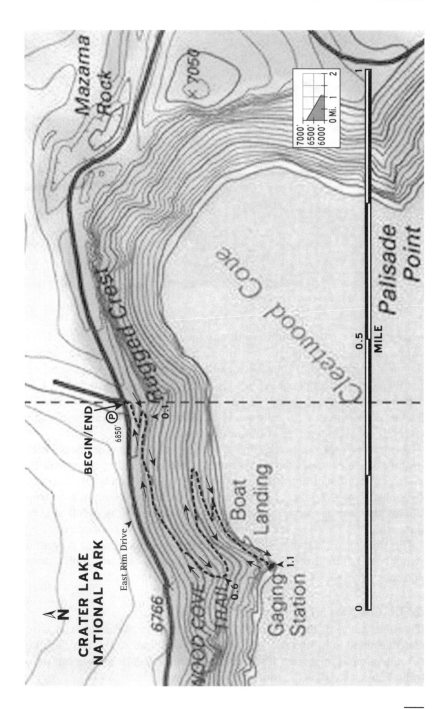

CRATER LAKE
NATIONAL PARK

N

Mazama
Rock

× 7050

Rugged Crest

BEGIN/END

6850'

East Rim Drive

6766

CLEETWOOD COVE
TRAIL

Boat
Landing

Gaging
Station

Cleetwood Cove

Palisade
Point

MILE

0.5

0

7000'
6500'
6000'
0 Mi. 1

2

Cleetwood Cove is the only trail access to Crater Lake.

make this trek every summer without incident. Take this advice from your ancient correspondent: rest often, drink water, and stop to enjoy the view at every opportunity. Remember, too, that you're walking a trail that is more than a mile above sea level. Oxygen is harder to find.

Before striking out, decide if you want to take the cruise to Wizard Island, which offers a 2.5-mile round-trip climb to the top of the island's crater. If so, plan to arrive at trailhead parking early.

The trail is rocky in places and not the sort of path that makes hiking in soft-soled shoes very pleasant. Lightweight hiking shoes will be more comfortable on the wide trail that begins immediately down to two switchbacks at 0.1 mile, then traverses for a half mile along the steep side of the Mazama crater where rock walls decorate the uphill side of the path.

The trail makes another wide switchback, then traverses to a second switchback before dropping to the boat landing. Hikers will find a steep and rocky shoreline with one viewpoint and the boat dock.

## GOING FARTHER

If you've got a ticket for the boat ride or tour to Wizard Island, you can ride there and hike the 1.1-mile one-way climb to the top and the 0.3 mile around the crater. It's about 800 vertical feet to the summit on a trail about as steep as the trail that got you here.

# 68. Mount Scott

| | |
|---|---|
| RATING | 👤👤👤👤👤 |
| DISTANCE | 4.4 miles round-trip |
| HIKING TIME | 3 hours, 30 minutes |
| ELEVATION GAIN | 1,250 feet |
| HIGH POINT | 8,929 feet |
| EFFORT | Knee-Punishing |
| BEST SEASON | Summer, fall |
| PERMITS/CONTACT | Daily or annual entrance fee required/Crater Lake National Park, (541) 594-3000, www.nps.gov/crla |
| MAPS | USGS Crater Lake East; National Park Service Crater Lake |
| NOTES | Dogs and bikes prohibited; carry water; trail usually snow-free by mid-July; road closed in winter |

## THE HIKE

This strenuous trek leads to the highest and most spectacular lookout in Crater Lake National Park.

## GETTING THERE

Follow Highway 62 from I-5 in Medford to Crater Lake National Park and turn left on East Rim Drive to Mazama Village. After stopping to pay a fee at the Annie Spring Entrance Station, continue 7.2 miles to the Rim Village and turn left on West Rim Drive. Follow West Rim Drive for 6.3 miles to the junction with the North Entrance Road. Stay right at this junction and drive 11.2 miles on the East Rim Drive to the trailhead on the left.

Alternate routes lead east from I-5 at Roseburg on Highway 230 and west on Highway 138 from Bend, then up the North Entrance Road. The trailhead is 7,690 feet above sea level. GPS coordinates: N42°55′46″; W122°01′45″

## THE TRAIL

Anyone in good physical condition can reach the top of Mount Scott if they remember to take their time, rest frequently, and drink plenty

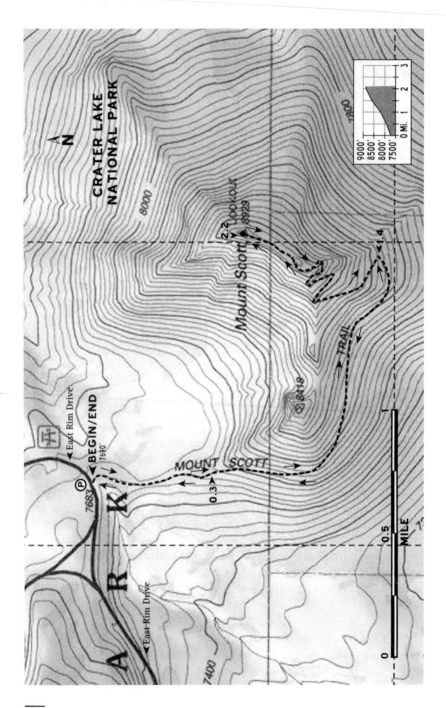

N

CRATER LAKE
NATIONAL PARK

8000

8000

LOOKOUT
8929

2.2

Mount Scott

8418

1.4

TRAIL

MOUNT SCOTT

0.3

East Rim Drive

BEGIN/END

7690

7683

P

A  R  K

East-Rim Drive

7400

MOUNT SCOTT

9000'
8500'
8000'
7500'

0 Mi.    1    2    3

0         0.5         1

MILE

Hikers at the Mount Scott lookout.

of water. The trail is in excellent condition and smooth, with a few mean rocks embedded in the trail surface to reach up and make you stumble. Pick up your feet!

After climbing above the trailhead, the path actually descends a bit, heading north toward the wide north bowl of Mount Scott for 0.3 mile before it begins to climb along the sunset-facing slope. This section of the trail climbs under whitebark pine, with views to the west through the trees.

The path begins climbing in earnest about 0.6 mile from the trailhead, traversing around to the south side of Mount Scott to the edge of a lava field 1.4 miles from the trailhead. It switches back at the rock and begins a series of five switchbacks in sparse pine woods to the sharp, rocky summit ridge. The trees finally give out on a broad, open saddle below the summit where you can look up to the lookout to the northeast.

This broad saddle makes an excellent spot for a picnic, with views in every direction. Before settling, however, climb the final 100 vertical feet and 0.1 mile to the lookout. Views include pointed Union Peak to the west, jagged Mount Thielsen to the north, and snowcapped Mount Shasta to the south.

# 69. Crater Peak

| | |
|---|---|
| RATING | 🚶🚶🚶 |
| DISTANCE | 6.8 miles round-trip |
| HIKING TIME | 4 hours |
| ELEVATION GAIN | 875 feet |
| HIGH POINT | 7,263 feet |
| EFFORT | Moderate Workout |
| BEST SEASON | Summer, fall |
| PERMITS/CONTACT | Daily or annual entrance fee required/Crater Lake National Park, (541) 594-3000, www.nps.gov/crla |
| MAPS | USGS Maklaks Crater; National Park Service Crater Lake |
| NOTES | Dogs and bikes prohibited; carry water |

## THE HIKE

Looking for a real workout? This is the hike for you, with distant views of the Klamath Basin and a shaded path much of the way that lacks the big Crater Lake crowds.

## GETTING THERE

Follow Highway 62 from I-5 in Medford to Crater Lake National Park and turn left on East Rim Drive to Mazama Village. After stopping to pay a fee at the Annie Spring Entrance Station, turn left to Mazama Village and continue 4.0 miles to Crater Lake National Park Headquarters and the junction with East Rim Drive.

Turn right at the junction and follow East Rim Drive 3.1 miles to Grayback Drive and turn right to the Vidae Falls picnic area and trailhead, 6,515 feet above sea level. GPS coordinates: N42°52′56″; W122°05′52″

## THE TRAIL

This hike begins with a pleasant, gentle downhill grade along Vidae Creek where wildflowers provide a showy display in summer. A hemlock and fir forest offers shade along the way as you cross the creek and traverse a steep hillside to Vidae Ridge, where you may find remnants of a spur trail leading up to the East Rim Drive, 0.7 mile from the trailhead.

The trail climbs to the crest of the ridge, then follows it along a mostly level path for almost 1.5 miles before arriving at a junction with a spur

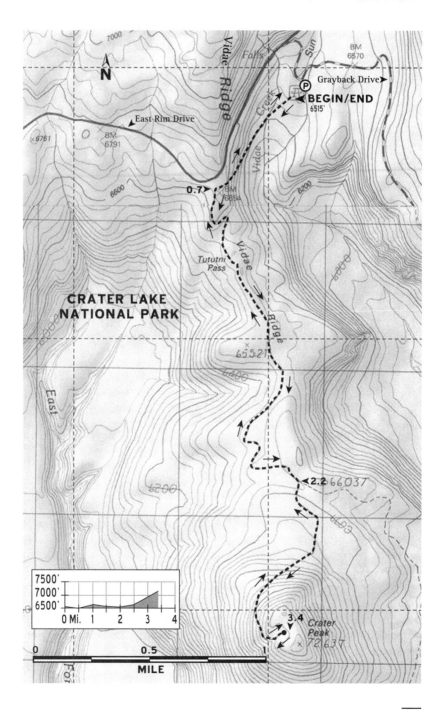

An interpretive sign shows the trail to Crater Peak.

trail leading to the summit block of Crater Peak. Turn right and begin the serious climbing—700 vertical feet in the next mile. The best view from the summit of this volcano is to the southeast; Crater Lake is not visible.

# 70. Sun Notch

| | |
|---|---|
| RATING | 𝍏𝍏 |
| DISTANCE | 0.8-mile loop |
| HIKING TIME | 30 minutes |
| ELEVATION GAIN | 150 feet |
| HIGH POINT | 7,104 feet |
| EFFORT | Stroll in the Park |
| BEST SEASON | Summer, fall |
| PERMITS/CONTACT | Daily or annual entrance fee required/Crater Lake National Park, (541) 594-3000, www.nps.gov/crla |
| MAPS | USGS Crater Lake East; National Park Service Crater Lake |
| NOTES | Dogs and bikes prohibited; wheelchair accessible with assistance; road closed in winter |

## THE HIKE

This short uphill walk provides the best view down to Crater Lake and its craggy rock formation, the Phantom Ship.

## GETTING THERE

Follow Highway 62 from I-5 in Medford to Crater Lake National Park and turn left on East Rim Drive to Mazama Village. After stopping to pay a fee at the Annie Spring Entrance Station, turn left to Mazama Village and continue 4.0 miles to Crater Lake National Park Headquarters and the junction with East Rim Drive.

Turn right at the junction and follow East Rim Drive 4.4 miles to the trailhead on the left, 7,000 feet above sea level. GPS coordinates: N42°54′0″; W122°05′42″

## THE TRAIL

Here's a wide, well-graded pathway that the National Park Service describes as "accessible to strong wheelchair users with assistance." It's a loop trail around a wildflower meadow that can be walked in either direction, but the trail to the right might not be quite as steep. It leads to the best spot to view the Phantom Ship, about halfway around the loop at the high point of the trail.

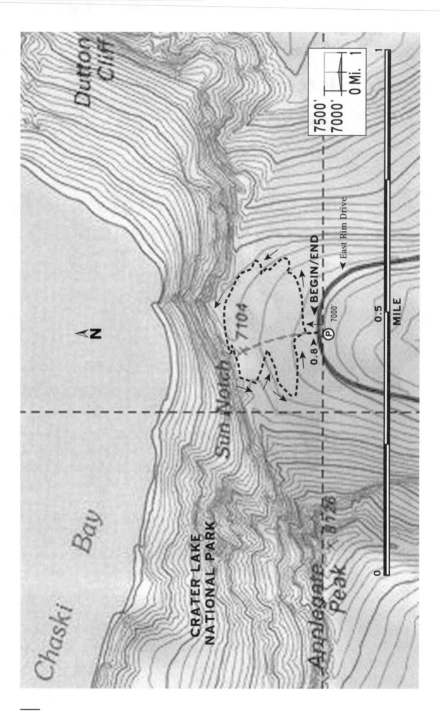

The Phantom Ship formation from Sun Notch.

# 71. Plaikni Falls

| | |
|---|---|
| RATING | 🚶🚶🚶🚶 |
| DISTANCE | 2.0 miles round-trip |
| HIKING TIME | 1 hour, 30 minutes |
| ELEVATION GAIN | 100 feet |
| HIGH POINT | 6,500 feet |
| EFFORT | Easy Walk |
| BEST SEASON | Summer, fall |
| PERMITS/CONTACT | Daily or annual entrance fee required/Crater Lake National Park, (541) 594-3000, www.nps.gov/crla |
| MAPS | USGS Crater Lake East; National Park Service Crater Lake |
| NOTES | Dogs and bikes prohibited; good family hike; wheelchair-accessible with assistance; road closed in winter |

## THE HIKE

Here's an excellent wildflower walk through forest to a meadow hillside and one of the most scenic and accessible waterfalls in the park.

## GETTING THERE

Follow Highway 62 from I-5 in Medford to Crater Lake National Park and turn left on East Rim Drive to Mazama Village. After stopping to pay a fee at the Annie Spring Entrance Station, turn left to Mazama Village and continue 4.0 miles to Crater Lake National Park Headquarters and the junction with East Rim Drive.

Turn right at the junction and follow East Rim Drive for 8.5 miles to a junction with the Pinnacles Road and turn right. Drive 1.2 miles to the trailhead, 6,390 feet above sea level. GPS coordinates: N42°54′06″; W122°03′37″

## THE TRAIL

The Plaikni Falls Trail is a great example of the future of trail building in a national park. Opened in 2011, it is a wide, flat, hard-surfaced path that meanders through huge old-growth fir and hemlock, accessible to those who hike in wheelchairs with assistance. The hike doesn't draw

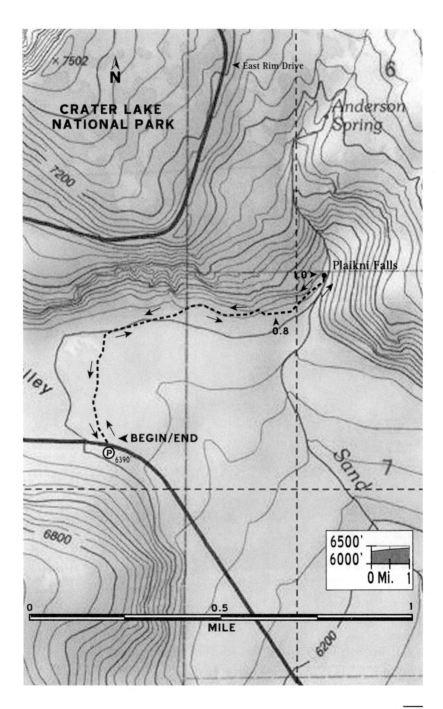

A sign at the Plaikni Falls trailhead outlines the hike ahead.

as big crowds as those along the crater rim, and an autumn walk might feel lonesome.

Another reason for taking this hike late in the season is to avoid the bugs of summer. Where people may not crowd the trail, mosquitoes and biting flies do. The trade-off is that the myriad wildflowers of summer won't be as showy in the fall, so take your pick: slap and snap flower flicks or walk and watch a waterfall.

The trail is a very gentle uphill grade for the first **0.8** mile in the forest, then emerges into the meadows of Sand Creek and climbs steeply to a viewpoint of the falls. *Plaikni* is a Klamath Indian word that describes "from the high country."

## MORE CRATER LAKE NATIONAL PARK HIKES

⚐ **Wizard Summit**, 2.2 miles round-trip, Prepare to Perspire. Trailhead on Wizard Island requires boat ride and hike to Cleetwood Cove.

⚐ **Fumarole Bay**, 1.8 miles round-trip, Easy Walk. Trailhead on Wizard Island requires boat ride and hike to Cleetwood Cove.

⚐ **Boundary Springs**, 5.0 miles round-trip, Moderate Workout. Trailhead off Highway 230, northwest of park boundary.

⚐ **Pinnacles**, 0.8 mile round-trip, Stroll in the Park. Mountain bikes welcome, wheelchair-accessible with assistance. Trailhead at end of Pinnacles Road.

⚐ **Stuart Falls Trail to Pacific Crest Trail**, 5.4 miles round-trip, Moderate Workout. Trailhead south of Lodgepole Picnic Area.

Oregon Caves entrance kiosk provides information on the monument.

# OREGON CAVES NATIONAL MONUMENT

The Oregon Caves National Monument in the Siskiyou Mountains grew by 4,000 acres in late 2014, making it an even better place to explore both underground and in the splendid high forest above the half-mile cave tour. Above ground, you'll hike to a Really Big Tree and see a forest populated by rare Port Orford cedars.

Although the caves—among the few marble caverns in the world—are the main attraction, the trails and history of the monument make it one of the areas not to be missed in the Northwest. Declared a national monument in 1909, the Oregon Caves became a popular tourist destination, and guides have led people into the caverns for more than a century. The area attracted the Civilian Conservation Corps in the 1930s, where they crafted the six-story Oregon Caves Chateau and Chalet, and built the rockery and gardens you see today.

The National Park Service assumed management of the monument in 1933, and now offers guided tours of the cave as well as longer day courses in basic spelunking. Haunted cave tours are popular in October, and although the monument is open throughout the year, the cave tours are only provided during the summer and fall.

The hikes outlined here include the basic cave tour and the loop walk to a giant Douglas fir, said to be the fattest fir in Oregon. Now that the monument is bigger, you'll discover pathways that lead to lakes and viewpoints beyond the borders of the old monument.

# OREGON CAVES
# NATIONAL MONUMENT

**72**  Oregon Cave Tour

**73**  Big Tree

# 72. Oregon Cave Tour

| | |
|---|---|
| RATING | 𝆏𝆏𝆏𝆏𝆏 |
| DISTANCE | 0.5 mile one-way |
| HIKING TIME | 1 hour, 30 minutes |
| ELEVATION GAIN | 230 feet |
| HIGH POINT | 4,220 feet |
| EFFORT | Prepare to Perspire |
| BEST SEASON | Summer, fall |
| PERMITS/CONTACT | Cave entrance fee/Oregon Caves National Monument, (541) 592-2100, www.nps.gov/orca |
| MAPS | USGS Oregon Caves; Oregon Caves National Monument maps |
| NOTES | Children shorter than 42 inches tall prohibited; dogs prohibited |

## THE HIKE
One of the most fascinating guided tours of a rare type of cave to be found anywhere, the walk through Oregon Caves is physically demanding.

## GETTING THERE
From I-5 in Grants Pass, follow Highway 199 southwest 33 miles to Cave Junction. (You'll know you're close when you pass the sign advertising "Sweet Cron.") Turn left and follow Highway 46 for 20 miles to the big parking and picnic area, 0.1 mile west of the Oregon Caves Chateau. The final 8 miles of the road to the monument are narrow, steep, and winding. Big recreational vehicles and trailers are not recommended, and free parking is available at the Illinois Valley Visitor Center near Cave Junction. The parking area at the monument is 3,980 feet above sea level. GPS coordinates: N42°05′49″; W123°24′46″

## THE TRAIL
This really isn't a trail but rather a walk through a twisting, turning underground passage that will make you feel like you've been on a hike. It's filled with all manner of interesting cave objects like stalactites and stalagmites, and creepy-crawly things like termite-looking springtails that can jump twenty times their body length. And bats. Park rangers

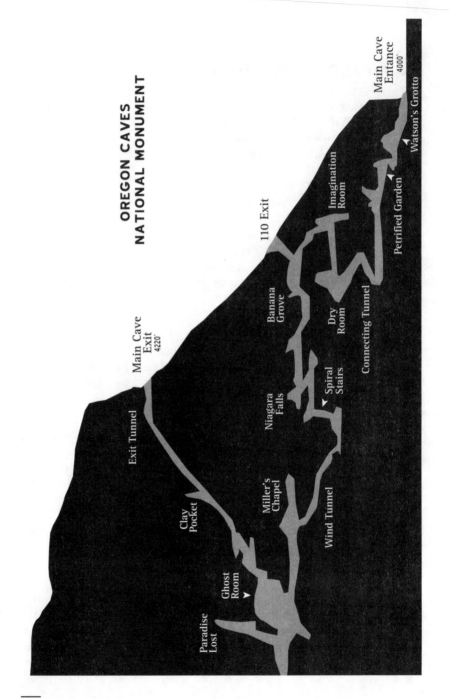

OREGON CAVES
NATIONAL MONUMENT

Main Cave
Entance
4000'

Watson's Grotto

Main Cave
Exit
4220'

110 Exit

Imagination
Room

Petrified Garden

Exit Tunnel

Banana
Grove

Dry
Room

Connecting Tunnel

Clay
Pocket

Miller's
Chapel

Niagara
Falls

Spiral
Stairs

Ghost
Room

Paradise
Lost

Wind Tunnel

Looking into the entrance of Oregon Caves.

warn that there are narrow passages and low rock ceilings upon which—I can regretfully report—at least one wide-eyed tourist bumped his head.

Other factors that might make one pause before taking this tour include some steep grades and five hundred stairs. The cave tour is well lit, but even in summer the cave temperature hovers around the mid-40s, so dress warmly and wear hiking shoes or boots with aggressive tread.

All of that said, if you're going to visit the Oregon Caves National Monument, you'd be remiss by not taking the cave tour. Get there early in the morning in the summer for a shorter wait.

# 73. Big Tree

| | |
|---|---|
| RATING | 🚶🚶🚶 |
| DISTANCE | 3.3-mile loop |
| HIKING TIME | 3 hours |
| ELEVATION GAIN | 1,100 feet |
| HIGH POINT | 5,180 feet |
| EFFORT | Prepare to Perspire |
| BEST SEASON | Summer, fall |
| PERMITS/CONTACT | None/Oregon Caves National Monument, (541) 592-2100, www.nps.gov/orca |
| MAPS | USGS Oregon Caves; Oregon Caves National Monument maps |
| NOTES | Dogs prohibited on trail; carry water |

## THE HIKE

Don't expect much company on this strenuous climb leading through beautiful forest to a record heavyweight Douglas fir, the best hike to see all the monument has to offer.

## GETTING THERE

From I-5 in Grants Pass, follow Highway 199 southwest 33 miles to Cave Junction. (You'll know you're close when you pass the sign advertising "Sweet Cron.") Turn left and follow Highway 46 for 20 miles to the big parking and picnic area, 0.1 mile west of the Oregon Caves Chateau. The final 8 miles of the road to the monument are narrow, steep, and winding. Big recreational vehicles and trailers are not recommended and free parking is available at the Illinois Valley Visitor Center near Cave Junction. The parking area at the monument is 3,980 feet above sea level. GPS coordinates: N42°05′49″; W123°24′46″

## THE TRAIL

You'll leave a lot of folks behind on this walk, because as you might guess, the big attraction here is the cave tour. This hike is worth taking anywhere, however, so walk under the arch entrance of the Oregon Caves Chalet. Turn left along a moderate grade under a forest of fir and oak, with a floor of wildflowers in the early summer. A quarter mile from the

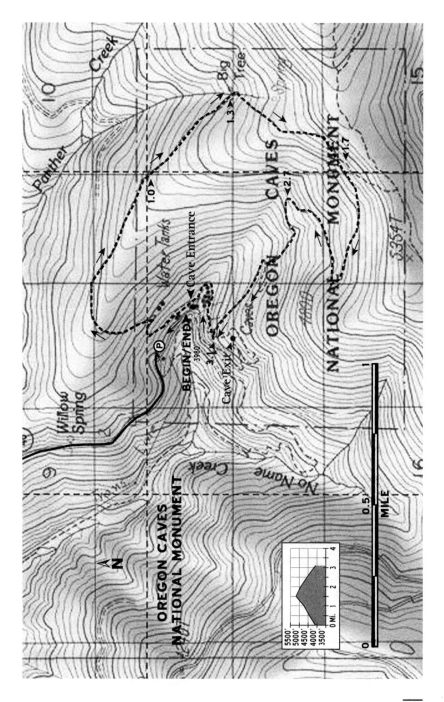

The Big Tree trail starts at the chalet and visitor center at the Oregon Caves National Monument.

trailhead, you'll reach a junction with the Old Growth Trail to the left. Switch back to the right and walk to a second switchback past the monument's water supply.

You'll climb steeply around a sharp ridge cloaked in old growth evergreens where rhododendrons color the understory in season. Once around the ridge, you'll continue climbing to the southeast under the crest of the ridge. At **1.0** mile, you should hear tumbling Panther Creek below the trail, and in another 0.3 mile, reach a fenced platform at the Big Tree.

Don't expect tall, since it looks like lightning has lopped off the leader of this Douglas fir at least twice. Instead, think corpulent—this ancient evergreen is more than 41 feet around and 13 feet in diameter.

Beyond the tree, the trail continues its steady climb for nearly a half mile to the high point of the hike near the junction with the Mount Elijah Trail, **1.7** miles from the trailhead.

Good news: it's all downhill from here. Walk along a hillside meadow to a switchback, cross a second meadow to another switchback, and enter the forest again, **2.7** miles from the trailhead. Continue down, rounding two sharp switchbacks to a junction with the Cliff Nature Trail and turn left to Vista Point, which provides a dramatic view down the Illinois River valley, **3.1** miles from the trailhead. You'll round three short switchbacks and pass the exit to the Oregon Caves before reaching the chateau.

## MORE OREGON CAVES
## NATIONAL MONUMENT HIKES

- **Cliff Nature Trail**, 1.0-mile loop, Prepare to Perspire. Trailhead at visitor center.

- **No Name Trail**, 1.3-mile loop, Prepare to Perspire. Trailhead at Chateau parking area.

- **Old Growth Trail**, 0.5 mile round-trip, Moderate Workout. Trailhead at visitor center.

- **Bigelow Lakes–Mount Elijah**, 9.2-mile loop, Knee-Punishing. Trailhead at chalet.

- **Cave Creek Trail**, 3.0 miles round-trip, Knee-Punishing. Trailhead at Chateau parking area.

A photo of Pilot Rock captured from the PCT.

# CASCADE-SISKIYOU NATIONAL MONUMENT

Established in 2000, the Cascade-Siskiyou National Monument is a 62,000-acre highland that begins along the border of Oregon and California and extends northeast through forest and ranchland along the crest of the Siskiyou Mountains. The Pacific Crest Trail cuts through the monument for 19 miles, providing access to high lakes and the Soda Mountain Wilderness.

Parts of the monument are separated by private lands, so hikers are asked to stay on trails and respect private property. The two trails outlined here show off different parts of the monument and provide a look at its diversity.

# CASCADE-SISKIYOU
# NATIONAL MONUMENT

74  Pacific Crest
    Trail—Pilot Rock

75  Pacific Crest
    Trail—Hyatt Meadows

# 74. Pacific Crest Trail—Pilot Rock

| | |
|---|---|
| RATING | 🚶🚶🚶 |
| DISTANCE | 7.5 miles round-trip |
| HIKING TIME | 4 hours, 30 minutes |
| ELEVATION GAIN | 850 feet |
| HIGH POINT | 5,180 feet |
| EFFORT | Prepare to Perspire |
| BEST SEASON | Summer, fall |
| PERMITS/CONTACT | None/Cascade-Siskiyou National Monument, (541) 618-2200, www.blm.gov/or/resources/recreation/csnm |
| MAPS | USGS Siskiyou Pass |
| NOTES | Carry water |

## THE HIKE

Walk to the base of an Oregon border landmark along a portion of one of the longest trails in the United States.

## GETTING THERE

Follow I-5 south from Ashland to exit 6 and take the exit, then continue on the west side of I-5 on the frontage road, crossing under the freeway in 0.7 mile. Drive another half mile to the PCT trailhead, a wide parking area on the left, 4,360 feet above sea level. GPS coordinates: N42°03′14″; W122°36′11″

## THE TRAIL

You can drive to within a mile of Pilot Rock, which is pretty much what all of the rock scramblers and Real Mountain Climbers do. So that means that your hike along the Pacific Crest Trail is more likely to be less crowded, and you won't have to dodge rocks dislodged by those rock scramblers at Pilot Rock.

Begin in a shaded forest by dropping to a gully and crossing a small creek that dries up in the fall, then turning northeast to a wide meadow sweeping down toward Ashland and yielding views of Mount Ashland to the west. Round a wide ridge and cross a tributary to Carter Creek 0.8 mile from the trailhead, then begin climbing up a ridge and

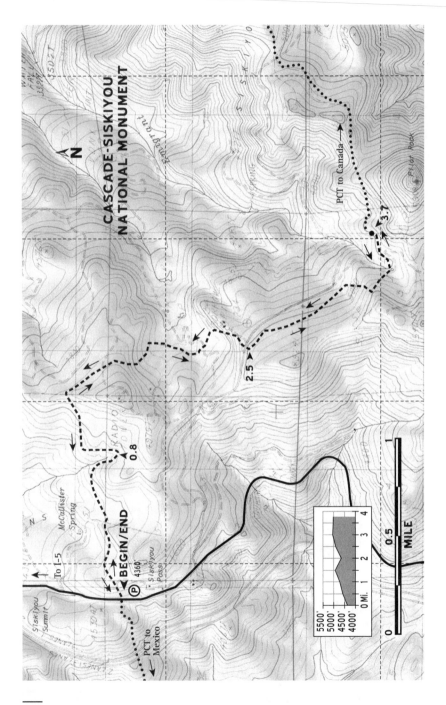

The Pacific Crest Trail passes by Pilot Rock on its way through Oregon.

switching back underneath a 4,900-foot hillside. You'll find a stock gate on the trail, which should be closed after passing.

The trail continues to climb and at 2.5 miles, crosses the Bureau of Land Management road leading to the Pilot Rock trailhead. Cross this road and continue for another 1.2 miles to the junction with the Pilot Rock Trail. This is your turnaround point.

## GOING FARTHER

The best way to extend this hike is to walk another mile or so along the PCT before turning around. The trail passes under the north face of Pilot Rock.

It's a steep 1.0-mile scramble to the summit of 5,908-foot Pilot Rock, which begins on a well-marked trail that ends at the base of the rock. If you're comfortable scrambling up steep rock, you can climb to the summit without artificial aid or rope. Peregrine falcons nest on the rock, and it is closed from February 1 to July 30.

# 75. Pacific Crest Trail—Hyatt Meadows

| | |
|---|---|
| RATING | ⅄ |
| DISTANCE | 7.2 miles |
| HIKING TIME | 5 hours |
| ELEVATION GAIN | 420 feet |
| HIGH POINT | 4,970 feet |
| EFFORT | Prepare to Perspire |
| BEST SEASON | Summer, fall |
| PERMITS/CONTACT | None/Cascade-Siskiyou National Monument, (541) 618-2200, www.blm.gov/or/resources/recreation/csnm |
| MAPS | USGS Hyatt Reservoir |
| NOTES | Carry water |

## THE HIKE
Climb through forest along the Pacific Crest Trail to a wide meadow near a popular recreation area.

## GETTING THERE
From I-5 in Ashland, follow Highway 66 east for 15 miles to the Green Springs Summit and PCT trailhead parking on the right, 4,560 feet above sea level. The trailhead is across the highway. GPS coordinates: N42°07′47″; W122°28′59″

## THE TRAIL
This trail isn't used as much as other parts of the Pacific Crest Trail because a road parallels parts of the route and heads to the same general destination. The downside to this is you cross roads several times; the upside is that you may find yourself or your party the only one on this path.

The hike begins at a gate marked with notes to PCT thru-hikers and other Cascade-Siskiyou monument information, where you should make certain to close the gate once past. The path then climbs along above the road through an open forest and around a hillside before climbing at a gentle grade for about a mile to cross the road to the Hyatt Lake Recreation Area, 1.3 miles from the trailhead.

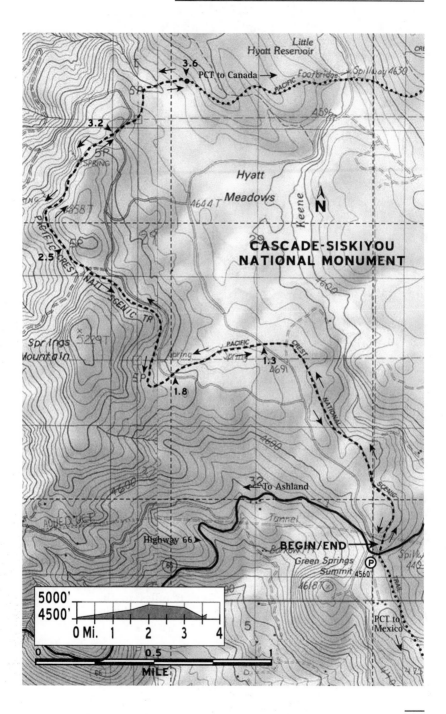

Parts of the Pacific Crest Trail pass through private property.

The trail then climbs another half mile and crosses a road leading to Green Springs Mountain, the 5,229-foot peak to the west. You'll climb above this road for another 0.8 mile before the trail begins descending, crosses a spur road, and drops to the final road crossing 3.2 miles from the trailhead. The Hyatt Meadows, a quarter mile beyond, is your turn-around point.

## GOING FARTHER
You can continue on the Pacific Crest Trail for another mile to the Little Hyatt Reservoir, or extend your walk 2.6 miles to the Hyatt Lake Recreation Area.

## MORE CASCADE-SISKIYOU
## NATIONAL MONUMENT HIKES

🚶 Pacific Crest Trail South from Green Springs Summit, 4–19 miles round-trip, Moderate Workout–Prepare to Perspire. Trailhead on south side of Highway 66, Green Springs Summit.

# INDEX

Annie Spring-Pacific Crest Trail,
   228
Ape Canyon Trail, 179
Ape Caves, 170
Be Careful, xix
   ten essentials, the, xix
   water, xxi
   weather, xx
   wildlife, xxi
Bench and Snow Lakes, 107
Benham Falls Trail, 185
Big Hump, 44
Big Tree, 278
Blue Basin Overlook Trail, 215
Boundary Trail, 167
Camp Handy, 55
Carbon River Road, 132
Cascade-Siskiyou National
   Monument, 283
   more hikes, 291
   Pacific Crest Trail—Hyatt
      Meadows, 288
   Pacific Crest Trail—Pilot
      Rock, 285
Cleetwood Cove, 256
Coldwater Lake Trail, 164
Comet Falls, 119
Crater Lake National Park, 223
   Annie Spring–Pacific Crest
      Trail, 228

Cleetwood Cove, 256
Crater Peak, 262
Crater Rim Trail, 246
Discovery Point Trail, 240
Garfield Peak Trail, 237
Godfrey Glen, 231
Lady of the Woods and Castle
   Crest Wildflower Loops, 234
more hikes, 271
Mount Scott, 259
Pacific Crest Trail North, 225
Pacific Crest Trail—Pumice
   Desert, 252
Pacific Crest Trail—Red Cone
   Spring, 249
Plaikni Falls, 268
Sun Notch, 265
Watchman Peak, 243
Crater Peak, 262
Crater Rim Trail, 246
Cutthroat Pass, 17
Discovery Point Trail, 240
Dosewallips Road, 48
Dungeness Spit, 66
East Bank Trail, 10
Elk Mountain, 74
Elwha Loop, 78
Emmons Glacier, 97
Garfield Peak Trail, 237
Geologic Time–Clarno Arch
   Trail, 218
Godfrey Glen, 231
Grove of the Patriarchs, 101

Harmony Falls, 149

Hummocks Trail, 161

Hurricane Hill, 70

Iceberg Point, 25

**John Day Fossil Beds National Monument, 213**

   Blue Basin Overlook Trail, 215

   Geologic Time–Clarno Arch Trail, 218

   more hikes, 221

Lady of the Woods and Castle Crest Wildflower Loops, 234

Lava Canyon, 174

Lava Cast Forest, 189

Little Crater Trail, 198

Lower Big Quilcene Trail, 51

Lower Gray Wolf Trail, 63

Mazama Ridge, 142

Mount Fremont Lookout, 93

**Mount Rainier National Park, 91**

   Bench and Snow Lakes, 107

   Carbon River Road, 132

   Comet Falls, 119

   Emmons Glacier, 97

   Grove of the Patriarchs, 101

   Mazama Ridge, 142

   more hikes, 145

   Mount Fremont Lookout, 93

   Naches Peak Loop, 135

   Nisqually Vista, 111

   Pinnacle Saddle, 139

   Rampart Ridge, 125

   Silver Falls, 104

   Skyline Trail, 115

   Trail of the Shadows, 122

   Westside Road, 128

Mount Scott, 259

**Mount St. Helens National Volcanic Monument, 147**

   Ape Canyon Trail, 178

   Ape Caves, 170

   Boundary Trail, 167

   Coldwater Lake Trail, 164

   Harmony Falls, 149

   Hummocks Trail, 161

   Lava Canyon, 174

   more hikes, 181

   Norway Pass, 152

   Smith Creek Trail, 155

   Windy Ridge, 158

Naches Peak Loop, 135

Newberry Crater Trail, 207

**Newberry National Volcanic Monument, 183**

   Benham Falls Trail, 185

   Lava Cast Forest, 189

   Little Crater Trail, 198

   more hikes, 210

   Newberry Crater Trail, 207

   Paulina Creek Trail, 195

   Paulina Falls, 192

   Paulina Lakeshore Loop, 201

   Silica and Big Obsidian Flow Trails, 204

Nisqually Vista, 111

**North Cascades National Park, 1**

Cutthroat Pass, 17
East Bank Trail, 10
more hikes, 21
Rainy and Ann Lakes, 13
River Loop Trail, 3
Thunder Knob, 7
North Fork, Skokomish River, 37
Norway Pass, 152
**Olympic National Park, 31**
Big Hump, 44
Camp Handy, 55
Dosewallips Road, 48
Dungeness Spit, 66
Elk Mountain, 74
Elwha Loop, 78
Hurricane Hill, 70
Lower Big Quilcene Trail, 51
Lower Gray Wolf Trail, 63
more hike, 89
North Fork, Skokomish
River, 37
Pacific Ocean Beaches, 86
Royal Lake Trail, 59
Shade Lane Trail, 41
South Fork, Skokomish
River, 33
Spruce Railroad Trail, 82
Oregon Cave Tour, 275
**Oregon Caves National
Monument, 273**
Big Tree, 278
more hikes, 281
Oregon Cave Tour, 275

Pacific Crest Trail North, 225
Pacific Crest Trail–Hyatt
Meadows, 288
Pacific Crest Trail–Pilot Rock, 285
Pacific Crest Trail–Pumice
Desert, 252
Pacific Crest Trail–Red Cone
Spring, 249
Pacific Ocean Beaches, 86
Paulina Creek Trail, 195
Paulina Falls, 192
Paulina Lakeshore Loop, 201
Pinnacle Saddle, 139
Plaikni Falls, 268
Rainy and Ann Lakes, 13
Rampart Ridge, 125
River Loop Trail, 3
Royal Lake Trail, 59
**San Juan Islands National
Monument, 23**
Iceberg Point, 25
more hikes, 28
Shady Lane Trail, 41
Silica and Big Obsidian Flow
Trails, 204
Silver Falls, 104
Skyline Trail, 115
Smith Creek Trail, 155
South Fork, Skokomish River, 33
Spruce Railroad Trail, 82
Sun Notch, 265
Thunder Knob, 7
Trail of the Shadows, 122

**Using This Guide, xv**
    best season, xvii
    distance, xvi
    effort, xvi
    elevation gain, xvi
    getting there, xviii
    going farther, xviii
    high point, xvi
    hike, the, xviii
    hiking time, xvi
    maps, xvii
    overall rating, xv
    permits/contact, xvii
    trail notes, xviii
    trail number and name, xv
    trail, the, xviii
Watchman Peak, 243
Westside Road, 128
Windy Ridge, 158